Contraception

Anne Szarewski is a Senior Clinical Medical Officer in
Family Planning at the Margaret Pyke Centre, a Family
Planning Doctor at the Marie Stopes Clinic, and Senior
Clinical Research Fellow in Gynaecological Oncology at
the Imperial Cancer Research Fund.

John Guillebaud is Medical Director of the Margaret Pyke
Centre and a consultant gynaecologist at the United
Elizabeth Garrett Anderson Hospital and Soho Hospital
for Women.

Contraception
A User's Handbook

SECOND EDITION

Anne Szarewski and John Guillebaud

OXFORD UNIVERSITY PRESS
1998

Oxford University Press, Walton Street, Oxford ox2 6DP

Oxford New York
Athens Auckland Bangkok Bogota Bombay
Buenos Aires Calcutta Cape Town Dar es Salaam
Delhi Florence Hong Kong Istanbul Karachi
Kuala Lumpur Madras Madrid Melbourne
Mexico City Nairobi Paris Singapore
Taipei Tokyo Toronto Warsaw

and associated companies in
Berlin Ibadan

Oxford is a trade mark of Oxford University Press

First published 1994 as an Oxford University Press paperback
Second edition published 1998

British Library Cataloguing in Publication Data
Data available

Library of Congress Cataloging–in–Publication Data
Szarewski, Anne.
Contraception : a user's handbook / Anne Szarewski and John Guillebaud.—2nd ed.
Includes bibliographical references and index.
1. Contraception—Popular works. I. Guillebaud, John. II. Title.
RG136.2.S96 1998   613.9'4—dc21   97–30323
ISBN 0–19–286195–6 (pbk.)

1 3 5 7 9 10 8 6 4 2

Typeset by Jayvee, Trivandrum, India
Printed in Great Britain by
Cox & Wyman Ltd.
Reading, Berkshire

Contents

Acknowledgements

We are indebted to our colleagues at the Margaret Pyke Centre and the Imperial Cancer Research Fund for their help and advice. Our editor Nicola Bion has been an invaluable source of good ideas, encouragement and constructive criticism. Finally, we would like to thank our families for their considerable patience and tolerance.

Introduction

> If it is not to generate children that the woman was given to the man as a helpmate, in what could she be a help to him?
>
> (Augustine, *The City of God*, 14.22)

Despite St Augustine, contraceptive methods of one sort or another have been used for thousands of years. Many ancient remedies were poorly effective and some downright dangerous. However, even with all our modern technology no one has yet managed to produce the perfect contraceptive method. In an ideal world, a contraceptive would provide complete protection against pregnancy, be entirely free of health risks and side-effects, not involve any action either during or immediately before intercourse, be completely reversible, not rely on the user's memory, and not involve the medical profession. Nowadays it would be welcome if, in addition to all these things, it prevented the transmission of sexually transmitted diseases. It is likely to take a very long time before this ideal becomes a reality.

Until then, we have to compromise and use less-than-perfect methods. They all have advantages and drawbacks. In general, it can be said that the more effective a method is, the more likely it is to have health risks or side-effects. Similarly, if a method is relatively free of health risks, it is likely to be less effective at preventing pregnancy.

At present, the most effective methods are the hormonal ones, such as the combined pill, injectable progestogens, and implants. Intrauterine devices (IUDs) are also very effective. These methods should be high on your list if it is very important that you do not become pregnant. Although they do have some side-effects and potential health risks, you may be surprised at how these have diminished in the last ten years.

If you are 'spacing' rather than 'avoiding' pregnancies almost all methods become worthy of consideration. Barrier methods, such as diaphragms and condoms, can be a good choice. Nowadays the condom may be advisable for protection against sexually transmitted diseases (such as HIV) even if you are also using a more effective method of contraception.

Some couples will need to take past or present medical problems into account: for example, a past history of a blood clot in a vein will exclude the use of the combined pill. Similarly, if a woman has frequent cystitis, the diaphragm is best avoided.

It is also worth considering how a method will fit into your life. If you travel a great deal you may prefer a method which does not mean that you have to remember to take pills every day very regularly. Or if you are having sex infrequently, you may prefer a method, such as a barrier, which you only use when you actually need it.

Contraception should involve both partners, not just the woman. Each couple has to balance the risks and the benefits, bearing their own medical histories and life-style in mind. These may change over time, and therefore they may wish to use several different methods at different times.

Where can you go for advice? Your GP may be knowledgeable and helpful. However, if you would prefer to see a different doctor (perhaps because your GP is male, or you feel inhibited because you have known him or her since childhood) you are entitled to see any other NHS doctor for family planning. This means you can see a doctor in a different practice, while still remaining registered for everything else with your own GP. Or you can go to a family planning clinic. Such clinics often have more female staff and may have more time and experience if you have a difficult problem. The Brook Advisory Centres provide a service for women and men under the age of 24 and specialize in teenage contraceptive and sexual issues. Clinics should be listed in your local directory: if you have problems finding them, contact the Family Planning Association or the Brook Advisory Head office, whose phone numbers are given at the end of the book.

It is unlikely that any consultation will be able to include every fact about every contraceptive method. Therefore you will almost certainly find it useful to have some idea beforehand about the options which are likely to suit you. Once you have narrowed the choices down you may again need more information in order to make the final decision. We hope that this book will be able to provide you with the facts, and dispel some of the myths which have accumulated over the years. Then you can make a rational and informed decision about what is best for you.

We have tried to make the chapters as self-contained as possible, so that you can 'dip into' the book as well as read it straight through. However, most readers will find it helpful to read Chapter 1, since this is where we discuss many basic concepts which it is impossible to keep repeating in full later on.

Conception: How it Happens

Most people—including many doctors!—have only a vague idea of how pregnancy occurs. And indeed, for something which is so 'natural' it is remarkably complicated. So we need to consider how conception happens before we can properly discuss how *contra*ception works.

The female reproductive system

The majority of a woman's reproductive 'parts' are to be found in her pelvis: the womb (uterus), Fallopian tubes, ovaries, vagina and cervix (see Figure 1.1). The ovaries produce eggs, which pass down to the womb through the Fallopian tubes. The egg is literally sucked into the open end of the tube by finger-like processes (called fimbriae). Once inside the tube, it is wafted down towards the womb by tiny little hairs called cilia. The womb itself is really nothing more than a box designed to hold a pregnancy. Meanwhile, the vagina (front passage) and cervix (the neck of the womb) provide a way for sperm to reach the womb and fertilize an egg which might be waiting there.

We all know that periods are somehow an integral part of being female and fertile. But the actual period is only the end result of a process which goes on throughout the month and is called the menstrual cycle ('menstruum' simply means 'monthly' in Latin). This cycle is under the control of the brain: of course, the brain is a long way away from the womb and ovaries, so it must have some way of communicating with them. It achieves this by means of chemical messengers, called hormones, which travel in the bloodstream and can reach all parts of the body.

The brain has a special area called the hypothalamus, which controls the release of a hormone called Gonadotrophin Releasing

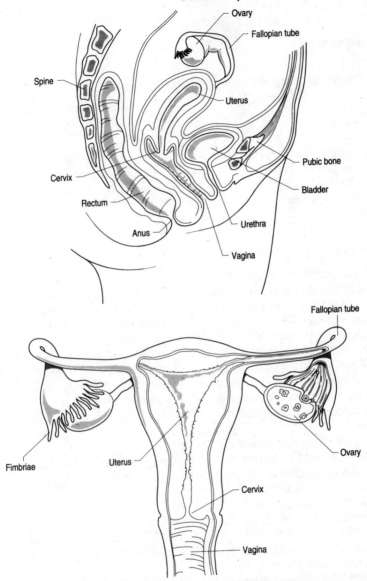

Figure 1.1 The female reproductive system

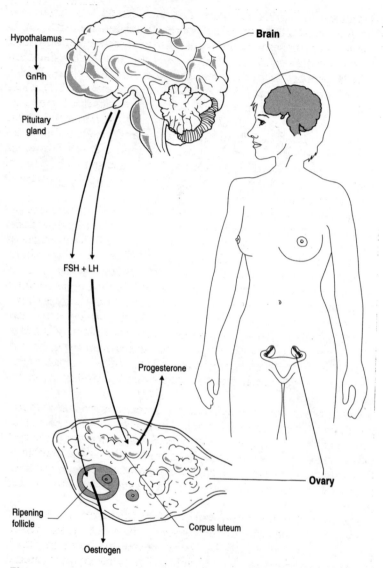

Figure 1.2 Hormones released from the brain to stimulate the ovaries
(*Source*: Szarewski, *Hormonal Contraception*, Macdonald Optima, 1991)

Hormone, or GnRH for short ('Gonad' means 'sex organ' and 'trophic' comes from the Greek for 'to stimulate or nourish', so the name means 'hormone which causes the release of something which stimulates the sex organs'). GnRH travels to the pituitary gland and here is responsible for the release of two further hormones, Follicle Stimulating Hormone (FSH) and Luteinizing Hormone (LH), which enter the bloodstream and are carried to the ovaries (see Figure 1.2).

At birth, every female child already has millions of small fluid-filled 'bubbles' or follicles in her ovaries, and each of these has the potential to develop into an ovum, or egg. No others are ever formed: in fact, they constantly disappear from this time on, so that by puberty there are only about 200,000 left: this is, of course, still far in excess of what any woman could ever need.

The function of FSH, as its name suggests, is to stimulate a number of these 'bubbles' or follicles to grow. One follicle will grow faster than the others, and this is the one which will actually become an egg. The follicles release oestrogen as they grow and this enters the bloodstream. Oestrogen is what makes women look like women: it causes the breasts to grow, and generally gives the body a more rounded shape than that of a man. It circulates throughout the body performing various functions, returning to the brain, where it has two important effects in the pituitary gland. In the first place, a high level of oestrogen halts the production of FSH, and this prevents the situation from becoming uncontrollable. This is called 'negative feedback' and works rather like the thermostat controlling a central heating system.

Oestrogen in the pituitary gland produces another effect: when it has risen to a certain level, it brings about a sudden increase in the release of LH. This is called 'positive feedback'. When this LH 'surge', as it is called, reaches the ovaries, it stimulates the largest 'bubble' or follicle to burst, releasing an egg. At this point, it becomes the business of the remaining follicles to help the egg to survive in the hope of meeting a sperm.

These follicles, under the influence of LH, form a small yellow area in the ovary, called the 'corpus luteum' (which just means 'yellow body' in Latin; Luteinizing Hormone means 'the hormone which causes the yellowness to happen'). Then the corpus luteum produces large quantities of another hormone, progesterone, in addition to oestrogen. Progesterone, like oestrogen, has various effects all over the body, but its principal function is to make a comfortable bed out of the uterus (womb) for the fertilized egg. (The

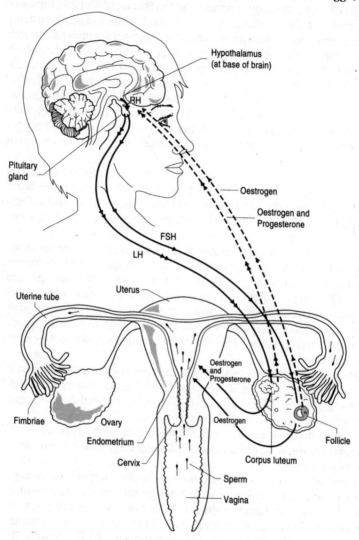

Figure 1.3 How ovarian and pituitary gland hormones affect each other

name comes from 'pro-gestation', which means 'towards pregnancy'.) It does this in two ways: first, it thickens the lining of the womb to make a kind of soft mattress, and secondly, it brings about a rise in the number of glands in the lining. These glands produce a fluid that makes the lining more comfortable and also provides nourishment for the potential embryo.

If the egg should be fertilized, the embryo will settle itself (or implant) into this nest in the womb, and then it must fight for its life: its nest is quite likely to be torn out and washed away with the next period. To protect itself, it produces a hormone called Human Chorionic Gonadotrophin (HCG), which instructs the corpus luteum to continue to send supplies of oestrogen and particularly progesterone; these keep the lining of the womb thick and prevent it from coming away. HCG also tells the pituitary that these high levels of oestrogen and progesterone are intended to support the embryo, rather than to cause another surge of LH (another egg might otherwise be released and a woman could have two simultaneous but separate pregnancies).

Despite these complex defences and preparations, the embryo often fails in its attempt. A large number of very early pregnancies are unable to survive: if they do not, or if the egg is not fertilized, the corpus luteum simply disappears. Then the levels of oestrogen and progesterone suddenly drop and the glands in the lining of the womb wither. The lining then comes off the walls, taking any unsuccessful embryo with it. This shedding of the lining is called menstruation, or a period.

The other effect of the drop in oestrogen and progesterone levels is that the production of FSH begins again, so that another group of follicles is stimulated, and the whole process starts again. This is called the menstrual cycle.

Other hormones are also involved in this extremely complex process. In addition to oestrogen, the follicles produce a hormone called inhibin, which is designed to block the action of FSH (another negative feedback mechanism). Inhibin will be important in later chapters, particularly in relation to the possibilities of a male contraceptive pill. The hormone prolactin, which stimulates the production of milk during breastfeeding, also has a function to perform, as do most of the hormones which travel around in the bloodstream. The process is in fact profoundly complex and even many doctors have only a partial understanding of it. A number of un-answered questions remain and much research into the subject is currently under way. However, the basics are quite easily compre-hensible and it is not hard to grasp the principle of the menstrual cycle.

'It really worries me that my periods are so irregular. My friends seem to have them regular as clockwork, every month. Mine can be anything from a month to six weeks.'

'My periods were completely regular for years. Then I went on holiday, travelling around Thailand and Malaysia for two months. I had no periods at all and spent the whole time panick-ing I might be pregnant. But soon after I got home they just started up again, as if nothing had happened.'

It is generally supposed that there is a standard, 'normal' menstrual cycle which lasts for twenty-eight days, from the first day of one period to the first day of the next. However this 'normal' cycle is a myth unless a woman is taking hormones. Many women have shorter or longer cycles, varying in length from one month to another: these are also completely normal. Many things can influ-ence the length of the cycle. As we have seen the brain is closely involved in the whole process. For this reason, stress, travelling, or a sudden shock many interfere with the regularity of a woman's periods, or may even stop them altogether for a time; this is com-pletely 'natural'.

'Every month I get a pain on one side, usually the right. It always seems to be around the middle of my cycle and just lasts a day or two.'

The only fixed time interval in the cycle is that fourteen days after the egg has been released the next period will take place, provided there is no continuing pregnancy. This is how long it takes for the corpus luteum to disappear and for the lining to begin to break down and this is why the 'rhythm' method of family planning is so liable to fail-ure: you cannot know the date of ovulation in advance, only in retro-spect. Only women who experience pain as the follicle bursts, releasing the egg, can tell when they are ovulating: the discomfort is probably caused by the stretching of the ovary. The technical name for this pain is 'mittelschmerz' (German for 'pain in the middle'). The pain will only occur exactly at mid-cycle if the woman has twenty-eight-day cycles, otherwise it will occur twelve to sixteen days before the next period.

You might wonder how it is possible to become pregnant in the first half of the cycle, if all the important events actually happen in the second half. The answer is that, unfortunately (or fortunately, depending on your viewpoint), sperm can survive in the womb and Fallopian tubes for four or five days, occasionally as long as a week. As a result even if you have sex several days before you ovulate, the sperm can be inside the womb, lying in wait for the egg to arrive.

The highly sensitive pregnancy tests which have come on to the market in the last few years are in fact based on the detection of the hormone HCG, which is produced by the embryo. Levels of HCG increase over time, and these tests can often detect a pregnancy by the time of the missed period, and sometimes even earlier. However, this is not always an advantage. Since so many early pregnancies are not viable, but are swept away as a normal or slightly late period, a great deal of worry (or false hope) can be caused unnecessarily.

Before we move on to look in detail at the role of sperm and to see how fertilisation occurs, we need to consider the reproductive system in men.

The male reproductive system

The male reproductive organs basically consist of the testes, the epididymis, the vas deferens, and the penis. There are two testes, each of which is about the size and shape of a walnut. They contain a huge network of tiny tubes, within which sperm production occurs. Although you can think of the testes as being equivalent to the ovaries in women, men are not born with all the sperm they will ever need: they have to keep producing new ones.

Once sperm have been produced in the testis, they move on to the epididymis, which is another tube attached to the testis. Here they are 'finished off' and become able to swim: all this takes about seventy days.

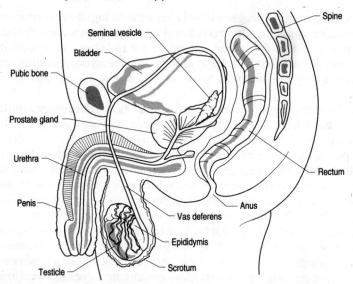

Figure 1.4 The male reproductive system

From the epididymis, they move on into yet another tube, called the vas deferens. This tube carries them past the seminal vesicles and the prostate gland, both of which produce secretions which may help to nourish the sperm, and make up much of the ejaculatory fluid or semen. When they reach the penis, the two tubes (one from each side) join up into one.

The penis has two functions. The first is that of passing urine. The second, and of more interest in our context, is that it facilitates entry of sperm into the vagina during sex. The penis becomes rigid and larger when a man is sexually aroused and ejaculatory fluid may appear at its tip quite soon: this is one of the reasons why condoms have to be put on very early during love-making, and also why 'withdrawal' can fail (see Chapter 13). Once ejaculation has occurred, the penis rapidly shrinks down to its original size again. As in women, much of this process is under the control of the brain. The effect of hormones in men is discussed in more detail in Chapter 13.

Meanwhile, during sex, millions of sperm are deposited in the vagina when the man ejaculates, although some will also enter earlier, which explains why withdrawal cannot be considered a very effective method of contraception. The vagina is an acidic environment, uncongenial to sperm, which therefore have to try to reach the womb, via the cervix, as quickly as possible. If they stay too long in the vagina they will die.

'I've noticed that I seem to get more discharge around the middle of the month. Just a clear discharge, not itchy or smelly.'

The woman can assist the sperm in some circumstances, because when she is sexually excited, especially around mid-cycle, glands in the vagina and cervical canal produce a particularly sperm-friendly mucus, which, since it is long and stretchy, provides an easy path into the womb. It is also thought that during orgasm, the sperm are actively sucked into the womb. Because of this, it is commonly believed that a woman who does not have an orgasm cannot become pregnant. In fact, since there are so many millions of sperm, there is a strong probability that one will still reach the womb even unaided.

When sperm enter the vagina they are not yet fully active and are not capable of fertilizing an egg. As they travel through the mucus they become activated, a process called 'capacitation' (that is, they now have the capacity to fertilize). Methods of blocking this capacitation process are now the subject of research into male contraception (of course, such methods would have to be used by women).

When sperm arrive in the womb they can survive for several days, and some will swim into the Fallopian tubes where they may meet an egg. Fertilization can and indeed often does occur in a Fallopian tube: however, as a rule the embryo passes into the main part of the womb before implanting itself in the thick, specially prepared lining. If for some reason it implants itself while still in the tube, it becomes an ectopic pregnancy (in Greek, 'ecto' means 'outside' and 'topos' means 'place', that is, a pregnancy outside the right place). This may occur, if, for example, the little hairs or cilia in the tube are damaged and do not move it quickly enough into the womb. The most likely cause of such a problem is an infection of the tubes (salpingitis, or pelvic inflammatory disease), so a woman who has had pelvic inflammatory disease has a greater risk of subsequently experiencing an ectopic pregnancy.

Ectopic pregnancies are dangerous because, of course, pregnancies need space to expand. The womb is specifically designed to expand when a woman is pregnant so it is an ideal place. The tubes are not, and will burst when the pregnancy becomes too big. The woman's life will then be in danger from internal bleeding and the possibility of subsequent infection.

If all goes well, however, fertilization will take place and the embryo will arrive safely inside the womb. Now it will implant itself in the lining of the womb and hope to survive. This has brought us full circle to the menstrual cycle, described earlier.

Contraceptive methods must obstruct this process at some stage, and most of them act in several different ways, to increase the chances of success. For example, some methods act as physical barriers, such as the diaphragm and sheath, since if sperm can be prevented from entering the cervix they will soon die in the vagina. However, it is usually recommended that spermicides are used with them; these are designed actively to kill or immobilize sperm so as to back up any deficiencies in the physical barrier. The intrauterine device (IUD) now usually contains copper, which seems to cause chemical changes in order to prevent fertilization in the first place; if that fails, it may prevent the fertilized egg (embryo) from embedding.

Hormonal methods are generally designed to disrupt the earlier stages of the process, by preventing or interfering with ovulation, but they often also have back-up mechanisms further down the line on which they depend to a greater or lesser degree.

The combined pill prevents ovulation from taking place; the brain is made to believe that the woman is pregnant. The pill does this by making use of the negative feedback process which is already set up naturally. As we have seen, in pregnancy, the high levels of oestrogen and progesterone are the signal for the pituitary gland to stop producing FSH and LH, thus ensuring that the woman does not ovulate a second time when she is already pregnant.

The levels of these two hormones in the pill are such that the brain is convinced that the woman must be pregnant, so it stops producing FSH and LH and ovulation does not occur, a very simple solution. The pill also thickens cervical mucus, which will make it harder for sperm to penetrate, but this is unimportant once ovulation has been blocked since no egg will be waiting even if they do get through.

CHAPTER 2

How the Pill was Developed

Hormonal contraception is not a new idea, although the earliest experimenters did not realize that was what they were trying to achieve. Swallowing things as contraceptives, rather than using barriers, was advocated in many ancient civilizations. In China, for example, women were advised to swallow live tadpoles! In India one prescription among many suggested that large quantities of three-year-old molasses should be eaten every day for a fortnight. If any woman succeeded in doing this she was supposed to remain childless for the rest of her life. Another way of becoming permanently childless was to drink a potion made up of the Kallambha plant mixed with the feet of jungle flies.

The Talmud describes the use of a 'cup of roots', which contained Alexandrian gum, liquid alum, and garden crocus, powdered and mixed with beer or wine. Although this was primarily intended as a cure for jaundice or gonorrhoea, it was acknowledged that a contraceptive or indeed sterilizing effect might occur. The cup of roots set a precedent in the Jewish faith for an oral contraceptive method and, as a result, the contraceptive pill is actually the most acceptable form of contraception for Jewish couples. In thirteenth-century Europe St Albert suggested the eating of live bees—it is impossible not to wonder whether this was in fact meant to punish a woman for daring to attempt contraception.

Almost every culture has used plant-derived mixtures for the prevention of pregnancy, and, although most of these are likely to have been useless, if not dangerous, some may well have worked. For many years scientists have been studying these herbal medicines, and some have been shown to contain hormones, or substances which would have been likely to induce a miscarriage.

It is not entirely surprising, then, to learn that we owe modern hormonal contraception to the Mexican yam. A substance called diosgenin is found in the roots of these yams, and it was discovered that progesterone could be produced from it. This was a major breakthrough because until then animals had been the only source of hormones. The time and expense of this method had seriously impeded the progress of research in this area: by the early 1930s both oestrogen and progesterone had been isolated, but they were of little practical use while literally tens of thousands of animals were required to produce enough hormone for a single human dose. In 1941 the Mexican yam changed all that, and the production of an oral contraceptive pill became a realistic proposition for the first time. Within ten years, synthetic preparations were available.

The first hormonal contraceptives were given by injection, but pills were soon introduced. The idea of combining both oestrogen and progestogen in a pill came later, though the doses were initially much higher than those used today. Reports of an increased risk of thrombosis led to the development of lower and lower dose pills and also to further refinements of the hormones used. In order to understand these developments better, we should now look at the functions of oestrogen and progesterone in the body, and then see how they are related to the effects of the hormones used in the pill.

The functions of oestrogen and progesterone

These two hormones are central to female development. They perform many complicated functions throughout the body, some of which are still not fully understood. The following explanation is naturally simplified, but it should be sufficient to clarify many of the actions and side-effects of hormonal contraceptives.

Oestrogen

The principal function of oestrogen (which is really a family of hormones) is to bring about the development of the female sex organs, the breasts, the pattern of body hair in women, and the distribution of fat around the body. Many stages in the menstrual cycle are directed by oestrogen. It encourages the growth of the endometrium (lining of the womb) early in the cycle, and makes the fimbriae (end) of the Fallopian tube move towards the ovarian follicle, to help guide the egg into the tube. It helps to make muscles contract, and thus aids the passage of the egg down the tube into the womb. At mid-cycle it is responsible for an increase in libido (sex drive) and it also makes the cervical mucus become particularly sperm-friendly. The mucus thins, and the sperm travelling through it will find their journey to the cervix much easier.

Another function of oestrogen is that it makes the skin supple and elastic, all over the body. This is particularly important in the vagina, since oestrogen makes it easier for it to expand in pregnancy, and also gives it the elasticity necessary for intercourse. Oestrogen also causes water retention by increasing the retention of salt; and it stimulates the liver to produce a number of hormones. For our purposes, the important ones are:

- sex hormone binding globulin (increased);
- high-density lipoproteins (increased);
- various factors which are involved in blood clotting.

High-density lipoproteins (also known as HDL cholesterol), which are blood fats, are protective against atherosclerosis (the so-called 'hardening of the arteries'). Oestrogen thus acts to protect women from the dangers of cardiovascular disease, for example strokes and heart attacks, and this effect is enhanced by the fact that oestrogen tends to cause a decrease in low-density lipoproteins (also called LDL cholesterol). LDL cholesterol, acting in opposition to HDL cholesterol, leads to an increase in the risk of cardiovascular disease: this can be neatly summed up by the phrase 'HDL good, LDL bad'. Clearly, since oestrogen both decreases LDL and increases HDL, from this point of view it is very good.

Sex hormone binding globulin will be discussed in the next section, on the actions of progestogens. The other, very significant function of oestrogen is that it helps maintain the structure of bones. After the menopause, when production of oestrogen by the ovaries stops, women tend to develop osteoporosis. In this condition bone material is lost from the body, due to the lack of oestrogen. This obviously makes the bones thinner and more liable to break; in addition, because of bone loss in the spine, women actually become shorter in old age. Deficiency of oestrogen is an important cause of both psychological and physical ill health after the menopause in women. However, these days the importance of oestrogen is understood, and hormone replacement therapy has been developed to try (as its name suggests) to replace the oestrogen which the body is losing, and to prevent the changes which would otherwise occur in both bones and skin.

Progesterone

This hormone is mainly responsible for preparing the body for pregnancy; we have already seen how, like oestrogen, it plays an important part in the menstrual cycle, especially in the second half, where its main function is to assist the survival of a pregnancy by maintaining the thickness of the lining of the womb. In conjunction with another hormone, prolactin, it also stimulates the breasts to produce milk.

Progesterone, in contrast to oestrogen, thickens the cervical mucus and makes it harder for sperm to penetrate. In further contrast, it tends to lead to a loss of salt from the body, and therefore to a loss of water. Because natural progesterone is destroyed in the stomach, oral doses are impossible, so the pill cannot contain natural progesterone: it contains instead a synthetic variety, called progestogen.

Progestogens

Progestogens, which are synthetic compounds, have many things in common with progesterone; but there are also many differences, most of which can be traced to the compounds from which progestogens are derived. Testosterone, the male sex hormone, is the source of most progestogens. Although this sounds strange, the difference between male and female hormones is not that great, and in fact 'female' hormones are being used in the development of the 'male pill', as is discussed in Chapter 13. In addition, all women do have a small amount of testosterone normally circulating in their bodies.

There is, however, one problem with the synthesis of progestogens from testosterone: it proved extremely difficult to remove all the 'male' characteristics. As a result the effect of these synthetic progestogens in the body was not identical to that of progesterone: they have also had 'androgenic' effects. Generally speaking, the term 'androgenic' is used to describe male characteristics as applied to women. This explains why progestogens are normally associated with side-effects such as acne and excess hair. They may also cause weight gain, since they can increase the appetite. (Oestrogen can cause weight gain, but by increasing water retention.) In certain women, these progestogens may reduce libido. The other very important effect of progestogens is a bad one: they raise LDL cholesterol and lower HDL cholesterol. This promotes the development of cardiovascular disease (such as heart attacks and strokes).

We mentioned above that oestrogens increase the production by the liver of sex hormone binding globulin (SHBG). SHBG tends to 'mop up' circulating testosterone and progestogens, thus reducing androgenic effects (acne, excess hair, etc.). Unfortunately, progestogens counteract the rise in SHBG caused by oestrogen. Thus, oestrogen and progestogen act against each other. When put together, as in the combined pill, whichever of the two is stronger (because of either a higher dose or a greater potency) will determine the net effect of a given pill (see below).

However, in the last few years scientists have produced a new 'generation' of progestogens which behave quite differently from the ones we have had up till now. In simple terms, it finally proved possible to get rid of the unwanted 'male' aspects of progestogens, thereby preventing the constant battle between oestrogen and progestogen. These new progestogens are described as 'highly specific': this means that they do not have the undesirable androgenic side-effects of the older ones. At this point we must remind you of an important concept:

Oestrogens and progestogens in the pill interact with each other, and therefore the actual observable effects will depend on the doses of both hormones and also the exact type of progestogen.

In this context, there is no point in considering them in isolation. In practice, this means that in certain combinations there will be an overall 'oestrogenic bias' or 'dominance' while in others there will be an overall 'progestogenic bias' or 'dominance'. This will govern, to a great extent, the kind of side-effects a woman will experience on a particular brand, and it may also affect potential health risks.

In those pill brands which contain the older progestogens, progestogen and oestrogen struggle against each other, as their effects tend to conflict. Whichever of the two is 'stronger' will determine the characteristics of that brand. In pill brands containing the new progestogens this effect is greatly reduced, since they basically lack a progestogenic bias and have very few, if any, androgenic effects.

One undesirable effect of modern pills (that is, those with less than 40 micrograms of oestrogen) which contain the older progestogens is that they tend to lower slightly a woman's HDL cholesterol. They also tend to slightly raise the blood sugar by affecting the hormone insulin. Both these changes might tend to increase the risk of disease of the arteries (discussed in the next chapter), but the effect is small. They also have a tendency to slightly reduce the effect of oestrogen on sex hormone binding globulin (SHBG); this too is undesirable, since it may increase the 'androgenic' side-effects. The newest pills, containing the latest progestogens (which are desogestrel, gesto-dene and norgestimate), do not behave in this way; indeed, the effects of the progestogen are barely noticeable. Women using these pills have normal, even slightly raised, levels of HDL cholesterol and SHBG and their blood sugar levels are much less affected.

In the next chapter we will look in detail at the suggestion that, despite their reduced metabolic effects, the pills containing the newest progestogens may increase the risk of deep vein thrombosis (blood clots in the veins). This whole issue has become very complex and it therefore merits a section of its own. Meanwhile, what has emerged is that, if we leave aside the issue of arteries and veins for a moment, these newer formulations produce fewer of the niggling, so-called 'minor', side-effects (which are not at all minor to the women who experience them). This is where the newest pills have their greatest advantage. We shall discuss the differences between individual formulations in detail in Chapter 4. In the mean time we must consider the risks and benefits of being on the pill.

The Combined Pill: Weighing up the Pros and Cons

More than sixty million women world-wide are on the pill, and 200 million are estimated to have used it since it was first introduced. No other medication has been taken regularly by so many women, nor has any medication been studied so closely. There are both risks and benefits in taking the pill, which you will want to consider, taking into account your own family and medical history, and the sort of life you lead. These are the kinds of things you will need to think about when making a decision about any form of contraception, not just the pill.

There have been numerous scares about the pill—some justified, but most blown up out of all proportion by the media. It is important to remember that there are positive health benefits as well as some dangers. We will look at the risks first, and then the benefits.

The possible health risks of the pill

Cardiovascular disease (heart and blood vessels)

The first reported serious health risk, in the 1960s, was the effect of the pill on blood-clotting, particularly in veins. Scientists at first believed that the risk was entirely due to the oestrogen in the pill, so they lowered the amount from 150 micrograms to 50 micrograms. In the 1970s it was however shown that a risk of clotting in the arteries remained; since the dose of oestrogen was now always 50 micrograms, it was possible to show that the critical factors which made one formulation more risky than another were the dose and type of progestogen. Companies therefore had to try to lower the dose of progestogen, and to improve the progestogens in use.

Early research missed one important factor: smoking. Smoking was very fashionable in the 1960s and 1970s, as its risks were not understood, and taking the pill was also a rather fashionable, avant-garde thing to do (a sign of the 'liberated' woman). Fashion-conscious women were therefore likely to be both taking the pill and smoking; astonishingly, this association persists today. Later studies showed that the single most important risk factor for developing disease of the heart and arteries is smoking: women under 50 who smoke are in fact three times more at risk of stroke than those who do not smoke. Early analysis of the risk due to the pill did not take smoking into account. However, when the analyses were redone bearing in mind the evidence relating to smoking, the risks resulting from the pill were greatly reduced. For non-smokers under the age of 35 they disappeared almost entirely. One should also remember that these studies were investigating pills which still contained 50 micrograms or more of oestrogen and more progestogen than is used in pills today. It is reasonable then to assume that the risks will be even less for women using low-dose pills.

The pill can increase the risk of cardiovascular disease in a number of ways, and although they are quite complex, we must consider them. Yet again the effects of oestrogen and progestogen, and what happens when they are combined, are the significant factors.

Disease of the heart and arteries develops through a combination of two elements. On the one hand, the blood acquires an increased tendency to form clots, which may block off a blood vessel and therefore starve part of the body of its food and oxygen. On the other, blood vessels increasingly tend to become 'silted up' and therefore narrower. This both reduces the amount of blood and therefore food and oxygen reaching that part of the body, and will also permit smaller blood clots than before to block the blood vessel totally and cut off supplies.

Exactly how much damage is caused by blood clots or narrowing of the vessels is dependent on the location of the vessels. The worst places are obviously the heart and the brain. If the arteries leading to the heart become narrowed, there will be a reduction in the activity of the heart muscle: this leads to angina. In addition, the heart will have to work harder to push blood out around the body, so the person's blood pressure will rise. If there is a blockage in one or more of those arteries leading to the heart, part of the heart muscle withers due to lack of oxygen and food, and a heart attack results. If the arteries leading to the brain become narrowed a person is likely to develop a clot and then vital oxygen and food supplies to that part of the brain will be cut off, resulting in a stroke.

Narrowing of arteries is called 'atherosclerosis', and a clot forming in a blood vessel is called a 'thrombosis'. Atherosclerosis appears to happen, and to have its significant effects, mostly in arteries, but thrombosis can occur in both arteries and veins. (Arteries bring fresh blood to a part of the body, while veins take the used blood back to the heart to be replenished with oxygen and food, before being pumped out again.)

Blood vessels can be affected in various ways by both oestrogen and progestogens. The effect of oestrogen tends to be an increase in the tendency of the blood to clot, particularly in veins. This is because oestrogen increases the production of various blood-clotting factors in the blood, although a simultaneous increase in some of the factors which cause the breakdown of blood clots partly offsets this. There seems to be a direct relationship between the risk of a venous thrombosis and the dose of oestrogen in the pill, and, until the 'scare' in October 1995, it had been thought that the type of progestogen did not have much effect (see below). It seems that the most important other factors leading to venous thrombosis are pregnancy, obesity, immobility and a genetic tendency to clotting, which will be discussed later. The most common manifestation of the increased risk is a venous thrombosis in the calf (called a 'deep vein thrombosis' or DVT): if you get a sudden severe pain and swelling of a calf you should always go to a doctor. The clot itself is not so hazardous; the real danger lies in the fact that it may become dislodged and move on. In such a case it might become trapped in the lungs and cause what is known as a 'pulmonary embolism', a dangerous, though rare, condition. Studies have shown that the lower the dose of oestrogen, the lower the risk of a venous thrombosis. What is more, the actual risk of a thrombosis in a woman using low-dose pills has been found to be very low, certainly half that of pregnancy. Furthermore, within a couple of weeks after the pill has been stopped the effect of oestrogen on venous thrombosis has been shown to disappear.

Arterial disease, such as heart attack or stroke, is more complicated, and we must take into account the effects of oestrogen, progestogens, and smoking. Oestrogen, as has been said, causes an increase of blood-clotting factors in the blood, although, since it also increases the substances which break down blood clots, this effect is partly nullified. Smoking prevents this increase in factors which help break down clots. As a result, if you both take the pill and smoke, your risk of developing a blood clot in an artery becomes higher than if you just took the pill or just smoked.

Then there is the question of the effects of oestrogen, progestogen, and smoking on blood fats. In Chapter 2 it was shown that oestrogen increases certain 'good' blood fats, the high-density lipoproteins (HDL), and at the same time decreases the amount of 'bad' fats, the low-density lipoproteins (LDL). HDL protects against atherosclerosis, whereas LDL tends to cause it. (The situation is actually much more complicated, as there are several kinds of both HDL and LDL, but this is beyond the scope of our book.) Progestogens, however (apart from the newest ones), tend to lower HDL and raise LDL. This means that while oestrogen is disposed to protect against atherosclerosis, the older progestogens would be trying to cause it. Smoking is another factor which lowers HDL and raises LDL, thus increasing the risk of atherosclerosis. Once again, it is clear that although in many cases the effects of oestrogen and progestogen may well balance each other out, the crucial extra risk factor is smoking. It nullifies the compensatory effects of oestrogen on blood-clotting and adds a further risk of its own.

Studies have in fact shown that there is virtually no increase in the risk of arterial disease for non-smoking women under 35 using low-dose pills of any kind. Indeed, there is little increase in the risk even above that age, which is why healthy non-smoking women are now allowed to continue with the pill up to the age of 50. Smokers are at greater risk, though, and must therefore stop taking the pill when they reach the age of 35. Their risk at that stage is greater than that of a 45-year-old non-smoker; that is, smoking effectively makes your arteries feel ten years older than their real age.

> *'My father and his brothers all had heart attacks while they were still quite young. My father had his when he was only 40, but luckily he survived. All the relatives on my mother's side were OK, though. I was very worried about going on the pill, but the blood tests all came back normal, so the doctor said it was OK.'*

Arterial disease is also associated with other risk factors, however, including a family history of a parent or sibling who has suffered a stroke or heart attack below the age of 45, severe obesity, and abnormal levels of blood fats (when not on the pill). If a woman who has these risk factors takes the pill, she may be at increased risk of arterial disease; for this reason it is vital that your full medical and family history are known before you start the pill. Such 'high risk' women should have a blood test to check their blood fats and sometimes blood-clotting factors before starting the pill. In general, however, it would not be considered necessary to do any blood tests unless there was something in your history to suggest that you might be at an increased risk. Since risk factors are cumulative, the risk for you would be higher if, for example, you had a family history of a parent who had a stroke at the age of 40, and you yourself smoke, than if only one of those factors were present. This needs to be taken into account when considering a woman's suitability for the pill.

Although all low-dose pills carry a low risk of arterial disease, it has long been speculated that the newest pills, containing the new progestogens—desogestrel, gestodene and norgestimate—should be associated with even less risk. As we mentioned previously, these, unlike the older progestogens, cause neither a lowering of HDL, a rise in LDL, nor any significant change in blood sugar. On the contrary, some studies have suggested that they actually cause an increase in HDL. This optimism was a major factor influencing the view that these pills can be taken up to the age of 50, provided the woman does not smoke and has no other risk factors for arterial disease. At last, we have confirmation that this is indeed the case. A recent study has shown that users of the newest pills were actually at one-third of the risk of one important type of arterial disease (heart attack), compared with users of pills containing the older progestogens. This is very reassuring, especially in view of the October 1995 'pill scare', which will be discussed below. It reinforces the view that such pills are to be preferred for women who have risk factors for arterial disease (e.g. smoking, family history of strokes and heart attacks and so on.) However, since smoking is such a strong risk factor in itself, the rule of stopping the pill at 35 if you smoke still holds for these pills.

The October 1995 'Pill scare'

In October 1995 the United Kingdom Committee of Safety of Medicines (CSM), which is a government 'watchdog', issued a statement saying that the risk of venous thromboembolism was doubled in users of gestodene and desogestrel-containing pills. (The term 'venous thromboembolism' or 'VTE' for short is a collective way of describing both venous thrombosis and pulmonary embolism, which have been discussed on page 23.)

TABLE 3.1 Risk of developing venous thromboembolism—yearly

	No. of cases per 100,000 women
Women not taking any hormones	5–11
Women taking levonorgestrel/ norethisterone (older progestogen) COCs	15
Women taking gestodene/ desogestrel (i.e. newest) COCs	30
Pregnant women	60
NB: in studies performed in the early 1980s, Women taking levonorgestrel/ norethisterone (i.e. older progestogen) COCs	30

The studies which the CSM looked at were carried out in the late 1980s and early 1990s, which were the years during which the newest pills came onto the market. They compared the current risk of venous thrombosis and embolism (VTE) with the newest pills (thirty cases per hundred thousand women a year) with the current risk of VTE with the older pills (fifteen cases per hundred thousand per year) and stated that the risk with the new pills was doubled.

What you will notice immediately from Table 3.1 is that until these new pills arrived, the older pills were thought to give a risk of VTE of thirty cases per hundred thousand women per year. So, in fact, the first thing to say is that the risk had not doubled with the new pills, but that the risk associated with the older pills seems, for some reason, to have *halved* in the last ten years. We think you'll agree that's not quite the same thing. Would women have gone into a panic, stopped their pills, got pregnant, because a group of pills had been found to be even safer? Would every newspaper in the country have carried the story on the front page? Doesn't sound so likely, does it?

We'll look at why the risk of the older pills might have halved in a moment. First of all, let's take the worst-case scenario: that it's actually true that the risk of VTE is thirty cases per hundred thousand new pill users per year. We'd like to point out to you that the vast majority of clots in the veins don't turn into anything else—admittedly, they are painful, you end up having treatment, and there are unpleasant results, such as having to use anticoagulant medication if you want to be pregnant. But they are very unlikely to kill you (in fact, the odds are 60 to 1 in favour of you surviving). Now look at Table 3.2, showing you the number of deaths due to various causes *per million* women between the ages of 15 and 44 (that is, who might use the pill).

TABLE 3.2 Deaths per million women aged 15–44 from various causes in 1992, England and Wales

Cause of death	Deaths per million
Acute myocardial infarction (heart attacks)	39
Strokes	8
Venous thromboembolism (VTE)	14
Ovarian cancer	'48
Pregnancy	60
Home accidents	40
Road deaths	80
Smoking-related disease, for women aged 35	1,670
Related to pill use	10 (approx)

As you can see, everything else pales into insignificance compared with smoking. But look at the other risks women take every day—car accidents, accidents at home, pregnancy—all greater than that of being on the pill. The other thing we would like you to notice is how few women die of venous thrombosis compared with arterial problems such as heart attacks and strokes. Remember that the newest pills are associated with only one-third of the risk of arterial problems, compared with the older pills. Now the equation looks a little different.

It has to be said that when the CSM reviewed the studies on the risk of VTE in 1995, they did not have available the results of the study actually showing the reduction in risk of arterial disease, although many experts throughout the world advised that it was likely this would be the case. At the time of writing, we still await their response in the light of the newer evidence. Most other parts of the world (including the United States and Europe) did not restrict the use of the newer pills, even though they had seen the same studies in 1995.

Now let's look at just why the older pills now appear to be safer.

First of all, it should be said that this is really the first time there has been a suggestion that progestogen has an effect on clotting in veins rather than arteries. Until now the evidence has all shown that the important factor for veins is oestrogen.

The first thing to look at is the women who were being prescribed the two kinds of pills. In the mid-1980s, the newer progestogens came on the market, complete with a fanfare of publicity about how safe they were going to be for 'heart disease', how good for side-effects and so on. Now, as you've seen, the situation regarding the difference between disease of the arteries and veins is pretty complicated, and it is likely that even many doctors were not entirely clear about it in their own minds. So there was a general assumption that these newer pills were 'safer'. But safer for what? We had all the indications that they would be better for arterial problems (better effect on lipids and blood sugar), but, of course, these things do not affect the risk of clots in the veins. In all the excitement, it was often forgotten that there was no earthly reason why the new pills should be any safer for clots in veins—after all, they contained the same amounts of *oestrogen* as the older ones, it was only that the progestogens were different.

So a tendency started to develop where all the women who had risk factors for any kind of arterial *or venous* disease would be put on the newer pills, whereas the older pills were reserved for those women who were perceived to be at less risk. What a surprise, then, that more clots in the veins appeared to occur in women on the new pills—they were at highest risk and some perhaps shouldn't have been on the pill at all.

Another trend was that doctors began to feel that actually all women would benefit by using the newest pills from the beginning—after all, why drive a Mini if you can have a Rolls Royce? They may both get you from A to B, but the drive in the Rolls will be much more pleasant. So first-time pill users started to be put straight onto new pills. This was very important. If you recall, during the height of the 'pill scare' there were a number of cases of deaths in young women made public. The most familiar scenario was 'my daughter went on the pill and within three months she was dead' or six months, or two months. The common factor was that these very unfortunate women generally developed a thrombosis quite soon (usually within six to nine months) after starting the pill. Why? It has been shown that there are a number of disorders of blood-clotting which may be present, either simply because they arise in that person, or because they are passed down in families. If a woman·already has a clotting disorder, the normally small effect of the pill is going to be greatly magnified.

Unfortunately, most young women are unlikely to be aware that they are at an increased risk. Unless they are aware (and tell their doctor) that close relatives have suffered from blood clots, there are no obvious signs. They will find out when one of three things happens to them: they become pregnant, they have an accident and are immobilized for a time, or they go on the pill. If a young woman is below or around the age of 20, the chances are that the first of those three things will be that she goes on the pill.

Any first-time user is at greater risk of having a thrombosis, as she is, as yet, an 'unknown quantity'. By the time you have been on the pill for a year or two without suffering a blood clot, the chances that you have a clotting disorder are very much reduced. So what was also happening in these studies was that the women on the new pills were much more likely to be 'unknown risk' first-time pill users. However, those on older pills were women who had been on them for a while, were happy on them and saw no reason to change—lower-risk by virtue of longevity, and the fact that those who had had a blood clot on their old pill were no longer allowed to take any combined pill, old or new (and so would not be present as pill-takers in any study).

Would these biases account for the apparent reduction in risk with the older pills? Unfortunately, we do not have any way of knowing, because sufficient information was not collected about this possibility in the studies. The apparent difference between the types of pills was an unexpected finding, and the studies had not been designed to look at this particular question. Certainly, it seems likely that there must have been some effect due to bias, but the nagging question is: exactly how much? While we wait for new studies, we have to live with this uncertainty and the possibility that part of the reduction in risk of VTE with the older pills may be real.

As we have seen, the latest research does show a benefit of the new pills with regard to arterial disease. In addition, they are often better for the minor 'nuisance' side-effects such as acne, weight gain, excess hair and so on, which will be discussed in detail in Chapter 4. At the time of writing, the guidelines which were introduced in

December 1995 have not changed. In effect, these state that if you take the pill or are about to take the pill, you should discuss the issue of thrombosis with your doctor. If you are an established user of one of the pills containing the newest progestogens, are happy on it and feel that you wish to continue, you can do so. If you are a first-time user, your doctor has been advised that, all other things being equal, you should start with one of the older pills, in case they really do have a lower risk of venous thrombosis. (Remember the first-time user is the 'unknown quantity' with regard to VTE risk.) However, this does not stop you from changing to one of the newer pills if, after trying the older one, you are not happy with the side-effects. Also, if you are perceived to have a risk factor for arterial problems (e.g. you are a smoker) in some cases you may be advised to use one of the newer pills straight away. The same applies if you have problems which may be made worse by the older pills, but improved by the newer pills, for example, if you suffer from acne or unwanted hair. The bottom line is that the choice is yours, after you have considered the pros and cons of both types of pill. Do not be alarmed by the fact that, if you do choose a newer pill (in any circumstances), the doctor will need to record that you have accepted the possibility of an increased risk of VTE—this is now a medico-legal requirement.

A word about Cilest and Dianette: Cilest is a new pill containing the progestogen norgestimate, while Dianette contains the progestogen cyproterone acetate, which is in many ways similar to a newer progestogen. The studies published so far have not really looked at use of these pills in any detail, and therefore no firm conclusions could be drawn about their effects on venous or arterial thrombosis. They were therefore not included in the ruling from the CSM in October 1995.

The effect of the pill on blood sugar

The level of blood sugar often increases during pregnancy, so it is hardly surprising that the pill may also have a slight effect. There is no evidence that the pill may actually cause diabetes; any increase in blood sugar that it may bring about seems to be slight and to occur particularly in women who have other risk factors for developing diabetes, for example, a family history, a history of diabetes during pregnancy, or severe obesity. Recent studies have examined low-dose pills, and have shown only very slight changes in blood sugar, which were still within normal levels (indeed, low-dose pills can be used even by a woman who is actually diabetic). It is thought that changes in blood sugar are due to progestogen; but the newest pills, which contain the new progestogens, have been shown to cause the least rise in blood sugar, so for women who are diabetic or have risk factors for diabetes these would be preferable.

The pill and surgery

'I was only going in to have a lump removed from my back, nothing serious, just a nuisance. When I got there and they found I was on the pill, they refused to operate. They sent me home.'

The question of when and if to stop the pill before having an operation has caused a good deal of confusion. The reason for stopping the pill before surgery is related to the risk of thrombosis. There is a risk of a deep vein thrombosis for anyone who is immobilized for more than a week or who has a long anaesthetic, whether or not they happen to be taking the pill, so it seems reasonable not to add even the tiny increase in risk which the pill may cause.

This only applies to relatively long operations which are likely to force one to remain in bed for more than about a week, so simple operations like sterilization, D & C, or abortions do not give rise to a risk of thrombosis. In these cases the pill may be continued quite safely right up to the day of operation (or, in the case of an abortion, one may begin on the day of the operation or the day after). However, when preparing for a bigger operation (or any leg surgery) it is sensible to stop the pill about four weeks beforehand; then, about two weeks after you have become mobile again, you can restart it. The same is true of either surgery or injection treatment of varicose veins: this is not a major operation, but it carries a higher than average risk of deep vein thrombosis, so it is best to avoid even the smallest extra risk. It is in fact best to wait for three months after the varicose vein treatment has finished before beginning the pill again; but remember to use an alternative method of contraception: pregnancy is also associated with an increased risk of thrombosis. Safe alternatives for this period would include the progestogen-only pill (see Chapter 6), injectable progestogens (see Chapter 7), or a carefully used condom.

Liver disease

One rare form of jaundice can be contracted both during pregnancy and on the pill. If induced by the pill, it usually develops within two or three weeks of starting the pill, and when the pill is stopped it will go away. However, the woman will not be able to use the combined pill again. Nor should the pill be used during any kind of active liver disease, such as infectious hepatitis. Only when tests of liver function have returned to normal and remained so for three months is it safe to use the pill.

Primary cancer of the liver (that is, cancer which actually starts in the liver, rather than spreading into it from elsewhere) is exceptionally rare: in this country it is found in only about one woman in a million. The pill can increase the risk, but the disease still remains extremely rare.

Trophoblastic disease (hydatidiform mole)

In this unusual condition a pregnancy goes 'out of control' and, instead of developing in the normal way, becomes a tumour, which may occasionally turn malignant. The pill does not cause this, but it would be inadvisable for a woman to use the pill while undergoing treatment for the condition since it is influenced by hormonal changes. However, once these associated changes have returned to normal, there is no reason why the pill should not be used. (The hormone Human Chorionic Gonadotrophin (HCG), which was discussed above in Chapter 1, is used as a criterion of the patient's condition. The 'out of control' pregnancy produces huge amounts of HCG, and these can be measured. Once the quantity of HCG has fallen to normal, that is undetectable, levels, the condition is considered cured.)

The pill and future fertility

'My friend stopped the pill and then couldn't get pregnant for over a year.'

'When I stopped the pill I didn't have any periods for months. We were having lunch with mother one Sunday and it came up; mother said she remembered the same thing happening years ago while I was sitting my A levels. I hadn't even started taking the pill then. I'd completely forgotten.'

The possibility that taking the pill may decrease chances of becoming pregnant at a later date causes many women anxiety; but there is no truth in it. It has been shown that, although after stopping the pill, a woman may take a few months longer to become pregnant, the same number of women will become pregnant in the end, whether or not they have used the pill. It is only necessary to stop the pill about one month before you would ideally like to become pregnant. However, since the pill enables women successfully to postpone having children until their late thirties, and since after the age of 30 there is a significant reduction in fertility, if a woman stops the pill at 36, her chances of becoming pregnant are lower than if she had decided to try for a baby ten years earlier. This is often forgotten, and the pill is blamed for any difficulties in becoming pregnant.

Another problem is that, while a woman is on the pill, her fertility will not be tested. If a woman is using a barrier method, such as the cap or sheath, it is quite possible that she may have an accidental pregnancy at some time, so she will know that she is fertile. Signs of reduced fertility are also more likely to be noticed: she may repeatedly take risks and not use contraception, yet not become pregnant, or she may stop having periods, and will therefore know that she is not ovulating. While a woman takes the pill all this is undetectable because the normal menstrual cycle is suspended altogether and the pill is so effective at preventing pregnancy. In this case too the pill may be blamed when the woman stops and finds it difficult to conceive, but the pill has merely masked a problem which was already there.

Another example of this phenomenon is 'post-pill amenorrhoea'. On occasion it takes more than six months for a woman's periods to return after she has stopped the pill. In fact, about 2 per cent of women stop having periods for six months or more when they are not on the pill. If they had such a tendency, it would have been concealed while they were on the pill; yet again, the pill is held responsible because the problem only becomes evident when it is no longer being taken.

Accidental pregnancy while taking the pill

A question that troubles many women is whether the foetus might be damaged if they became pregnant while taking the pill. Indeed, some women worry that a baby might be abnormal even if they had stopped the pill, but became pregnant shortly afterwards. Evidence on this latter point all goes to show that there is no increased risk of miscarriage or of an abnormal baby. Nor is there any tendency for an increased likelihood of male or female babies. For women who conceive while actually still taking the pill the evidence is also reassuring, although, because this is such a rare event, there is correspondingly less evidence available. About 2 per cent of all babies born are abnormal, and there does not appear to be any increase in women who conceive while on the pill. If you find that you are pregnant, you should of course stop taking the pill, but there seems no reason to fret over any possible effects on the baby.

Cancer of the cervix

Cancer of the cervix is increasing, especially among young women. There has been much research into this cancer during the last twenty years, but there are still many gaps in our knowledge of its causes and of how it may be prevented. Sex is the only definitely known causal factor: that is, roughly speaking, if you never have sex, you will not develop cervical cancer. This is of course an impractical option for most women. The relation of sex and sexual behaviour to cervical cancer is an extremely complicated matter. The original, simple theory, that the earlier a woman starts to have sex, and the more men she has sex with, the more likely she is to get cervical cancer, was abandoned when it was found that some women who had only ever had sex with one man had still developed cervical cancer. In an attempt to discover the reason for this, the concept of the 'high-risk male' was generated. This can be summarized as follows: the more women a man has sex with, the more likely that some of these women might get cervical cancer. Thus the number of sexual partners men have is just as important as the number of partners a woman has.

Unfortunately, we still do not know what it is about sex that is so risky, although a number of suggestions have been made, from sperm to bacteria to viruses. At present, the genital wart or human papillomavirus (HPV) seems to be the most likely candidate; yet it cannot produce cancer on its own. When a papillomavirus causes cancer in animals there is always another factor involved. For example, bovine papillomavirus can cause stomach cancer in cows, but only if they eat bracken as well. Increasing amounts of evidence suggest that in women smoking may often be the extra factor.

Smoking was not considered in the early pill studies of cervical cancer, just as it was ignored in relation to the risks of arterial disease. However, as has already been stated, women who use the pill are known to be more likely to smoke than non-users. Pill users are also unlikely to use sheaths, which are known to protect against cervical cancer, presumably because they help prevent the transmission of some sexually acquired diseases. They will clearly be at risk, in comparison with users of barrier methods, if there is any effect of semen or sperm (although there is no proof of such an effect), since the cervix of a woman on the pill is still exposed to semen. It has also been shown that women who smoke are more likely to have sex more frequently than those who do not smoke, and that women who take the pill are also likely to have sex more frequently than non-users. Other evidence shows that pill users tend to have more sexual partners than non-users.

This complex network of risk factors has not yet been fully studied. It is clear that the pill is intimately related to sexual behaviour and to smoking habits, so to separate the effects of these from that of the pill is something of a problem. One should therefore be wary of accepting studies which implicate the pill as a risk factor for cervical cancer without qualification; smoking has a greater effect. To account for all the other factors in a single study would be a formidable task; among other things it would be necessary to find out how many partners each of the men in a particular woman's life had had in the past, and how often the subjects of the study had had sex during the last ten years.

The pill is therefore implicated as a weak risk factor in some studies, but no really strong evidence has been forthcoming; if you wish to lower the risk of cervical cancer it is more practical to give up smoking. Regular cervical smears (at least every three years) are also imperative, as for all women; these will detect changes in the cells of the cervix before they can develop into cancer, regardless of whatever made those cells start to change abnormally in the first place. That is, we now have a means of preventing cervical cancer, despite the fact that we still cannot really tell what causes it.

Breast cancer

Again there is an extremely complicated relationship between the pill and breast cancer, and one which is full of contradictions. Breast cancer appears, as we shall see, to a great extent to share the same risk factors as both ovarian and endometrial cancer. An association with the early onset of periods, late menopause, and lack of children is common to all three and breast cancer, according to some studies, also appears to be less common in women who breastfeed for a long time. The common factor here is periods, and therefore ovulation. The evidence suggests that the more periods you have, and therefore the more times you ovulate in your life, the higher your chances of developing cancers of the breast, ovary, and endometrium (lining of the womb). Those women who breastfeed for a long time frequently have no periods until they stop, which reduces the total number of times that they ovulate. It is also accepted that the pill will protect to a considerable extent against cancer of the ovary and the endometrium, presumably because it prevents ovulation; in addition, as we shall see, it provides strong protection against the development of benign (non-cancerous) breast disease. Theoretically, the pill should therefore protect against breast cancer: yet there is no evidence for this. Indeed, since the early 1980s much alarm has been generated by studies which actually suggested that the pill posed an increased risk of breast cancer.

As yet, little is known about the causes of breast cancer. Associations have been made between the diet of the Western world (high in saturated fats—that is, red meat and dairy products) and an increased risk of breast cancer. No proof that this is actually a cause of cancer exists; but there is a much lower level of risk for women who live in the developing world. Further evidence in this respect is that there is a very low incidence of breast cancer among Japanese women living in Japan and eating a diet which is low in saturated fat; but when these women emigrate to the United States and presumably adopt a Western diet, there is a dramatic rise in their risk of breast cancer.

Breast cancer seems to differ from ovarian and endometrial cancers in that the risk of a woman developing cancer increases if either her mother or sister have developed it. However, so far no studies have suggested that taking the pill may increase the risk still further; a family history of breast cancer puts women at increased risk, but it does not seem that the pill actually adds to this risk. It is difficult to draw firm conclusions about any aspects of breast cancer, since other as yet undiscovered risk factors may well exist.

It is probable that many of the women observed in any study of the relationship between the pill and breast cancer previously took high-dose pills, which are no longer in use. Until recently, the general consensus was that pill use did not increase the risk of breast cancer in women over the age of 35. Even in young women, newer studies suggested that low-dose pills did not increase the risk and that it was confined to users of high-dose pills.

TABLE 3.3   Relative risks of breast cancer for low-dose pills
(*Source*:   UK National Case Control Study, *Lancet*, 6 May 1989)

Brand	*Oestrogen (mcg)*	*Progestogen (mcg)*	*Total woman-months of use*	*Relative risk*
Brevinor/ Ovysmen	35	500 norethisterone	711	1.18
Logynon/ Trinordiol	32	90 levonorgestrel	1490	0.83
Eugynon 30/ Ovran 30	30	250 levonorgestrel	14941	1.00
Microgynon/ Ovranette	30	150 levonorgestrel	15348	1.08

It can be seen that not only is there little or no increase in risk for low-dose pills, but, indeed, one brand (Logynon/Trinordiol) actually appears to be protective. However, since relatively small numbers of women were using this pill, we cannot draw any conclusions from this, and the same is true for the apparent very slight increase in risk in women using the Ovysmen/Brevinor brand. The other two brands, which had by far the greatest number of woman-months of use, are probably more reliable indicators: there was no alteration either way in the risk for these (a 0.08 difference is not significant). Women currently using, or thinking of using, the modern low-dose pills can therefore take some reassurance from the results of this study.

In 1996, a large overview of almost all the studies to date was published. This meant that all the data from these studies were pooled and analysed together. Their results did not match with what had been thought previously.

They showed a small increase in the risk of breast cancer of 24 per cent for current pill users (of any age, who had used the pill for a year or more) and a progressively declining risk during the ten years after stopping, with no increased risk thereafter. However, two things stood out as being odd. First, they showed no effect of duration of use: this means that a woman who had taken the pill for twenty years would have the same increase in risk as one who started last year. In addition, no effect of pill dose was seen (i.e. high-dose pills appeared to carry the same risk as low-dose pills).

TABLE 3.4   Risks of breast cancer found in the study by the Collaborative Group on Hormonal Factors in Breast Cancer

(*Source*: *Lancet*, 22 June 1996: 1713–27)

	Increase in risk (% age)
Current user	24
1–4 years after stopping	16
5–9 years after stopping	7
10+ years after stopping	0

Another interesting finding was that the breast cancers diagnosed in pill users were less advanced than those in never-users, and were less likely to have spread beyond the breast. This would suggest that *deaths* from breast cancer might actually be reduced in pill users.

The authors of this overview themselves stated that the lack of both a duration of use and a dose-response effect makes it seem unlikely that the pill has a causal effect. There are two plausible explanations for these results, either or both of which may play a part.

First, it is possible that the pill accelerates the growth of tumours which were already present, thus making them obvious earlier. This would explain an apparent increase in risk, because it means more cancers would be found at a younger age, when breast cancer should be less common. A second possibility is that of surveillance bias, i.e. that women who take the pill are more 'breast aware' and are also more likely to be seeing doctors and nurses regularly, allowing the opportunity for advice and examinations. This would explain the earlier diagnosis (and therefore possibly better chance of cure) in pill users compared with never-users, who may be less exposed to medical contact.

However, let us look at the worst case scenario—that the findings of the overview are indeed due to pill use.

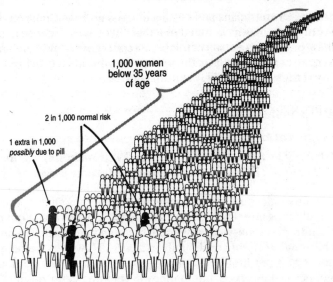

1,000 women below 35 years of age

2 in 1,000 normal risk

1 extra in 1,000 *possibly* **due to pill**

Figure 3.1 Chance of being diagnosed with breast cancer for young women aged up to 35

Think of a concert hall holding 1,000 women (see Figure 3.1). Imagine it is filled with one thousand pill-takers, all aged 45, but having used the pill for varying durations of time and then stopping when they reached 35 (a common scenario). The (cumulative) number of cases of breast cancer would be eleven in that concert hall. However, imagine the same hall is filled with one thousand non-users of the pill, also all currently aged 45; there would still be ten cases. In other words there is only one extra case linked with pill-taking, allowing for both the current and ex-use risks in Table 3.4.

Meanwhile, the remaining 989 past users of the pill in the first audience will have no extra risk of breast cancer, because it is ten years since they stopped the pill. This should be reassuring to women who have taken the pill in the past. And even then, the cancers diagnosed in women who have taken the pill will tend to be less advanced than those of non-users.

As always, an individual woman needs to assess the particular risks and benefits of the pill in relation to her own needs and medical history. However, both the Faculty of Family Planning of the Royal

College of Obstetricians and Gynaecologists and the Committee of Safety of Medicines have stated that there need be no change in prescribing practice as a result of this breast cancer overview. Let us now look at the health benefits of the pill, so that you can decide for yourself what the balance is likely to be in your case.

Health benefits of the pill

Prevention of pregnancy

> *'I thought I'd have a break from the pill, use something else for a while. I didn't think it would be so easy to become pregnant.'*

This is the single most important health benefit though it is perhaps not an obvious one. The pill has a failure rate on average about one per hundred woman-years (meaning that one in a hundred women will become pregnant accidentally in a year). However, the range is from 0.3 to 3 per hundred woman-years. You may not think that pregnancy is dangerous, but in many developing countries it is the most significant cause of death among women. Even in Britain, being pregnant is nearly ten times more dangerous to your health than being on the pill, if you are young and do not smoke. (If you do smoke and you are under 35, your risk from the pill is only the same as if you were pregnant.)

Prevention of ectopic pregnancy

An ectopic pregnancy is a pregnancy in the Fallopian tube (see Chapter 1), and is extremely dangerous: if not treated early enough it can cause death. Because the pill stops you ovulating and is so effective, it obviously protects against ectopic pregnancy.

Protection against pelvic inflammatory disease (PID)

Pelvic inflammatory disease (salpingitis), or PID, is the term used to describe an infection of the Fallopian tubes. There may be no symptoms for some time, but then pain and sometimes fever may develop. The inflammation can cause the sides of the tubes to stick to each other, thus becoming blocked.

Women using the pill have only half the risk of developing PID compared with non-users. This is probably because it thickens the cervical mucus, preventing not only sperm from getting through, but also bacteria that might cause infection. It may at first seem odd, but since PID is a major cause of infertility, taking the pill can actually protect your fertility.

Fewer problems with periods

'I had terrible problems with my periods before I went on the pill. Every month I was laid out for two days, could hardly move. The doctor gave me pain-killers, but they weren't much help. Now I hardly notice periods at all.'

'My periods were so heavy I had to change my super-absorbent towels every hour in the day, and wear two together at night. It was so embarrassing: I couldn't go anywhere if I wasn't sure I'd be able to find a loo at regular intervals, and then there was the problem of carrying all this stuff around. Eventually I begged the doctor to let me try the pill as I'd heard friends say their periods were lighter on it. I can't begin to tell you how it changed my life: now I can go anywhere, do anything. My confidence has increased—not to mention the money I save each month!'

The pill has been shown to help 90 per cent of women who have painful periods (dysmenorrhoea). It also reduces the blood flow and so helps to prevent anaemia: women on the pill lose only about half as much iron from their blood because of their lighter periods.

Relief from pre-menstrual syndrome (PMS)

'John used to dread the last week of every month. He said he could tell the minute it started. I'd be irritable, fly off the handle at the slightest thing. I didn't want him near me. I felt bloated, my breasts were sore, I couldn't cope with anything. The first month on the pill was almost worse, as I felt bloated and had sore breasts most of the time. But since then things have settled down and I really hardly have a problem any more, just in the day or two when I stop the pill, before the bleeding starts. And even then it's nothing like before.'

Monophasic pills (which have the same dose all month) can dramatically improve PMS symptoms. Triphasic pills (see Chapter 4), however, are less likely to help.

Prevention of ovarian cysts

Non-cancerous ovarian cysts, although not usually dangerous, can rupture and lead to pain and hospitalization. The pill gives about a 90 per cent protection against the development of this kind of cyst by making the ovaries inactive. In fact, the pill is sometimes given as a treatment to women who have a condition known as 'polycystic ovary syndrome' in which the ovaries form a large number of small cysts.

Prevention of benign breast disease

For women taking the pill there is a 50 to 75 per cent reduction in benign breast disease (also called mastitis): that is, they are less likely to develop benign (non-cancerous) breast lumps or lumpy, tender areas. This effect is probably similar to that of the pill on the ovaries, that is, there are fewer fluctuations in hormone levels and so there is a sort of 'calming' effect, with the breast tissue becoming less active. This very considerably reduces the number of women who have to have breast biopsies taken; as this procedure is both unpleasant and traumatic for the woman concerned, the pill is of great benefit here.

Reduced likelihood of developing fibroids

'My mother and my sisters all had fibroids, so I knew when my periods started to become heavier that I was next in line. My mother had to have a hysterectomy when she was 40, they got so big. I saw the doctor and had a scan which confirmed I had early fibroid changes in the walls of the womb. I was surprised when the doctor suggested I go on the pill, but I've been on it for five years now. I had a scan two months ago, which showed they were not bigger. I was very relieved.'

Fibroids are swellings of the muscle which makes up the womb. Women of African or West Indian origin are more likely to develop them, although it is not known why. They do not become cancerous, but they can grow to the size of a football, and because the amount of muscle and lining in the womb is increased, heavy and painful periods may result. If they become large, problems arise because of their sheer size. Since they can actually cause a visible swelling they can make you feel fat; they can also press on the bladder, resulting in a need to pass urine more frequently, and can cause constipation by pressing on the bowel. They are also associated with an increased chance of having a miscarriage. Women on the pill are actually about 30 per cent less likely to develop fibroids. In addition, the pill can slow down the growth of one which has begun to develop. In such cases a progestogen-dominant pill (see Chapter 4) should be used.

Relieving the symptoms of endometriosis

> '*It took them a long time to figure out what my problem was due to, but eventually they said I had endometriosis. I was bleeding in places I shouldn't. They gave me this medicine to take, but I felt so awful on it. I put on weight, I grew hair on my face but started to lose it on my head, my skin was terrible. . . . after six months I said I'd had enough. I asked if there wasn't anything else I could try, especially as the endometriosis hadn't been too bad. So I went on the pill. I take it all the time, have a break once or twice a year rather than stop every month. I feel—and look—so much better.*'

Endometriosis is an unpleasant gynaecological condition which results in very painful, heavy periods, as well as pain before and after the period. The pill is not the most effective treatment for endometriosis, but it can certainly keep it under control and remove the symptoms associated with periods. Besides, some women cannot tolerate the side-effects of the more effective treatments. For such purposes a woman should take the pill without any breaks, to avoid bleeding, and a progestogen-dominant brand (see Chapter 4) should be used.

Reduced risk of duodenal ulcers

A number of studies have suggested that those women who use the pill are less likely to suffer from duodenal ulcers. As no detailed work has been done in this field, we cannot yet be sure how true this is.

Reduction in rheumatoid arthritis

There are now several studies which show that pill users are protected against the more severe forms of rheumatoid arthritis, perhaps by a factor of up to 50 per cent. The reason for this is not known and research is continuing.

Improvements in skin and hair

> *'I had acne from when I was a teenager, but I did think it would have gone by the time I was 25. Nothing doing. It made me very self-conscious, I would always wear foundation and power to try and cover it up. I didn't think of the pill for that reason. My boyfriend and I decided to live together and I thought we might as well stop relying on the sheath. The doctor saw my face and said she would give me a pill that would help my skin. Within two months almost all the spots had disappeared.'*

Dermatologists frequently use the pill as a treatment for acne. It can be most effective, and can also help stop the growth of excess hair on the body (hirsutism) and improve greasy hair. For all these cases, an oestrogen-dominant pill should be used (see Chapter 4). Dermatologists sometimes use special pills (brand names Diane and Dianette) for severe acne: these were around before the advent of the third-generation pills (see Chapters 2 and 4) and have a type of progestogen, cyproterone acetate, which does not have androgenic effects. However, nowadays the pills containing one of the new progestogens (e.g. Marvelon or Cilest) are often just as good.

Protection against ovarian cancer

The pill has been proved to give a 40 per cent reduction in the chance of developing ovarian cancer. Better still, one need only take the pill for a year to be protected (though the longer it is taken, the greater the effect), and the protection lasts for up to fifteen years after stopping (it would have to do so, as ovarian cancer is most common in women over 50). It has been shown that both the older high-dose pills and the lower-dose ones used in recent years have this protective effect. Since ovarian cancer is a major cause of death in older women (about twice as many women die of ovarian cancer as of cervical cancer), this is a very important health benefit of the pill.

Protection against endometrial cancer

Taking the pill has likewise been shown to bring about a 50 per cent reduction in the risk of developing cancer of the endometrium (the body of the womb, as opposed to the cervix, or neck of the womb). As with ovarian cancer, protection begins when the pill has been taken for a year, and is greater the longer it is taken, with the protective effect lasting for up to fifteen years. (This is again relevant as endometrial cancer is also most common in women over the age of 50.) The protective effect holds for both high- and low-dose pills.

This effect of the pill as a protection against both ovarian and endometrial cancer has been proved beyond doubt, and is very marked. Both these cancers have the same risk factors (that is, things which make a woman more likely to develop them): a woman is more likely to develop both if she starts to have periods young (under 12), stops having them late (that is, has a late menopause), has no children, and never takes the pill. The common factor between all these things is periods. Apparently the more periods a woman has in her lifetime (and therefore the more often she ovulates), the more likely she is to develop ovarian and endometrial cancer. More intriguingly, the risk factors for breast cancer are exactly the same, so it is puzzling that the pill appears to give no protection against breast cancer.

Risks versus benefits

One long-term study began in 1968 and has observed over 17,000 women, some of whom use the pill, while others use different methods of family planning. Some results of this study, which is still continuing, were published in December 1989: they looked at the causes of death in these women, comparing pill users with non-users. It was discovered that pill users were overall slightly less likely to have died, compared to non-users (the relative risk for pill users was 0.9). This low level of risk was largely due to the effect of the pill as a strong protection against ovarian and endometrial cancers. This benefit far outweighs all the other potential health risks which we have considered. Furthermore, it must be borne in mind that this study concerned women who, for the majority of the period in question, would have been taking high-dose pills. It is certainly a reassuring result.

Statistics are all very well, but you have to weigh up the risks and benefits in your own personal circumstances. If you feel the need of further information, your doctor should be able to help.

CHAPTER 4

Which Pill will Suit me Best?

What to do about side-effects

> *'It did seem silly, wanting to come off the pill because of a few spots on my face—but I had to live with them every day, every time I looked in the mirror.'*

> *'What's the point of being on the pill when I'm not interested in sex while I'm using it?'*

In this chapter we will consider the so-called 'minor' side-effects of the pill, which are of course not at all minor to those who experience them. Indeed, women often do stop the pill not because of worries about health risks, but precisely because they are fed up with some nagging, 'trivial' side-effect. So, in fact, these side-effects are of great importance. In most cases the balance of oestrogen and progestogen in a particular pill formulation is responsible: we saw in Chapter 1 that each of these hormones has its own specific effects in the body, although these are modified when the two are combined in the pill. Your experience of any given brand will depend on which of the two hormones is dominating the combination. Effects of oestrogen are:

- breast enlargement;
- breast tenderness;
- bloating;
- weight gain due to water retention;
- nausea;
- non-infective vaginal discharge;
- some headaches;
- chloasma (brown patches on the face);
- photosensitivity;

Effects of progestogen are:
- acne;
- greasy hair;
- hirsutism (excess hair);
- weight gain due to increased appetite;
- depression;
- loss of libido;
- vaginal dryness.

These effects are not caused, or are caused to a much lesser extent, by the new progestogens: desogestrel, gestodene, and norgestimate.

It is not uncommon for two friends to be using different pills, and to find that a swap does not suit either of them. Why should this be? In the first place every woman will react to the pill in a different way: everyone has her own unique hormonal balance, and although the pill stops most of her own hormone production, a certain amount continues, in a balance specific to her body. Each woman's body is therefore accustomed to its own natural oestrogen dominance or progestogen dominance.

> *'Jane was given Ovysmen and was absolutely fine on it. In fact she commented how good her skin was. But when I went on it I got such sore breasts I could hardly wear a bra.'*

Various things may happen if you change to an oestrogen-dominant pill after being used to a progestogen-dominant one. The oestrogen bias may cause you to develop breast tenderness, though this may pass off after a while. Feelings of bloating are another possibility. On the positive side, you may discover that your acne has improved, your hair is less greasy, and you have more interest in sex. A combination of positive and negative effects is also possible.

Equally, if you are used to being oestrogen dominant and are then given a progestogen-dominant pill, certain changes are likely to occur. Your breasts may become less tender and you may experience fewer headaches, but then after a few weeks you could start to get spots. In many cases, these problems will disappear in time, as the body achieves a new sense of balance. About three months is a reasonable period to allow for such adaptation.

Side-effects may also occur during the first couple of months if you change from a relatively progestogen-dominant pill to a relatively oestrogen-dominant one, or vice versa. Consequently, if you are starting the pill for the first time or restarting after a long break, it is important to consider your personal characteristics. Do you often have tender breasts? If so, a progestogen-dominant pill might suit you better. On the other hand, if you have a tendency to acne or greasy hair, an oestrogen-dominant pill may improve them, though you may pay the price of some breast tenderness at first. Another factor that should be taken into account is your medical history. For example, a progestogen-dominant pill would be more appropriate for women with a history of benign (non-cancerous) breast lumps, endometriosis, or fibroids. Each woman's history and characteristics are different, so it is quite likely that you will be given a different pill from those of your friends and acquaintances.

> *'Years ago when I was on the pill I got a lot of bleeding. So they changed my brand, which stopped the bleeding, but then I got spots. So they changed it again and the spots went but my breasts were very sore. Will they ever find one that suits me? I'm getting so fed up.'*

Any previous experience you have had of taking the pill will be valuable. If you can remember which pills you have taken, and what effect they had on you, it will be easier to decide what you should take in the future.

One important discovery has been the finding that there is a three-fold variation in the way that different women absorb the pill. This means that if you give a group of women the same pill at the same time of day, there is likely to be a threefold difference between the ones with the lowest and highest blood levels when measured after the same time interval. These women will consequently experience varying side-effects, even though they are taking exactly the same pill. It may be better, as a result, to give the woman who has the highest blood levels a lower dose of pill, while the woman who has the lowest levels may need a higher dose of pill. Although these two women will then presumably have similar blood levels, they will in fact be taking different strength pills.

The personal preferences of your doctor introduce a further variable. Different doctors have their own 'favourite' pills with which they are most familiar: after all, there is now a large choice of pills, and doctors who do not specialize in family planning may not be really familiar with the effects of each one. Furthermore, as newer, better pills become available, or a doctor realizes, through experience, that a different pill gives fewer problems, so the personal favourites may change.

Your first time on the pill

Within certain limits it is not very important which pill you are given at first if you are a young, healthy non-smoker, although you should check that the pill prescribed for you does not contain more than 35 micrograms of oestrogen (unless there is a specific reason, such as an interacting drug; see Chapter 5). As a result of the October 1995 'pill scare' you are now likely to be offered one of the older low-dose pills as first choice, unless there is a reason to do otherwise (see Chapter 3). It is likely that a common choice will be Microgynon/Ovranette or Ovysmen/Brevinor, which are the most widely used of the older pills: their formulations are given below:

Microgynon/Ovranette	30 mcg. ethinyloestradiol + 150 mcg. levonorgestrel
Ovysmen/Brevinor	35 mcg. ethinyloestradiol + 500 mcg. norethisterone

Each pill is made by two different manufacturers, which is why each one has two different names. Of these two formulations, Microgynon/Ovranette gives better cycle control, but is more progestogenic, that is you are more likely to have problems with acne or unwanted hair. Ovysmen/Brevinor is much less progestogenic, and is therefore good for acne, but often gives problems with breakthrough bleeding. In that case, Norimin or Trinovum might be tried.

If there is a reason why it would be better for you to use one of the newer pills, you may be offered one of the following:

Cilest	35 mcg. ethinyloestradiol (oestrogen) + 250 mcg. norgestimate
Minulet/Femodene	30 mcg. ethinyloestradiol + 75 mcg. of gestodene
Marvelon	30 mcg. ethinyloestradiol + 150 mcg. desogestrel

Mercilon	20 mcg. ethinyloestradiol
	+ 150 mcg. desogestrel

The above list shows that Marvelon and Minulet/Femodene (which are identical, just made by different companies) contain 30 micrograms of oestrogen, in combination with different progestogens. The level of the dose of progestogen is not comparable, so it can be disregarded. In fact, the 150 micrograms of desogestrel in Marvelon are not quite as strong as the 75 micrograms of gestodene in Minulet/Femodene. Cilest has 35 micrograms of oestrogen, but the difference between 30 and 35 micrograms is so small as to be meaningless by the time the progestogen has been added. Cilest contains the latest of the new progestogens, norgestimate, which at this dose is probably more comparable in 'strength' to 150 micrograms of desogestrel than to the 75 micrograms of gestodene.

Mercilon contains only 20 micrograms of oestrogen, combined with the same amount and type of progestogen as Marvelon. You may wonder why you should not start with Mercilon, since it is a lower dose; in fact this is not always a good idea, for the following reasons. Many, if not most women when they first start the pill have side-effects. These are usually nausea, feeling a little bloated, odd aches and pains, some headaches. These are, you will realize, very similar to the problems women often have in early pregnancy; and this is hardly surprising, since, as we have seen, the pill works by making the brain think the woman is pregnant. Such problems usually settle down in a pregnant woman after the first two or three months, and this is equally true for the pill; but some women suffer great discomfort during the first couple of months, and whether they started off with 20 micrograms of oestrogen or 30 does not seem to make any difference. The significant factor is merely the adaptation process to being on the pill. You may also be a bit anxious when you first start the pill, since you do not know what to expect and tend to fear the worst. Whenever you have a headache, you may be uncertain whether it is due to the pill, and all this worry does nothing to help you tolerate side-effects.

'When I started taking the pill I was pretty worried and it wasn't helped by my mother telling me how unhealthy it must be to take artificial drugs. In the first month I had quite a lot of headaches

*and I felt bloated. Then in the second month I started to get bleed-
ing, not heavy, but enough to have to wear a tampon. It just
merged with my period when I stopped the pill. When I started
the third packet it seemed better for a while, but I still felt bloated
and occasionally I had some spotting. I was beginning to get fed
up, I thought the pill was supposed to make your life easier.'*

When you go and see the doctor, how will you feel if you are simply
reassured that things are likely to improve within a couple of
months? Some women grit their teeth and carry on, but others feel
they can no longer stand the side-effects and simply decide to stop
the pill. They want a change to something different, and preferably
now. At this point, changing 'downwards' to Mercilon usually helps
quite rapidly. You feel better quickly and are reassured both physically and psychologically. If, however, you had begun with Mercilon,
you might well be feeling the same as on a 30-microgram pill, but
what option would you have? You could hardly change upwards to
Marvelon, and there is no lower-dose alternative available. You
would have no choice but to put up with the situation.

What about those women who are given a 30-microgram pill and
have no problems with it? You may wonder about the risks of staying
on a higher dose. There is in fact no evidence that it is any safer to take
Mercilon in the long term than to take Marvelon. The effects of both
pills on blood fats, sugars, and clotting factors are very similar. It is
possible that once a certain dose level has been reached, even if you
lower it further, there is no difference in health risks (which by now
are extremely small). Many women may also be happy on a slightly
more 'oestrogenic' pill, since this is likely to give them a very good
complexion. (If, of course, they develop side-effects at any time, they
can always then change to Mercilon.) However, we do tend to recommend changing to Mercilon for women over 40 who wish to stay
on the pill, simply because it seems reasonable to give them the lowest dose possible, despite a lack of any real supporting evidence.

Whichever pill you start with, you should give it at least two
months, and preferably three, to discover whether or not it is going to
suit you. If you are not happy your next pill can be chosen to correct
the particular side-effects which still trouble you. We will discuss the
common ones first.

Breakthrough bleeding

This is bleeding which occurs other than during the pill-free week, when you have your period. It may sometimes be heavy or it may be just spotting. One cause of anxiety among women seems to be the appearance of dark, apparently old blood. This is quite meaningless and does not have any sinister implications.

What causes breakthrough bleeding?

The usual cause of this is that there is an insufficiently high level of hormones present in the blood to keep the endometrium (lining of the womb) firmly under control; but it is not an indication that you are at risk of pregnancy. Higher hormone levels are needed to keep the endometrium 'quiet' than those required to prevent ovulation, so there is sufficient hormone present to avert pregnancy, even if breakthrough bleeding does take place. However, the latter is a sign that you have a smaller margin for error, so, if you should then forget to take pills, or take interacting medicines, you might well be at risk of pregnancy.

What causes your hormone levels to be insufficiently high? The most obvious explanation is that your pill is not strong enough for you. As was stated above, there is a threefold variation in blood levels between different women, which means that in some women either less is being absorbed from the gut or more is being destroyed in the liver. Absorption may be reduced if you have a stomach upset, or if you take broad spectrum antibiotics like penicillin or tetracycline. (A detailed discussion of this appears in the next chapter.) Certain bacteria in the gut normally help to increase the amount of oestrogen which is absorbed, but broad spectrum antibiotics are designed to kill as many bacteria as possible, regardless of whether they are helpful or malevolent ones, so these helpful gut bacteria disappear along with the rest. It is interesting to note that vegetarians also seem to have fewer of these bacteria, so they sometimes require a stronger pill to give adequate blood levels. Additional contraceptive precautions should be taken if you have a stomach upset or are taking a course of antibiotics; Chapter 5 contains full instructions for this eventuality. Breakthrough bleeding resulting from such causes will stop when you are recovered or have finished the antibiotics.

Forgetting to take one or more pills is another common cause of less hormone being absorbed. Breakthrough bleeding resulting from this often occurs several days, or even a week, after the pill has been missed; forgetting a single pill can lead to a week of breakthrough bleeding. When high-dose pills were being used, women could forget several pills without either bleeding or becoming pregnant (although this was at the cost of side-effects and health risks). Nowadays, the very low-doses of hormones produce fewer side-effects, but also give little margin for error. What you should do if you miss a pill is discussed fully in Chapter 5.

It is not uncommon for breakthrough bleeding to occur when you first start a new pill. Unless the condition is really unbearable, you should try to wait for it to settle down—a couple of months should be enough. If things do not improve, and there is no obvious reason why you are absorbing too little hormone, it is probable that your liver is getting rid of it rather fast.

> *'My friend Sue and I have both been given Marvelon. Sue's been absolutely fine on it but I've been getting bleeding in the last week of the packet.'*

The enzymes in the liver which destroy the pill work at different rates in different people. It is, however, impossible to know in advance whether a woman has fast enzymes or slow ones. Both are quite normal; but if a woman has fast enzymes she will need a higher dose of hormone to achieve the same blood level as a woman who has slow enzymes. Even though she may take a higher dose, she will not suffer from more side-effects or health risks, since her body will only be able to use the same amount as a woman who is on a lower-dose pill, but has slower enzymes.

Certain medicines, especially those used to treat epilepsy and tuberculosis, can cause an artificial acceleration of the liver enzymes. Women to whom this applies will need to be on a higher-dose pill. This is discussed fully in Chapter 5.

> *'I went to the doctor because I was suddenly getting bleeding with my pill. I've been on it three years without any problem so I couldn't understand what had gone wrong. I'm meticulous about taking them every day. And the irony is I've been having*

a real health binge: everyone at work has been going down with colds and I decided I wasn't going to be the same. I started going to the gym and drinking grapefruit juice—well they say that's a really good way of getting vitamin C and there's all this stuff about taking vitamin C to prevent colds, isn't there?'

It used to be thought that taking high doses of vitamin C (over 400 mg.) within four hours of the pill could increase the absorption of oestrogen, effectively turning a low-dose pill into a high-dose one. More research has shown that this does not appear to be true. However, it has been shown that grapefruit juice can have exactly this effect, but because of other substances (called flavinoids) which it contains. So, if you drink a lot of grapefruit juice within four hours of taking your pill, it could be converted to a higher dose that day. If, next day, you drink the juice at a different time (i.e. more than four hours apart from your pill), or don't have any at all, your pill will be at its usual lower dose—and this is how breakthrough bleeding can occur. The simplest solution is just to try not to drink grapefruit juice within four hours of taking the pill.

The antibiotic Septrin (Cotrimoxazole), which is often used to treat cystitis, can sometimes increase the dose of the pill, though in a rather different way. It works by slowing down the liver enzymes, with the result that more hormone can enter the system. Here, too, when you stop taking the antibiotic you may find you get breakthrough bleeding. It is possible that another antibiotic, called metronidazole, or Flagyl, may have the same effect. Taking the tablets at different times will not have any effect here.

'I had breakthrough bleeding on the pill once before, so when it happened this time, I just thought I'd better see if I need a different pill. But when the doctor examined me she said I was bleeding because of an infection.'

If breakthrough bleeding occurs without any obvious explanation, and persists even after a change of pill, it would be a good idea for your doctor to examine you, to ensure that the bleeding has no other cause. Although this is unlikely, there is always the possibility of infections (for example, chlamydia) or other gynaecological conditions (perhaps related to your cervix—have you had a cervical smear recently?).

Once all other causes of breakthrough bleeding have been excluded and it really does seem that it is down to your hormone blood levels, what should you do? Obviously, you will need to discuss your individual case with your doctor, but here are a few guidelines. The first action to take, as a rule, is to increase the strength of the progestogen, whilst leaving the oestrogen dose unchanged. If this is still unsatisfactory, then the dose of oestrogen should also be increased. Each change of pill should be tried out for two or three months to see if the problem has been solved. It is quite safe to increase the dose as long as you are still getting breakthrough bleeding, since this means that the pill is not yet strong enough for you.

If your breakthrough bleeding always occurs in the first week of your packet, one option would be to shorten the pill-free week, from seven days to perhaps four. This means your hormone levels will not be allowed to drop so low before you restart. Sometimes a triphasic pill helps to settle the bleeding pattern without having to resort to a higher dose, but you may then have other problems (see the section at the end of this chapter).

It is unfortunate that we do not have higher-dose pills (with 50 micrograms of ethinyloestradiol) which contain the new progestogens. This means that if your problem is not solved by one of the above suggestions, you are left with pills containing the older progestogens, which may give rise to other side-effects. A slightly controversial possibility is to double up on the new pills. This means that if you take two tablets of Mercilon a day, you will have a 40-microgram oestrogen pill. Or you could take one Mercilon together with a Marvelon or a Minulet/Femodene to reach 50 micrograms. This would allow you take a higher-dose pill while still using one of the new progestogens. However, it must be said that there have not been large studies to make absolutely sure there are no health risks with this approach. In addition, the position with regard to the October 1995 'pill scare' (see Chapter 3) has made this a difficult situation from the medico-legal point of view. Your doctor may be worried about prescribing higher doses of the newer pills, or, at the very least, will be doing so as a 'special case', keeping a careful record of what is being done and why, and making sure you are happy to do this.

Here are some suggestions for dealing with breakthrough bleeding (BTB) on specific pill formulations:

Mercilon, Marvelon, or Cilest (*there is not enough difference between them to warrant changing from Mercilon to Marvelon*).
Change to Minulet/Femodene; but if this still does not work, a triphasic sometimes helps. If you want to try one of the older pills, go for Microgynon/Ovranette in the first instance, then to Norimin or Loestrin 30. Otherwise, you will need one of the older 50-microgram oestrogen pills, or you might try the 'doubling up on new pills' approach.

Ovysmen/Brevinor (*which contain 35 micrograms of oestrogen, plus 500 micrograms of norethisterone*).
On this formulation it is almost more common to suffer from BTB than to escape it; and the missing of withdrawal bleeds is equally frequent, especially in women who have had BTB. This pill suffers from being very oestrogenically biased (good for skin, but breast tenderness is another common problem). A change to Marvelon or Cilest is usually enough, and if this is no use, follow the rules for BTB on Marvelon.

Microgynon/Ovranette (*which contains 30 micrograms of oestrogen plus 150 micrograms of levonorgestrel*).
This is unusual, but if it occurs, try Minulet/Femodene first. If that does not work, you can try Loestrin 30, or a new triphasic, but otherwise you will need a higher-dose pill.

Older triphasic pills (*Trinordiol/Logynon/Logynon ED, Trinovum/ Trinovum ED*).
One of the newer triphasics, such as Tri Minulet or Triadene, may be enough. Or try Minulet/Femodene, or Loestrin 30, and then move on to higher doses.

Norimin (*35 micrograms of oestrogen plus 1 milligram of norethisterone acetate*) or **Loestrin 30** (*30 micrograms of oestrogen plus 1.5 milligrams of norethisterone acetate*).
If this occurs, one possibility is Minulet/Femodene, but there is no guarantee that it will be strong enough. You may need a higher dose regimen.

Loestrin 20 (*20 micrograms of oestrogen plus 1 milligram of norethisterone acetate*).

Since this is almost universal, this pill has never been very popular. It will probably be sufficient to change to Mercilon, but if not you can work up from there. Within the next year there may be a new 20 microgram pill containing 100 micrograms of levonorgestrel as its progestogen (i.e. a slightly lower-dose version of Microgynon/Ovranette). It is hoped this might have better cycle control than Loestrin 20.

To clarify all this, there follows a list of the formulations of the various types of pill, and whether they are progestogen- or oestrogen-dominant.

Older type of pill: oestrogen-dominant

Ovysmen/Brevinor	35 mcg. ethinyloestradiol + 500 mcg. norethisterone
Neocon/Norimin	35 mcg. ethinyloestradiol + 1mg. norethisterone

Older type of pill: progestogen-dominant

Loestrin 30	30 mcg. ethinyloestradiol + 1.5 mg. norethisterone
Microgynon/Ovranette	30 mcg. ethinyloestradiol + 150 mcg. levonorgestrel
Loestrin 20	20 mcg. ethinyloestradiol + 1 mg. norethisterone acetate

Triphasics: oestrogen-dominant

Trinovum	21 tablets of 35 mcg. ethinyloestradiol + 500 mcg., 750 mcg., and 1 mg. norethisterone (7 tablets of each)

Triphasics: progestogen-dominant

Trinordiol/Logynon	6 tablets containing 30 mcg. ethinyloestradiol + 50 mcg. levonorgestrel, 5 tablets containing 40 mcg. ethinyloestradiol + 75 mcg. levonorgestrel, and 10 tablets containing 30 mcg. ethinyloestradiol + 125 mcg. levonorgestrel.

Newer triphasics

| Tri-Minulet/Triadene | 6 tablets containing 50 mcg. gestodene + 30 mcg. ethinyloestradiol, 5 tablets containing 70 mcg. gestodene + 40 mcg. ethinyloestradiol, and 10 tablets containing 100 mcg. gestodene + 30 mcg. ethinyloestradiol. |

Among the newest pills, none exhibits real progestogenic side-effects, but all vary in their oestrogen dominance and control of bleeding. In descending order of oestrogen dominance they are:

- Cilest/Marvelon;
- Minulet/Femodene;
- Mercilon.

Best cycle control is given by Minulet/Femodene; Cilest is next in order and then Marvelon and Mercilon.

Missed withdrawal bleeds

'I'd always had periods on the pill, regular as clockwork. Then they started to get lighter, but that didn't particularly bother me. But last month I didn't have one at all. I was in a terrible state, I was sick with worry.'

'It was completely ridiculous. I bled for the last two weeks of the packet and then when I stopped, I didn't bleed at all.'

Although most women are anxious when they do not see a bleed it is very unlikely that this is due to pregnancy. Indeed, even during pregnancy it is possible to have withdrawal bleeds. It is probable that, because insufficient lining has built up in the womb, there is nothing there to come away. Blood does not 'build up inside'. None the less, for the sake of certainty it is worth having a pregnancy test if you normally have withdrawal bleeds on a particular brand.

It is also quite likely that you will have no withdrawal bleed if you suffered from breakthrough bleeding during the last packet, since what lining there was has already been shed. In that case, assuming you do not have further breakthrough bleeding, you will probably have a withdrawal bleed after your next packet.

There is no danger in missing withdrawal bleeds; in fact there is the considerable advantage that you do not have the discomfort of bleeding, despite being able to have your normal pill-free week. It is inadvisable to try to induce withdrawal bleeds by changing brands, as there is no guarantee this will work. Nor is it certain that a more progestogen-dominant pill, or a triphasic pill, will achieve this, although they may do so. If you are otherwise happy with your pill, it is better to stay on it unless you find the absence of bleeding very upsetting.

Breast tenderness/enlargement

'When I first went on Marvelon, my breasts just ballooned. I went up two bra sizes. They got a bit smaller by the third month, but I still wasn't happy. My doctor changed me to Minulet and now I'm almost back to the way I was before.'

When a woman begins to take the pill, this is a fairly common side-effect, but it should settle within two or three months; otherwise a change of pill should work. A more progestogen-dominant pill will be needed, as breast tenderness and enlargement are oestrogenic side-effects. Ovysmen/Brevinor is particularly likely to cause breast tenderness, and a change to Marvelon may be enough to sort out the problem. However, since Marvelon itself is quite oestrogenic, that may not be sufficient; Minulet/Femodene should be tried, or, if that is unavailable, Microgynon/Ovranette. It would also be possible simply to reduce the dose of oestrogen by changing to Mercilon (but preferably not to Loestrin 20, as you may well then suffer from BTB). Breast tenderness in the last week of a triphasic pill will often improve if you change to a monophasic pill (that is, one which has the same dose of hormones all month), although you should be careful not to choose one which itself has a tendency to cause breast tenderness.

'When the doctor mentioned it, I realized that, because I'm vegetarian, I eat an awful lot of cheese and yoghurt. It was quite difficult to adapt my diet, but you can get hard cheeses now with only half the fat and, of course, low fat yoghurts. It has made a difference.'

Diet may also be a factor and, if no changes of pill help the condition, and you wish to continue taking the pill if possible, you should take this into consideration. There seems to be an association between breast tenderness and a diet containing a high level of saturated fats (found in dairy products and red meat). Try to cut down on these, and, if you do eat dairy produce, try to use low-fat versions of milk, cheese, and yoghurt. Evening primrose oil, a mixture of polyunsaturated fats, has been shown to be of additional benefit if you are already cutting down on saturated fats. Vitamin B6 has also proved helpful to some women, usually in doses of around 50 milligrams per day. As a rule some solution to breast tenderness on the pill can be found. However, if nothing seems to help, you may need to stop the combined pill and perhaps try the progestogen-only pill (see Chapter 6) or an injectable progestogen (see Chapter 7).

Milky discharge from the nipples

If you get a milky discharge from the nipples, this may be due to a harmless increase, induced by the pill, in the production of the hormone prolactin, which stimulates milk production in the breasts. However, you should not ignore this condition or assume that it is harmless, since an extremely rare tumour of the pituitary gland can also be the cause of a large increase in the production of prolactin. Although this kind of tumour never spreads to other parts of the body, it can cause serious problems in the brain solely on account of its size. You should therefore consult a doctor, who will take a blood sample in order to check your prolactin level and will perhaps arrange for you to have a skull X-ray, as this can sometimes successfully detect the tumour. If it emerges that you do have a pituitary tumour, specialist treatment and monitoring will be needed (the treatment itself normally consists of a medicine called bromocriptine, which shrinks the tumour). The pill used to be held responsible for making such tumours worse, but with the modern low-dose pills this is no longer so. You may indeed be permitted by the specialist endocrinologist to carry on taking the pill, even while you are under treatment.

If it is shown to be a harmless condition it may get better on its own. Sometimes a change of pill may help—usually to a more progestogenic type.

Bloating/water retention

'I can feel it building up every month. My tummy gets larger and I feel more lethargic. It gets better in the week I'm off the pill.'

Since this is caused by oestrogen the solution as a rule is to reduce the dose of oestrogen and/or use a more progestogen-dominant pill. The 'carpal tunnel syndrome' is an occasional manifestation of this particular side-effect, although it is more common in pregnancy, and is due to the water retention which occurs then. The wrists swell, and this puts pressure on a nerve which has to pass through a narrow space in the wrist called the carpal tunnel. The squashing of the nerve brings about a gradual tingling and numbness in the fingers, in particular in the thumb and first two fingers, since they are the ones supplied by this particular nerve. The condition should improve if the dose of oestrogen is reduced.

Weight gain

'The thing I'm most worried about is, will I put on weight? My mother said she put on half a stone when she used the pill.'

With the high-dose pills used in the past, weight gain was common, but today, with the newer low-dose pills, it is almost unknown. There are two possible reasons for its occurrence. In the first place it may be due to water retention caused, as we have seen, by oestrogen, in which case a lower-dose pill can be tried. Progestogens can cause an increase in appetite, and clearly an increase in weight may result from this. However, this would be unusual on low-dose pills, and is even less likely with the new progestogens: the problem may thus disappear if you try changing to one of the newest pills.

Headaches/migraines

Water retention can often cause a worsening of simple headaches and migraines, and again it is a good idea to turn to a progestogen-dominant pill.

'I never get headaches except in the week I'm not taking the pill. Then I have them every day.'

If the pill-free week is the only, or almost the only, time when you are affected by headaches, you could go straight from one packet to the next, and simply avoid having a pill-free week. A probable result is that you will not have a withdrawal bleed, but this is not important. It is the drop in hormone levels during the pill-free week which may bring on headaches or migraines, so avoiding this may be effective. A good compromise is tricycling, that is, taking three or four packets in a row before taking a week off; in this situation you will have only three or four pill-free weeks a year in which to have your headaches. If you should suffer from headaches or migraines during the last week of a triphasic pill it will usually suffice to change to a monophasic pill (one with the same dose throughout the packet). If the problem should continue, and you have tried all the above solutions, it is best simply to try the lowest-dose pill possible which does not give breakthrough bleeding.

Special cases

You should not take the combined pill if you suffer from such serious migraine that you regularly have to take specific medication for it containing a substance called ergotamine (rather than merely painkillers such as aspirin or paracetamol). Ergotamine constricts the blood vessels which supply the brain, and this creates an increased risk of thrombosis. Since migraine sufferers already have a slightly increased risk of a stroke, the pill might increase this risk slightly again. Although the chance of this happening on modern low-dose pills is extremely small, it would be better to avoid taking unnecessary risks.

It is possible that you may develop migraine for the first time ever while on the pill, or may develop a severe migraine which continues to grow worse and worse over a long period; in such a case it would be advisable to stop the pill, as you may well be excessively sensitive to its effects.

'I thought I'd better see the doctor because I had this really weird headache. It started off like a normal one, and I took a couple of

paracetamols, but it wouldn't go away. Then suddenly, I could only see if I looked right at something, I couldn't see anything around it. I think a friend of mine has migraines a bit like that, but I'd never had one. It lasted a few hours, but it worried me. When I saw the doctor she said I had to come off the pill straight away.'

Women who suffer, or who have ever suffered, from what is called focal migraine should not take the combined pill at all. Unfortunately most people (including many doctors) do not know the difference between a normal migraine and a focal migraine. A normal migraine is a severe headache, often on only one side of the head, combined with nausea and/or vomiting, aversion to light, generalized flashing lights in front of the eyes (not restricted to one area), blurring, and therefore disrupted sight. A focal migraine always causes one or more of the following symptoms: a loss of vision restricted to one side, as though half the field of vision had been obscured, temporary paralysis, numbness, a distinct tingling in one side of your body (that is in one arm and one leg on the same side, or just in one arm or in one leg). The other visual aspect is so-called 'tunnel vision': in this situation the sufferer feels as though she is looking through a small central hole, like a tunnel, with everything around it dark. On occasion a bright light may appear at the edge of the dark areas; this light will be distinguishable from the more generalized 'flashing lights' described above. If any of these symptoms should ever affect you, you should consult your doctor at once, and in the mean time stop taking the pill. Unless some other explanation can be found, you should never take any oestrogenic medication again. However, it will be quite safe to use progestogen-only contraception in all these situations (see Chapters 6 and 7).

Raised blood pressure

While you are taking the pill, you should have your blood pressure checked at least once a year, since some women can develop raised blood pressure due to the pill. If your doctor is not accustomed to checking your health while you are on the pill, but merely signs each new prescription when the time comes, you may be well advised to find a new doctor.

Blood pressure is extremely changeable, and has no one ideal level, but rises and falls depending on your general health and the level of stress you are experiencing. The doctor should therefore check your blood pressure several times, not just once, and on different days, before stating that it really is high; and even then, 'high' is a relative term. Blood pressure has two components, diastolic and systolic. Diastolic blood pressure measures the pressure when the heart is relaxed, whereas systolic blood pressure reflects the pressure generated when the heart muscle contracts at each beat.

The official measurement of blood pressure consists of two figures, written like a fraction, with the systolic first, or at the top, and the diastolic second, or at the bottom. The ideal (textbook) blood pressure would be written as 120/80; but a wide range of blood pressure is considered normal. The systolic may go as high as 140, and the diastolic can reach 90, before anyone becomes seriously concerned. Low readings, for example 90/60, can also be considered normal: there is no danger in low blood pressure, although it may cause you to feel faint if you get up quickly. However, if your blood pressure is consistently around 140/90 you should probably consider changing to the lowest-possible-dose pill, preferably one which contains one of the new progestogens as well. If your blood pressure should rise even higher, it might be better to give up the combined pill and turn to a progestogen-only method.

Depression

'I'd been feeling low for some time. Things weren't going well at work, nor at home for that matter. Jeff was in danger of being made redundant so he was on a short fuse. But then I just couldn't drag myself out of it any more. I wondered if it might have something to do with the pill, though I think I knew I was clutching at straws.'

It is never easy to discover the true causes of depression. Nearly everyone will feel 'depressed' from time to time, but some people find that the condition grows so serious that it may disrupt their lives; yet the roots of this depression are hard to disentangle from the many superficial worries in life. If you are on the pill and you lose your job, which of the two has caused your depression? The pill is often suggested as a cause, merely because most people hope to find a simple cause, and therefore a simple solution, to their problems.

> *'I never realized I wasn't 'right' on the pill until I came off it—*
> *I felt so much more positive, happier.'*

None the less it is true that some women genuinely feel happier when they give up the pill, and they may indeed be helped by a change in type. In this respect the pills containing the newer progestogens may be the most useful; changing to a less progestogen-dominant pill, or just one with a different progestogen, has sometimes been known to help. As the new progestogens have no 'progestogenic' side-effects, they should give better results. Doses of vitamin B6 are also a possible solution. Evidence has been produced that some women who suffer symptoms of depression on the pill have lower than normal levels of this vitamin in their blood. If vitamin B6 is given to such women (but not the ones with a normal level of the vitamin in their blood) their depression will improve. As measuring blood levels of vitamin B6 is not usually practicable, it is simpler just to take the vitamin for a time (a dose of 50 micrograms per day should be sufficient), and see if it works. You should persevere with this for at least two months or you will not be able to tell whether it is really of any use.

If you are taking triphasic pills, and you suffer from a kind of premenstrual syndrome, possibly combined with depression, during the last week of the packet, you will probably find that changing to a monophasic pill (same dose all month) will improve things.

Loss of libido

This means a loss of interest in sex: although of course effective, it is a rather extreme form of contraception. However, there are many causes of this, the principal ones being stress, overwork, fear of unemployment, guilt, and 'falling out of love' with one's partner. Very few people nowadays would say that they have no fears or anxieties, and it is therefore difficult to say how far the pill is really responsible for a woman's loss of sex drive. All the same, changing your pill may have an effect; you should try a pill containing one of the new progestogens, or even just a more oestrogenic pill.

'I just wasn't interested in sex anymore. I still loved John, but he couldn't understand that I could love him but not want to have sex. He was hurt, he asked if I was seeing someone else. Fat chance with the hours I was working. Of course, that only made him suspicious: was I really staying late at the office to work?'

If the change seems to make no difference, giving up the pill altogether for a while may be a solution, but there is no guarantee of this, as we have said. If there is no change for the better, try to consider what stresses and anxieties in your life might be affecting your sex drive. If necessary your doctor could refer you for psychosexual counselling.

Dryness during sex

This is connected to the previous problem as a rule, although on occasion a woman may really want to make love, but just finds she is dry. A pill containing one of the new progestogens, or a more oestrogenic pill, may do the trick; but you should also consider the problem of stress, discussed in the last section. If you know that your present circumstances are stressful, but that this is likely to be only temporary, you may find it helpful to use a lubricant, like KY jelly or Senselle, which can be bought over the counter at the chemist.

Increase in body hair

'When I started the pill, after a couple of months I noticed I was growing a moustache! I was horrified and rushed back to the clinic. They said it sometimes happened on this pill and gave me a newer one. Thank goodness the moustache has gone.'

The medical term for this is hirsutism. On rare occasions it may be due to the pill, but it can also occur in women who are not taking the pill and is more evident, of course, in those with dark hair. If the pill is responsible, it is an effect of progestogen, and can be solved by changing to a more oestrogenic pill or, better still, to a brand which contains one of the new progestogens. Cilest may be the best pill currently available for this problem. In fact, women who develop hirsutism while not on the pill are sometimes given one of these new brands as treatment, whether or not they need contraception. However, those whose problem is very marked and unrelated to the pill often need specialist treatment.

Greasy hair

Again, progestogen may be responsible for this, so an oestrogen-dominant brand should help, or one of the brands containing the new progestogens. Even with one of the latter you will find oestrogen helpful, so Cilest, Marvelon, or Minulet/Femodene are likely to be better than Mercilon.

Acne

'I just wanted to go on the pill for contraception. I was surprised when the doctor said my acne would improve, but it really has. I hardly ever get a spot now.'

'When the doctor gave me Microgynon, I was quite happy, as two of my friends were on it and seemed OK. But within a month my skin had broken out. It was like being a teenager again. I went back and asked if it could be due to the pill. So he changed me to Cilest which has been fine, the spots have gone.'

Acne is yet another effect of the progestogen in the pill, and the response is the same as before: change to an oestrogen-dominant pill or, even better, to a brand containing one of the new progestogens (Cilest or Marvelon are likely to be the most successful). Once again, these new pills have proved so successful that they are often used as treatment for women who suffer with bad acne.

Chloasma

This is an uncommon condition, also occurring during pregnancy, in which brown patches appear on the face. It occurs in approximately 0.3 per cent of women per year. The pill probably accounts for 0.1 per cent. Any woman affected by it will have to stop taking the pill (although she can still take the progestogen-only pill). The condition is not dangerous, and there is no need to stop in the middle of a packet, but changing to a different brand, or even lowering the dosage will not improve matters, as the problem is due to oestrogen. It will fade gradually although it is possible that it will never completely disappear. Sunbathing will make it much worse; and it will also recur if you become pregnant. If you developed it for the first time during pregnancy, you should not take the combined pill.

Photosensitivity

'I used to be able to sit for hours in the sun and I'd go brown really quickly. But I've noticed that I burn much more easily now.'

One rare result of being on the pill is that some women find that sunbathing will give them a red, blotchy rash instead of the usual brown colour. This is not of course confined to pill users, but it does seem to be more common among them. Unfortunately the only effective treatment is to give up either the combined pill or sunbathing.

Problems with Contact Lenses

Contact lenses may become uncomfortable if the shape of the eye is affected by the slight water retention sometimes caused by oestrogen. The first thing to do is to ensure you are taking the lowest-dose pill possible (that is, the lowest dose that does not cause breakthrough bleeding). If no improvement occurs, you should see your contact lens specialist, who may alter your prescription slightly; or you may need to change from hard lenses to soft lenses. It may take a while before you discover the correct solution, but nowadays it is unusual for any woman to find it impossible to combine the pill with contact lenses.

Pre-menstrual Syndrome (PMS)

'In the last week of the packet I would always get irritable and my breasts were sore, just like when I wasn't on the pill. Then my period would come and I'd feel better. I didn't really think anything of it, I'd tried lots of things for PMS anyway and found evening primrose oil helped the breast tenderness, so I kept

taking it. I was at the clinic once when it was particularly bad, so I mentioned it, just to see what the doctor would suggest. I couldn't believe it was all just down to changing my pill. Since then I've been on one where I take the same dose all the time—I've stopped the evening primrose and I feel good all month.'

Since the pill stops you ovulating, and therefore stops you menstruating (withdrawal bleeds are of course merely artificial), there should be no reason for a woman on the pill to suffer from PMS, unless she is taking one of the triphasic pills. These mimic the so-called natural cycle so closely that they will even give PMS to women who have never had it before. The solution, therefore, if you are getting PMS-like symptoms (breast tenderness, bloating, depression) on a triphasic pill, is to change to a monophasic one (same dose all month); this will probably dispose of the problem.

However, if you are one of the minority of women who find that the monophasic pill has no beneficial effect on their PMS you should try a pill with one of the new progestogens, and you should also take as low a dose as possible. If you find that the PMS symptoms come just in the pill-free week, it may be a good idea to run several packets together (tricycling, see page 62, section on headaches). In this way, at least you will only get the problem three or four times a year, instead of twelve. There will still unfortunately remain a very small number of women whose PMS cannot be improved by the pill; some indeed may find the condition worsens. If you are one of these, you should consider giving up the pill altogether and turning to a non-hormonal method of contraception. There is no single accepted theory as to what causes PMS, and there are therefore various treatments available. Even if the first you try does not help you, you should persevere, since all of them have proved to be of use to some women.

Nausea

During the first couple of months of pill taking this is quite common, but it should stop after that. If it fails to do so you might perhaps try taking a lower-dose pill, since nausea is usually related to oestrogen. Some women find that taking the pill at night prevents nausea, but the opposite can also be true for some people. At any rate, changing the timing of your pill taking may help. Another source of nausea can be taking medication on an empty stomach, so check whether this might not apply in your case.

> *'When I went to the clinic for the first time, they saw I was on Ovranette and said it was fine for me to carry on. They said they could give me Microgynon which was exactly the same, just made by a different company. That seemed quite reasonable, so I took my packets and went home. But every day after that I felt sick after taking my pill. It didn't matter when I took it. After a fortnight I went back. It turned out that I must have an allergy to the yellow colouring in the Microgynon tablets: when they put me back on Ovranette, I was fine.'*

Another, though less common, cause of nausea (and some other side-effects) is allergic reaction to a colouring used in a pill. The best-known allergy to colour additives is to tartrazine, which is a yellow colouring, and it may be worth changing brand, keeping the formulation the same, and seeing if it helps. Some women will be better off on a white rather than a coloured pill, even though the hormone content and type are the same.

Vaginal discharge

For some women taking the pill may increase the amount of their 'normal' discharge. This sort of discharge is usually colourless or white, and causes no itching or odour. If a discharge should be itchy or smelly it is probably due to some kind of infection, and it would be advisable to have a check-up in a genitourinary medicine ('special') clinic.

Non-infective discharge may increase when you take the pill, if this should cause what is known as a cervical erosion or ectopy (a harmless condition of the cervix). This condition is more common in women who are young, pregnant, or on the combined pill. It results from the soft, columnar cells which line the inside of the womb spreading outwards on to the surface of the cervix. Because these cells have a good blood supply they produce a reddish appearance, and when this condition was first observed it was for this reason described as looking like a graze or 'erosion'. These cells also have a great many mucus-producing glands amongst them and therefore they produce discharge. Although the condition is harmless it may be a nuisance. It is not necessary to be a pill user to suffer from it, as it can occur in any young woman, but the combined pill (not the progestogen-only pill) does make it more likely.

'The discharge was bothering me so much that I decided I had to have something done. The clinic said they could freeze the area for me and it wouldn't hurt. I made a special appointment and had to lie on a couch with my legs up a bit: I think that was the worst thing. The doctor took a smear and said she would just have a quick look at my cervix through a special type of microscope to make sure that there were no abnormal cells on it. I felt some fluid going on, which felt a bit cold, and then she said everything was fine. It just felt strange but didn't hurt. It didn't seem to take any time at all. The whole appointment was over in less than fifteen minutes.'

If necessary the problem can easily be treated by freezing the surface of the cervix (cryotherapy): this treatment can be done in an out-patient clinic and takes only a few minutes. Beforehand a cervical smear will probably be taken and sometimes a special examination of the cervix called a colposcopy will be made (this will be done in the same out-patient clinic just before you have the treatment). This must be done to ensure that any abnormal cells on the cervix are not accidentally masked by the cryotherapy. Although an ectopy is easily treated, if you continue to take the combined pill it may recur, so those women who have found the discharge to be a serious problem may decide to change to a progestogen-only method.

Thrush (candida, monilia)

This is a common yeast infection which often causes itching and a creamy white discharge. It is particularly prevalent when conditions are hot and humid, or when a woman is run down, for example just before a period or if she is suffering from a cold, and unfortunately it will also occur frequently if a woman takes antibiotics.

'I'm terrified of taking antibiotics now, as I know it'll give me thrush. But I have found that changing my soap and not using bubble bath has helped a bit. I've even changed to a non-biological washing powder. I'll try anything!'

In normal circumstances this yeast, which is present in the vaginas of all women, is controlled by a woman's immune system and by the bacteria in the vagina. However, when her immune system is weaker than usual (for example if it is engaged in dealing with an infection elsewhere), then thrush finds conditions to its liking. Taking antibiotics, which kill off the bacteria, will also help thrush to multiply, as will anything which makes the normally acidic vaginal environment (unfavourable to thrush) become more alkaline. Bubble baths and perfumed soaps can be responsible for this.

It is fairly simple to cure thrush; all that is required is a course of Canesten pessaries and cream, although a single pill, called Diflucan, has now been developed, and this is as effective as the pessaries and cream, but less messy. Recurrences of the infection remain a problem, however. Although scientific studies do not confirm this, many women, and many doctors too, believe that taking the pill creates a higher risk of thrush. Thrush is very common, and since pill taking is also extremely common, there will inevitably be an overlap between the two. The majority of women find that stopping the pill does not prevent them from getting thrush.

However, some women suffer very badly from thrush: no sooner do they get rid of it than it returns. For such women, the experiment of stopping the pill may have some value, since they will not afterwards feel that any possible solution has been ignored. Besides, occasionally coming off the pill does seem to help. Other suggestions for helping recurrent thrush include the use of a Canesten pessary routinely every week, or after every time you have sex; but by the time you have reached this stage you would be best advised to seek specialist advice, usually from a genitourinary medicine clinic.

Cramps in the legs

'I never used to get cramps, but I've had several since starting the pill. They don't seem to happen at any particular time of day, I haven't been doing anything out of the ordinary.'

This complaint is very common among women who are taking the pill, especially when they are new to it; but after a few months it generally passes. If the pain is severe and the leg becomes swollen, you should consult a doctor just to make certain that you are not suffering from a deep vein thrombosis (DVT). If this turns out to be the case you will need to stop the pill (see Chapter 3), but it is most unlikely, and it is far more likely that there is no serious cause.

Some pains in the legs may be the result of varicose veins; if you are developing these, you should avoid high-heeled shoes and be careful not to remain standing for long periods. Contrary to what many people think, varicose veins are not caused by the pill; and occasional cramps in the legs when you are taking the pill do not appear to have any particularly worrying significance. Their causes are on the whole unknown, and they will usually go away on their own, again for no apparent reason.

Gallstones

The pill cannot cause gallstones to form, but it appears to hasten their formation if they are developing from some other cause. However, if you have had a cholecystectomy (removal of the gall-bladder) due to gallstones, it is perfectly possible for you to take the pill. There can be no risk of the pill affecting you in such a case, since without a gall-bladder no gallstones can form in the first place.

The immune system

Since the immune system itself is still poorly understood, it is not surprising that there is as yet little firm knowledge concerning the effects of the pill on it. Allergies and eczema seem to be more common in pill users, although this may simply be because women who suffer from allergies have chosen the pill in preference to other methods which may cause them still more trouble. For example, spermicides, which are used in conjunction with sheaths and caps, are a common cause of allergy. Thus a woman who has a tendency to allergies or eczema might choose the pill because she has already discovered an allergic reaction to spermicides, or is afraid that she might do so. There is no evidence that the pill has any effect on asthma sufferers; and in the case of certain immune-related conditions, such as rheumatoid arthritis, it seems to be beneficial. However, others, such as the condition known as systemic lupus erythematosus (SLE), may be made worse.

Because of this variety of effects—and because the science of immunology is constantly changing—if you suffer from a condition which affects the immune system you should check with your specialist about the possible effects of the pill.

A word about triphasic pills

Triphasic pills have been coming up again and again in this chapter as a cause of problems and side-effects. Their original purpose was to reduce the level of progestogen in the pill as much as possible, without sacrificing good cycle control; but the invention of the new, monophasic pills containing the new progestogens, which achieve the desired result without the necessity of changing the dose three times a month, means that they are seldom a first choice. In rare cases it might be better to use one of the newer triphasics rather than to move to a higher-dose pill, but in general this will not be a preferred solution.

> *'I knew my friend had just run her pill packets together when she went on holiday so she didn't bleed that month. I thought I'd do the same, but it didn't work. I bled right through the week.'*

Frequent confusion is caused by the nature of the three different doses in triphasic pills, and muddles over pill taking can of course result in pregnancies. If you wish to miss a period, you should remember that you must continue taking the last row of the packet until you want to bleed. Those women who do not realize this, and just try to run the two packets together, are likely to be disappointed: there is a high chance they will bleed anyway, since the dose at the beginning is lower than at the end. Even if you do manage to get it right, you will use up your packets very fast and very wastefully, since only the last row of each will be of use to you. A possible alternative is to choose a monophasic pill which has the same composition as the last week of the packet, but this may not always work, and anyway means that you will have to pay extra visits to your doctor.

A further unfortunate feature of triphasics is that women taking them tend to experience pre-menstrual-syndrome-like symptoms. Breast tenderness, bloating, depression, and headaches are all quite common in the last week of the packet. Since most women have also experienced these symptoms before going on the pill, they regard them as quite normal and do not bother to consult their doctor. However, since the purpose of the pill is to prevent women from having real cycles, and therefore real periods, they should not need to suffer the symptoms of PMS; and in fact taking the pill, if it is the same dose all month, should relieve most women's PMS. It seems a shame to remove two of the tangible benefits women can experience while on the pill—being able to skip periods at will, and getting rid of their PMS. Although there is no reason for you to stop your triphasic if you are perfectly happy on it, if you are having any of the above-mentioned problems, a change to a monophasic pill will almost certainly give an improvement.

In conclusion

We hope you will have found help or reassurance to cover any annoying problems you may be experiencing on the pill, or anything that is causing you anxiety. This book is of course too small to deal with everything, but we have tried to include all the common problems, as well as the well-documented rarer ones. If you need more information, have a look at the Further Reading list at the end of the book. However, it would be advisable to turn to your doctor or family planning clinic if you feel that you may need help.

CHAPTER 5

Practical Aspects of Taking the Combined Pill

'*My doctor gave me a leaflet about the pill, which I read in the clinic. But then I got home and looked at the leaflet that came in the packet: it had completely different instructions! I checked with my flatmate. She had a leaflet she'd been given a while back—that was different as well. Which one is right?*'

The failure rate of the combined pill (COC) is only 0.2–3 per hundred woman-years. This means that, if 100 women take the pill for a year, at most only one will become pregnant. It is, therefore, extremely effective; but of course, like all methods, it must be used correctly.

However, as far as instructions go, many different leaflets exist, and they often contradict one another. Those produced by the manufacturers give different instructions from those of the Family Planning Association (FPA); and the latter may even differ among themselves, since the FPA leaflets have been brought up to date over the years. However, it is possible that old FPA pill leaflets are still in circulation. With so much varied and unreconcilable information about, it is not surprising that women are confused and mistakes occur.

There are several reasons for this. In the first place, our knowledge of how the pill works keeps advancing, and it is necessary to try to keep the leaflets up to date; but it is less easy to ensure that only the up-to-date ones are still being handed out. Pharmaceutical companies take much longer than everyone else to change their information sheets. They too have various problems to deal with, since, when a company applies for a licence to bring a pill on to the market, the information sheet they supply at that time becomes a legal document. They are virtually compelled to apply for a new licence each time they need to change the information sheet, and this, as you may imagine, is extremely time consuming and costly. However, they are making every effort to produce more user-friendly as well as accurate leaflets.

How to take the pill

Pills come in blister packs, usually containing twenty-one pills. These packs may have the days of the week printed beside the pills, so that you can remember whether or not you have taken one on a particular day. All you need to do is to be careful to choose a pill which corresponds to the day when you begin the packet. In order to help you remember some manufacturers provide a means of noting down the day on which you always start your packet, The most unhelpful system is that in which numbers instead of days are printed on the packs; this makes it much harder to keep track of whether or not you have taken your pill.

In general, the instructions are simple: you should take one pill a day until you have finished the packet. With the COC you do not need to take the pill at the same time each day, provided you do not let more than thirty-six hours pass between pills: that is, you can be up to twelve hours late taking your pill without needing to worry. When you come to the end of the packet you should go for exactly seven days without taking a pill, and then start your next packet on the eighth day.

During this break most women have their withdrawal bleed, although some women never have withdrawal bleeds at all and others miss them from time to time. This is of no importance, as withdrawal bleeds are merely artificial; their purpose is to make women feel that they have had a period. However, they in no way fulfil the same function as periods: missing them does not mean you are pregnant, since taking the pill prevents you from ovulating. Equally, it is quite possible to have a withdrawal bleed while you are actually pregnant. It is important that you should restart your pills on the eighth day as usual, whether or not you have had a withdrawal bleed. By all means consult your doctor if you are worried, but, meanwhile, do not give up your pills. Otherwise, you may really become pregnant even though you were not before.

A few pills come in an ED (Every Day) format. These packs contain twenty-eight tablets, of which seven are 'dummies' and contain no hormones. The advantage of this idea is that there is no need to remember to restart the next packet after the seven-day break, because a pill is taken every day, and there is no break between packets.

How to start taking the pill

You should begin taking the pill on the first day of your period, as a rule, and you will have immediate protection, with no need for additional contraceptive precautions such as the sheath, diaphragm/cap, or abstinence. The latest FPA leaflet says that you should use extra precautions if you start at any time after the first day of your period. However, on the evidence available, we would suggest that you only need to take extra precautions if you start later than the third day. The extra precautions should then be used for seven days.

In the case of Logynon ED you are advised to start your packet with the 'dummy' pills; you must however remember to use additional precautions for the first seven days, even if you start on the first day of your period, since you will not be protected. Trinovum ED is more sensible, because with this format the dummy pills are to be taken last, and you begin with active pills. You will thus be protected straight away, as with ordinary pills, and need no further precautions.

If you have had a miscarriage or abortion, you should start the pill on the same or next day (no additional precautions will be necessary); but if you have just had a baby, it is advisable to wait until twenty-one days after delivery. During pregnancy and for a short time afterwards the risk of thrombosis (blood clots) increases and it is obviously best not to add yet another risk, even if this is a very small one. However, as ovulation has not been known to occur before the end of the fourth week after delivery, if you begin on the twenty-first day, you will have full protection and will need no additional precautions. If you start later, you will need to use extra precautions for seven days. None of this will be relevant if you are breastfeeding: in this case you should not use the combined pill at all, but can safely use the progestogen-only pill (see Chapters 6 and 12).

When you change from one combined pill to another of an

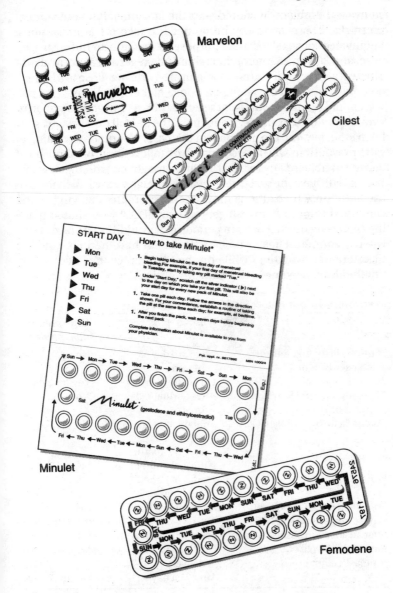

Figure 5.1 Various packets of combined oral contraceptive pills

equivalent dosage you should start the new one after your normal seven-day break; there will be no need to take extra precautions. ('Equivalent dosage' for these purposes refers only to the oestrogen dose, and 30 and 35 micrograms should be regarded as equivalent.) This will also apply if you are changing from a lower-dose to a higher-dose pill; but if you are changing from a higher-to a lower-dose pill, you should not take your usual seven-day break but go straight on to your new pill: for example, if you finish the old pill on Tuesday, start taking the new one the next day (in this case, Wednesday). Again, no extra precautions will be necessary if you follow this procedure; but if you are unable for any reason to follow straight on with the new pill, you can still have the seven-day break, although you will then need to use additional precautions for a week. If you are changing to the combined from the progestogen-only pill (POP), you should make the change on the first day of a period, and no additional precautions will be required. Those women who do not have periods (and are therefore not ovulating) while on the POP can change over at any time, without needing to use extra precautions.

TABLE 5.1 Starting routines for the combined pill

	When to start	*Extra precau-tions needed?*
Starting pill for first time or after a break	1st to 3rd day of period	No
	On or after 4th day	Yes, for 7 days
Changing to COC of same or higher dose	After normal 7-day break	No
Changing to lower-dose COC	Straight after last pill of previous packet, i.e. no 7-day break	No
	If normal 7-day break	Yes, for 7 days
From POP to COC	1st day of period (no break)	No
From POP to COC when you have no periods on POP	Any time (no break)	No
After an abortion or miscarriage	Same or next day	No
After childbirth (if not breastfeeding)	On 21st day after delivery	No
	After 21st day	Yes, for 7 days

Note: Rules for Logynon ED are different; please see text.

What to do when you forget a pill

Because of continuing research the rules have been changing in this field also, and a clear understanding of the pill-free week is needed in order to explain this.

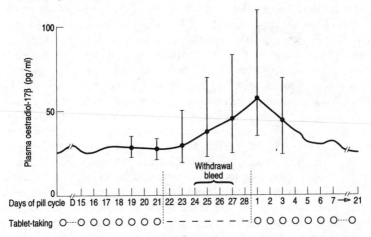

Figure 5.2 Blood oestradiol (oestrogen) levels during the pill-free week. Note the progressive rise, which is only halted by starting the next packet.
Source: Filshie and Guillebaud, *Contraception: Science and Practice*, Butterworths, 1991)

We should begin by stating clearly that pill users remain protected during their pill-free week, even though they are not taking any pills. However, as can be seen from Figure 5.2, the levels of natural hormones produced by the ovary rise quite rapidly during the pill-free week, although they drop again when you restart pill taking on the eighth day. If you happened to forget to restart, the rise in the hormone levels would continue, and could eventually reach a point at which the LH surge (see Chapter 1) would be triggered and ovulation would begin. You would need to be only a couple of days late to produce a risk of pregnancy, and a similar danger occurs if you forget to take pills at the end of a packet. If you were to omit the last three pills, and to follow this by your normal pill-free week, you would of course leave a gap of ten days during which ovulation may occur.

> *'I missed a few pills last month, at the end of the packet, but I had a period so that must have been OK. But I'm worried now, as I've missed the 12th pill—isn't that the most risky time?'*

The beginning and end of the packet are in fact the crucial times: it is far more damaging to forget a pill at one of these times than it is to forget an odd one in the middle. If, for example, you were to miss your twelfth pill, nothing serious could occur, since your ovaries are completely dormant after seven days of pill taking, and they will probably need at least a week without pills before there is a risk of pregnancy. It is of course inadvisable to grow careless and miss several pills at a time, but it is far more risky to extend the pill-free week at either end.

The rules for missed pills have changed to take account of this new understanding. If you are less than twelve hours late taking a pill, you need only take the one you forgot and continue as usual, taking your next pill at the normal time, even if by this you take two pills in one day. No other precautions are necessary. If, however, you are more than twelve hours late, you should take the pill you forgot immediately, and then the next one at the usual time, but you will have to take extra precautions for the next seven days, as you cannot rely completely on the pill during this time. If this occurs when less than seven pills remain in the packet, then as soon as you finish your packet you should go straight on to the next one on the following day, and have no pill-free interval at all. Missing a pill will have weakened the effect so this would not be a good time to stop it completely for seven days. You may find that you have no withdrawal bleed that month, but, as we have said, this has no significance. If you are taking a triphasic pill, in which the dose at the beginning of the packet is lower than that at the end, you may well experience breakthrough bleeding; this too, although a nuisance, does not matter. Figure 5.3 displays these rules in a clearer, more diagrammatic form.

If you are taking an everyday (ED) pill, you should check how many active pills are left in your packet. If there are fewer than seven you should not take the dummy pills at all during this cycle, but move straight on to a new packet (taking active pills, of course), as soon as you run out of active pills.

> *'I went on holiday and forgot to take a new packet with me. My old one finished ten days ago and I couldn't start again till today. I did try to be careful, but we got carried away last night.'*

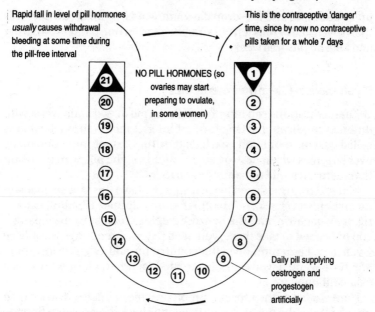

Rapid fall in level of pill hormones *usually* causes withdrawal bleeding at some time during the pill-free interval

This is the contraceptive 'danger' time, since by now no contraceptive pills taken for a whole 7 days

NO PILL HORMONES (so ovaries may start preparing to ovulate, in some women)

Daily pill supplying oestrogen and progestogen artificially

Figure 5.3 The pill cycle (21-day system)

If you realize that you have forgotten to start a new packet when the pill-free week is over, and have had sex in the last couple of days without taking any further precautions, it might be wise to ask for emergency contraception (the 'morning-after pill')—see Chapter 11.

If you have a stomach upset

Since a stomach upset may cause loss of the pill before it is absorbed, you should treat the problem as one of a missed pill. There is a chance of a pill not being absorbed if you have vomited within three hours of taking it. Unless you are vomiting frequently (in which case there would be no point), you should try to take another one. If you have very severe diarrhoea, it is less easy to decide whether the pill is likely to have been properly absorbed, or whether it has been wasted. It would be best to take no chances, but assume you have missed pills on any days that it occurs. Mild diarrhoea is unlikely to affect absorption of the pill. Take extra precautions for as long as the stomach upset lasts, and also for seven days afterwards; again, if you have less than seven active pills left, go straight on from one packet to another and take no pill-free week.

If you have to take other medicines

Other medications can interfere with the pill in two main ways, with different implications. One form of interference is through what is called enzyme induction, in which the drug hastens the action of the liver enzymes which destroy the hormones in the pill, with the result that there is less pill remaining to do its job.

Many of the drugs used to treat epilepsy have this kind of effect on the pill. However, exceptions are sodium valproate (Epilim), Lamotrigine, Vigabatrin, and the benzodiazepines such as Clonazepam: if you only need to take these, you need pay no attention to the advice given here. Less common in this country, but still a significant group, are those women who are being treated for tuberculosis with a drug called Rifampicin.

Here is a list of the most common enzyme-inducing drugs which interfere with the pill (you may need tho check the packet to find the 'proper' name of the drug, as there are several trade names for each of these):

drugs used in the treatment of epilepsy	barbiturates
	Phenytoin
	Primidone
	Carbamazepine
	Topiramate
	(but not sodium valproate)
antibiotics	Rifampicin
antifungal drugs	Griseofulvin
diuretics	Spironolactone
strong sedatives/tranquillizers	chloral hydrate
	Dichloralphenazone

You should consult your doctor if you have any doubts about your own medication; if your doctor is not sure either, he or she can contact either a hospital pharmacy or the pill manufacturers themselves. Their names, addresses, and telephone numbers are listed at the end of this book.

The majority of those women using an enzyme-inducing drug will probably be taking it over a long period: if this is the case for you, you will probably need to take a higher than average dose of the pill. Although this has traditionally been done using 50-microgram pills, none of these contains the new progestogens; a possible alternative would be to take two lower-dose pills each day, as discussed in Chapter 4. You need to increase the dose until you stop having break-through bleeding.

The high dose of hormones that you will be taking in such circumstances is nothing to worry about: most of the dosage is being destroyed by your liver almost as fast as you can swallow it, so you are not actually using the whole amount of hormone. The size of the dose is merely to allow for the extra wastage caused by the interactive medication: the dose your body actually makes use of will be identical to that which you would receive if you were on a normal strength pill and taking no other medication. Under these circumstances, you are further advised to take three packets in a row and then have a gap of only four pill-free days (see section on tricycling later in this chapter). Because the effect of the hormones is not so long-lasting the possibility of ovulation will arise much earlier, and a whole week off the pill could expose you to a risk of pregnancy. The effect of an enzyme-inducing medicine will not wear off at once, so if you stop taking one you still need the higher-dose pill for two to four weeks afterwards.

Rifampicin is such a strong enzyme inducer that it has its own special rules and these apply to both long and short courses of treatment. Even if you are using a high-dose pill, it is still recommended that you use another method of contraception as well. And when you have stopped the Rifampicin, you should continue to use extra precautions for four to eight weeks afterwards. All in all, if you have to take this drug on a long-term basis, you may wish to consider using an injectable progestogen (see Chapter 7), which would be far simpler.

If you know that you will only be taking an enzyme-inducing medicine for a short time, you may think it is not worthwhile changing to a higher-dose pill; but if you make this decision you should use extra precautions while you are taking the medication and for seven days afterwards, if necessary omitting the pill-free week.

The second kind of interference from medication is caused by broad spectrum antibiotics, such as penicillin, the tetracyclines, and neo-mycin. All these kill off the bacteria which normally live in the gut, and a side-effect of this is the lowering of the hormone dose received from the pill. The bacteria in the gut have a part to play in the enterohepatic cycle which is the name given to the movement of oestrogen and progestogen from the gut to the liver and back again. The process works as follows: oestrogen and progestogen, having been absorbed from the gut, pass on to the liver, where they are attacked by the liver enzymes. A proportion of both hormones is then converted into by-products, and these are dumped back into the bowel as waste, where they await disposal. The bacteria which live in the bowel then get to work on them, and can reconvert oestrogen into a useful form which can be reabsorbed into the blood and used, although there is nothing they can do with the progestogen, and so it is lost.

The bacteria are thus contributing to the quantity of oestrogen which is available for the body to use, and if these bacteria are

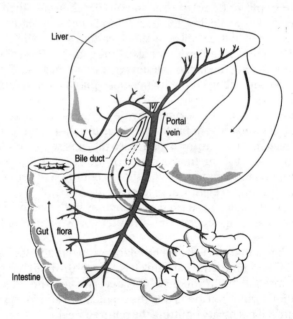

Figure 5.4 The enterohepatic cycle, showing the recycling of oestrogen

destroyed by antibiotics, the extra oestrogen will be disposed of along with the progestogen, thus lowering the amount available to the body. Although the quantities involved are very small, the result may be significant for those women whose oestrogen levels are only just being maintained at an adequate level by the action of the bacteria. There may be a risk of pregnancy for such women if they take these antibiotics, but, unfortunately, we have no way of predicting who they are. All women are thus advised to use extra precautions when they are taking courses of these antibiotics, and for seven days afterwards, following the rules described above.

However, if you are on a long course of such antibiotics (for example, tetracyclines for acne), these extra precautions will only be necessary during the first two weeks. Thereafter the bacteria become resistant to the antibiotics and can then continue to function normally, so the oestrogen level will rise again. In fact, if you have been taking tetracycline for your acne over a period of several months, and you then begin to take the pill, there will be no need for you to take any extra precautions, since the bacteria will have long since developed a resistance to the antibiotic. Extra precautions will however be required for the first fortnight if you are on the pill and then start a course of, for example, tetracycline, intending to continue using it for several months.

Moving periods

'I travel a lot, so having periods is a drag. I just run the packets on if I'm going to be away, it saves such a lot of bother.'

'I'd worked out that my period was due exactly in the week of the wedding. I really didn't need that to complete a perfect day. So the doctor said I should carry on taking the pill. It was that simple.'

One of the advantages of being on the pill is that it is possible to alter the timing of your periods to suit yourself. You can either avoid a period altogether or postpone it to a more convenient time. If you are taking a monophasic pill, and you would like your withdrawal bleed to occur a few days, or a week, late, just continue to take pills until it becomes convenient to have a bleed, and then stop. To prevent a period altogether you have only to miss out your pill-free week and carry on with the next packet.

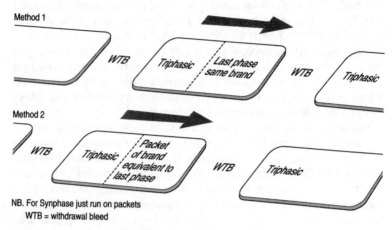

NB. For Synphase just run on packets
    WTB = withdrawal bleed

Figure 5.5 Postponing bleeds using a triphasic pill

It is not quite so easy to postpone withdrawal bleeds if you are using a triphasic pill (see Figure 5.5). You will have to keep taking the last row of pills for as long as you wish to put off the bleeding, and, of course, this means you may have to waste a lot of pills, as only the last row of each packet will be of use. Furthermore you will run out of pills sooner than usual and have to visit your doctor more frequently. It is not advisable to run the packets together, as with the monophasic pill, because the dose at the end is higher than the dose at the beginning, and therefore the withdrawal bleed may still occur.

It should be emphasized that withdrawal bleeds are merely artificial bleeds produced by stopping the pill. They are not related to ovulation, and even a pregnant woman may have them. It is completely safe to move them around, and indeed it is in no way necessary to bleed every month since there is nothing which needs to be washed away. Some women do however find that they feel bloated and uncomfortable if they omit the pill-free week. This may be partly psychological, but since the pill can cause slight water retention, this may be enough to make certain women uncomfortable unless they have a break (during which time it presumably improves). There are no problems for most women in missing the occasional withdrawal bleed.

Why have withdrawal bleeds at all?

One reason for withdrawal bleeds was given in the last section: that some women do find that they feel bloated if they do not have a break from the pill. It is also suggested that women may be reassured by regular, supposedly 'natural' bleeding. Indeed, pill-free weeks were originally advised not for any valid scientific cause but because the man who invented the pill felt that women would be happiest seeing a regular, though artificial, period. Naturally, because this break has become the norm, all the research studies looking at the pill have worked with women who had a pill-free week, and there is no evidence as to whether taking the pill continuously would have any effect on the findings. One major change that would result from giving up pill-free weeks is that three extra packets would be taken each year, but it is not clear whether this would pose any new health risks in the long term.

A few studies made using old, high-dose pills showed that the lowering of HDL cholesterol (see Chapter 1) caused by the pills was to some extent reversed during the pill-free week; the implication of this is that the risks of cardiovascular disease may be reduced if a break is taken between packets. However, low-dose pills, particularly those containing the newer progestogens, have far fewer effects on HDL cholesterol, and other metabolic parameters, so the argument may be less relevant.

If the advantages of a pill-free week are dubious, there is no doubt about the disadvantages. One of the worst is that women forget to restart, and this of course may lead to pregnancies. Withdrawal bleeds, however 'reassuring', can be a nuisance. Some women even get side-effects, such as headaches, or a kind of pre-menstrual syndrome, during their breaks.

> *'Once I realized the periods on the pill were basically just a con-trick, to make me somehow feel more normal as a woman, I thought "blow this" and stopped having them. Who needs to bleed all the time anyway? I stop occasionally, when it suits me, but otherwise I live a period-free life.'*

'I found that I was more likely to have epileptic fits during my pill-free week, so the doctor suggested I take the pill continuously. It's made an enormous difference, I hardly have any problem with fits now.'

There are some gynaecological conditions, such as endometriosis, in which continuous pill taking is to be preferred, since bleeding is to be discouraged. As hormone fluctuations may encourage epileptic fits to occur, women liable to this condition may also be advised to omit the pill-free week.

However, there is no one right answer for everyone, and the disadvantages should be measured against the advantages, both real and theoretical. In the end, each woman must decide for herself, and this will partly depend on how serious the disadvantages of the pill-free week have been for her. One possible compromise is the concept of tricycling.

Tricycling

This means taking three, or sometimes four, packets in a row before having a pill-free week. Women who suffer side-effects related to the pill-free week, for example headaches which occur only or mostly at that time, may be advised to try this method, and it can also be useful for women who have heavy and/or painful withdrawal bleeds. As we have said, it is also recommended for women who are taking enzyme-inducing drugs, since the pill-free week can reduce hormone quantities to a dangerously low level.

If you are tricycling you only need to suffer the discomforts of the pill-free week three or four times a year, instead of every month, but at the same time you will still have a few pill-free weeks rather than none at all. (As we said above, it is not yet clear whether there are any health advantages to this.) Any woman may tricycle, if she wishes to; it is not limited to those who have already experienced unpleasant side-effects.

Breaks from the pill

'I thought I should have a break from the pill every couple of years. After all, it can't be good to stay on it all the time, can it?'

There is no medical reason why it should be necessary to take a break from the pill; after all, every time you have a pill-free week, you are effectively having a break for seven days. The main disadvantage of stopping the pill for a while is that unwanted pregnancies may occur, and this is liable to be far more damaging to a woman's health, both physically and psychologically.

Monitoring your health while you are on the pill

Before starting you on the pill (or, indeed, any method of contraception) your doctor should find out details of your medical and family history, to ensure that there is nothing which needs investigating before you begin, and no reasons why it would not be safe for you to take it. Blood pressure and weight should be tested, and everyone should be encouraged to ask questions, not just about the pill, but about any methods of contraception.

Three months after you have started a new pill the doctor should see you to deal with any problems or new questions that may have arisen, and to check your blood pressure again. Women often feel that they should not bother their doctor over 'minor' side-effects, which is why a three-month visit should be made automatically, to prevent people from feeling that they need to ask specially to be seen. After this, when you are settled and happy on a particular brand, you should be seen by the doctor every six months. If your doctor merely leaves a prescription for you to pick up, you should change to a new doctor, as this gives you no opportunity to discuss any new side-effects or to ask questions. Your weight and blood pressure need to be checked at least once a year.

There is no need for you to be examined before you can go on the pill, but it is strongly advised that you should have a cervical smear taken at least every three years, and an internal examination at the same time. This advice applies to all forms of contraception, not just to the pill. If you find that your own doctor is unsatisfactory in any of these respects, or you cannot see a female doctor at your practice, you have a right to consult a different doctor or family planning clinic for family planning services, even if you wish to remain registered with your original GP for other purposes.

CHAPTER 6

The Progestogen-only Pill

'The mini-pill? That must be like my pill but a lower dose. So why am I on a higher dose?'

As its name suggests, this type of pill contains no oestrogen, and it is thus completely different from the combined pill. Its old name, the 'mini-pill', unfortunately implies that it is merely some kind of low-dose combined pill, but this is certainly not true. In this book, we shall instead refer to the progestogen-only pill as the POP. Far too little use is at present being made of the POP, because few women, or even their doctors, know anything about it. In actual fact it is a very useful method of contraception, especially when there is some reason why a woman cannot, or does not, want to take oestrogen.

How does the POP work?

Unlike the combined pill (COC), the POP will not certainly stop ovulation (release of the egg). Evidence suggests that only about 20 per cent of women will cease ovulating altogether when taking this type of pill; another 40 per cent will experience some disruption of ovulation, but the remaining 40 per cent will continue to ovulate normally. If it is not reliably stopping ovulation, how does it work? In the first place it affects cervical mucus, thickening it so that it becomes more difficult for sperm to get through. At mid-cycle, when you are most fertile, the mucus has very large gaps between the microscopic strands, so that the sperm have plenty of room to swim through. However, four hours after you have swallowed a POP, the strands are pushed closer together to form a dense mesh. Unfortunately, this effect only lasts a short time: in some women it begins to wear off after about 27 hours. The trouble with this is that with the POP it is therefore important to remember to take the pill within three hours of the same time each day.

The POP also works by altering the lining of the womb and reducing the number and size of its blood vessels; if it is very thin it is less likely that implantation (the embedding of a fertilized egg) will be able to take place. Thus even if a woman has ovulated, and a sperm has succeeded in penetrating the cervical mucus, with any luck this effect on the lining will be able to stop the pregnancy from taking place.

How effective is the POP?

The POP does not have such a high success rate as the combined pill, since it does not always stop ovulation, but it does not compare badly: its failure rate ranges from 0.5 to 4 per hundred woman-years (that is, if 100 women took the POP for a year, at most four would be likely to become pregnant). Like any method of contraception which allows you to ovulate, the success rate improves as you grow older, since you will ovulate less frequently and the 'top up' needed will become less. Figure 6.1 shows a graph of failure rates related to age, so that you will be able to decide for yourself whether to try it now, or wait till you are older.

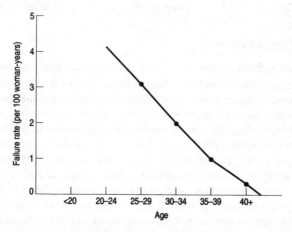

Figure 6.1 Graph showing failure rates for the progestogen-only pill by age of user

(*Source*: Vessey et al., *British Journal of Family Planning*, 10 (1985), 117–21)

It is clear that the failure rate above the age of 30 is quite accept-able, at under two per hundred woman-years. However, as regards younger women, under the age of 25, the failure rate is around four, and the graph rises rapidly. The failure rate in teenagers may there-fore be too high for it to be a good choice. It is therefore better not to turn to the POP unless you are at least over the age of 25, and prefer-ably over the age of 30. By the age of 35 the failure rate has become comparable to that of the COC (one per hundred woman-years), so the POP is recommended for those women who smoke and are there-fore compelled to stop taking the COC at this age (see below).

What types of progestogen-only pills are available?

From Table 6.1, which shows the composition of the most common POPs in use, it can be seen that the dose of progestogen used in each of these brands is lower than that used in the combined pill.

TABLE 6.1 Composition of progestogen-only pills

Femulen	Ethynodiol diacetate	500 mcg.
Micronor/Noriday	Norethisterone	350 mcg.
Microval/Norgeston	Levonorgestrel	30 mcg.
Neogest	Norgestrel	75 mcg.

Advantages of the POP

The principal advantage of the POP is that it contains no oestrogen, so those women who have been advised not to take the combined pill because of their family medical history, their own medical history, or because they have experienced side-effects on it can almost certainly take the POP. The POP does not affect blood pressure or increase the risk of heart disease, and since it does not affect blood-clotting or the blood levels of HDL cholesterol (see Chapter 5), it is even possible for a woman who has had a thrombosis (blood clot) to take it. For this reason there is no need to set an age limit for taking this pill, even for smokers, who are compelled to stop taking the combined pill at the age of 35; with this pill they can continue until the menopause. You can also safely take the POP even if you have to take tablets to lower your blood pressure.

The POP can be used by diabetics because it does not increase the likelihood of heart attacks, a risk which diabetics already face. Nor does it matter if you are very overweight; the POP will not make you put on any more, or increase the risk to your health. However, studies of newer low-dose progestogen-only methods suggest that, if you weigh more than 70 kg. (11 stone), the failure rate of the method may be increased (see Chapter 15), possibly even doubled. There have been relatively few studies specifically looking at this effect with the POP, but one did suggest a possible reduction in efficacy. Until further studies have been made, if it is crucially important to you not to get pregnant—and especially if you are under 30 years old—it might be worth discussing with your doctor whether you should perhaps take two tablets a day instead of one.

As for the side-effects and health risks, those of the combined pill do not generally occur on the POP. Therefore, if you have experienced raised blood pressure on the combined pill, or if you suffer from headaches or migraine (including 'focal' migraine; see Chapter 4), or if they become worse, on the combined pill, you can take the POP (even though the headaches or migraines may persist, you will not be placed at greater risk of a stroke, as might be the case with the combined pill). If you change over to the POP because you have put on weight, felt bloated, or had breast tenderness, you should find you improve. If you have developed chloasma (brown patches on the face) you can still take the POP, though the problem itself may not entirely go away—at least it should not become worse. It might also be worth experimenting with the POP if you suffer from depression and loss of interest in sex, despite the fact that these are not usually oestrogenic side-effects; the dose of progestogen is so small that you may find that the effect vanishes.

If you are breastfeeding, it is quite safe to use the POP, since this neither stops the production of milk, nor has any effect on the baby. The dose of progestogen in the pill is extremely small, and only a tiny amount of that actually passes into the milk; in fact it has been calculated that if a woman took the POP every day while breastfeeding for two years, at the end of that time, the baby would have absorbed the equivalent of just one tablet. In addition, breastfeeding in conjunction with taking the POP raises the effective protection against pregnancy to almost 100 per cent, since breastfeeding itself gives a contraceptive effect. (This is of course an improvement over the protection given by the POP alone.)

The POP will not continue to affect your fertility in any way after you have stopped taking it; even the 20 per cent of women who stop ovulating, and therefore have no periods, will find that these return rapidly when they stop. Nor is there any need to give up the POP a few months before attempting to get pregnant.

As regards health risks, of course the evidence is limited since not as many women have taken the POP as the combined pill, and therefore it has not been as extensively researched; but it has not been shown conclusively to have either a good or a bad effect on any kind of cancer.

Disadvantages of the POP

The pill-taking routine

> *'The doctor told me because I'm 35 and I smoke, I can't take the pill any more. So he gave me this other pill, the progestogen-only pill. He says it's safe but I've got to be really careful about taking it at the same time every day. I've tried everything. I tried taking it in the morning, but I get up late at weekends. I tried taking it at night, but that was hopeless. I tried taking it at lunchtime, but then I had to keep going to the loo if I was with colleagues or friends—well, it doesn't look nice, does it, taking a pill in front of people?'*

A principal disadvantage is that, as we have already stated, it is necessary to take it at the same time (or at least within three hours of the same time) every day, or else its effect may wear off. This can clearly be a problem, but in the end most women manage to cope with it.

Breakfast time is convenient and easy to remember for many people, the only difficulty being that they may get up very much later at weekends. If you do so, you could perhaps keep a set of pills in the office and take one when you arrive; then your timing will be easier to match at weekends. Other solutions to timekeeping problems might be to keep a spare packet at work or in your handbag; or, if you have a digital watch, you could set the alarm as a reminder to take your pills. Time zone changes can also be a problem if you travel frequently. The important thing is to make sure you do not leave a gap of more than 24 hours, and since the dose is so low it is better to take two pills within a day than to risk taking a pill late. Keeping a packet of pills permanently in your suitcase, in case you should happen to forget to pack your current one, is also a useful piece of insurance.

Period problems

As we have seen, since about 40 per cent of the women who take the POP will continue to ovulate normally, there will be no change to their periods. A further 20 per cent will, however, stop having periods altogether. This should not cause any anxiety about pregnancy, since it is due to the fact that in these women ovulation has completely stopped, and thus pregnancy is virtually impossible (this group is enlarged of course by those who take the POP while fully breastfeeding). This means you would be as well protected as if you were taking the combined pill, without the possible health risks or side-effects. As for all POP takers, there will be no extra difficulty for you in becoming pregnant after stopping. On the first occasion that you miss a period, you do not of course know the cause: you may have forgotten a pill, or had a stomach upset, and in fact become pregnant. Therefore it is sensible to have a pregnancy test about a week after your missed period, and, if this should be negative, and you have still not had a period, have another test a couple of weeks later. By this stage, if the tests still prove negative, you may be fairly confident that you have stopped ovulating. After that you know that you are very unlikely to become pregnant, so—unless you really start to have pregnancy symptoms—you do not need to keep having tests.

> *'Neurotic? I was a wreck! Every time my period didn't come, there was that nagging worry. Had I forgotten any without realizing?'*

Some women find the lack of periods disconcerting, and remain constantly anxious about the cause, especially if they know that they have a tendency to be forgetful over taking their pill. If this is the case with you, you should consult your doctor, as it is sometimes possible to bring the periods back simply by changing the brand of POP.

The worst period problem, which affects about 40 per cent of women who take the POP, is that periods become in some way irregular. This is a considerable nuisance, and can range from infrequent periods to periods every three weeks or to constant spotting. There is unfortunately no way of predicting who will be affected, or what form the irregularity will take in any individual case. However, in many cases the problem only occurs when a woman first starts taking the POP, and after a couple of months it will settle down, so do not give up immediately. Again, a change of brand can be enough to improve the situation: it does not matter what brand you are on, just changing to any one of the others may help.

These three types of period pattern may in fact all happen to the same woman at different times. When she first begins to take the POP she may have irregular periods for a few months, and then they may return to regularity for a year or several years. Later, for no apparent reason, she may again have irregular periods, or indeed they may stop altogether for a while. Any of these patterns may continue to recur. The causes of this are still fairly obscure, but it seems that irregular periods may occur when the usual hormone-producing routine of the ovaries is slightly disrupted. Regular periods thus return if the routine is re-established and, of course, if she stops ovulating altogether, she will no longer have periods. Irregular periods can of course occur for other reasons, and can affect women who are not using any type of hormonal contraception: common causes are stress or the disruption brought about by travelling.

Ovarian cysts

There appears to be a slightly greater chance that women who take the POP may develop non-cancerous (benign) ovarian cysts. There is no need to worry about these, since as a rule they are small and cause no symptoms; they would probably not even be noticeable, and usually disappear without the need of treatment. On rare occasions a larger one may develop, and this may cause some pain: stopping the POP will generally be enough to make the cyst disappear. However, if you have already had an ovarian cyst which needed treatment you would be better advised not to use the POP, as you may be already slightly more at risk of developing another one. You should consider using a method which actually lowers the risk of an ovarian cyst, like the combined pill or injectable progestogens.

Ectopic pregnancy

An ectopic pregnancy is a pregnancy which occurs outside the womb itself—in other words, in the wrong place. When this happens it is usually in one of the Fallopian tubes. The tube is not made to expand in the way the womb is, so when the pregnancy reaches a certain size, the stretching causes the tube to burst. This is dangerous and can even be life-threatening. The most common reason for an ectopic pregnancy is that the tubes have been infected in the past. Infection damages the tubes so that the eggs take longer to travel down them, rather like an obstacle course. This also means there is more time for sperm to travel further and reach the tube, where fertilization can then take place.

The POP is good at preventing pregnancies within the womb itself, but does allow ovulation to happen in many women. Thus, those who already have slightly damaged tubes will still have their 'normal' pregnancies prevented, but not their ectopic ones. This means that, although overall there are very few pregnancies of any kind on the POP, those that do occur are slightly more likely to be ectopic. Some doctors would not even prevent a woman from taking the POP if she had already suffered an ectopic pregnancy, although in such a case she would be known to be at higher risk of another one. However, since the matter of risk due to the POP cannot at present be proved either way, and since no woman who has had one ectopic pregnancy should take even the slightest chance of increasing her likelihood of a second, it seems wiser to avoid the POP in these circumstances. There are in fact methods of contraception which actually decrease the risk, such as the combined pill or injectable progestogens, so these would be a more sensible choice.

If you have not had an ectopic pregnancy, then there is no need to worry about it if you are taking the POP. If indeed there is any increased risk, it is very, very small.

Other uncommon side-effects

Because the POP is such a low-dose pill, side-effects are extremely rare; but occasionally women on the POP find they feel bloated (although they have not put on weight), or they may develop acne or slight excess hair growth. It is not even entirely certain that the POP is responsible for these developments, since some women find that there is no change at all when they stop taking the pill; but if you do suffer this kind of side-effect you should at least consult your doctor. For many years we have asked for a POP containing one of the new, specific progestogens in order to try and minimize these problems. The market has been considered too small and unviable for a pharmaceutical company to justify the enormous investment required. However, at long last, it does look as though a desogestrel POP may be available within the next year or two.

How to take the POP

When you begin to take the POP for the first time, you should start your packet on the first day of your period; in these circumstances you will need no further precautions but will be protected straight away. If you have previously been using the combined pill you should begin your POP as soon as you have finished the COC packet. Do not take the usual seven-day break. Once again, no additional contraceptive precautions are required. The POP should be taken every single day of the month; unlike the combined pill, there is no pill-free week between packets. This is on the whole an advantage, since women taking the COC find it all too easy to forget to restart a packet after the break. In addition, as we have said before, the POP must be taken at about the same time every day. You cannot afford to be more than three hours late taking this pill. If you should find that you are more than three hours late you should take it as soon as you realize what has happened, and then continue to take the rest of your pills as usual. You will however need to take extra precautions for the next seven days, for instance the sheath or diaphragm. You will also need to take precautions for seven days if you have missed a couple of pills: in this case you should take the ones you missed and continue with the rest of the packet as usual. If you should forget the pill and fail to take any precautions when having sex, you should ask your doctor to give you the emergency contraception pill (see Chapter 11).

> *'When I started the POP, I was given a leaflet which said I should use extra precautions for fourteen days. Than I was told it was only necessary for forty-eight hours, though the leaflet in the packet still said fourteen days. Now you say seven days. What on earth is going on?'*

Unfortunately, pill-taking rules keep changing, usually because research shows that a new rule is simpler or safer. At one time women were advised to use additional precautions for fourteen days if they missed a pill, as well as when they first began to take it. Eventually it was discovered that, although the cervical mucus effect wears off within 36 hours, it builds up again equally rapidly. This is why a 48-hour rule was introduced. It has been shown that ovulation is most unlikely to occur before the seventh day of the cycle (day 1 is the first day of a period), and by this stage both the cervical mucus effect and the thinning of the lining of the womb will have occurred. So as long as you start on the first day of your period, you will not need to take any additional precautions.

Unfortunately, science and legal bureaucracy do not go well together. It takes a very long time for manufacturers to be able to change the instructions on their leaflets, as they have to go through a lengthy official procedure. Also, manufacturers do not want the slightest possibility of their advice being found to be wrong, even in a few cases, because then they can be sued. Thus, until recently, the manufacturers' leaflets were still advising fourteen days' extra precautions, while the Family Planning Association (FPA) leaflets said 48 hours.

Having several sets of conflicting instructions around at the same time helps no one. In an effort to achieve consistency, the FPA and the manufacturers have been negotiating to see if they can find a common ground. In the end they decided that the best compromise was to make the basic rule for the combined pill and the POP the same (that is, seven days). At least all the leaflets will now say the same thing. It could also be argued (though without scientific proof) that for the 60 per cent of women who do not ovulate on the POP, seven days does allow more time for the ovary to be completely 'switched off', as in users of the combined pill. However, no increase in avoidable pregnancies was demonstrated when the 14-day rule was replaced by the 48-hour rule.

If you have a baby

If you wish to begin taking the POP as soon as you have had a baby, there is no reason why you should not. However, studies have shown that problems with irregular bleeding are less likely to occur if you wait for between four and six weeks after the birth. A compromise that the FPA adopts is to advise starting on day 21 after the birth. Equally, it is quite safe to use the POP during breastfeeding; it is also much more effective then. In fact, it is our view that as long as a breastfeeding woman is not having periods, she need only use extra precautions if she is more than *twelve* hours late taking her pill.

You are not at risk of becoming pregnant again until the fourth week after delivery; later if you breastfeed, because of the contraceptive effect of the breastfeeding itself. So either start the POP then, or use a condom, for example, for a week. But you can start earlier if all this seems too complicated (see Chapter 12 on contraception while breastfeeding).

After a miscarriage or a termination of pregnancy

You can start the POP the next day, without the need for extra precautions.

Antibiotics and the POP

Although the combined pill is affected by a number of antibiotics, the POP, despite its low-dose, escapes most of these problems. The reason for this is based on the enterohepatic cycle, which was described in Chapter 5. When oestrogens and progestogens have been absorbed through the stomach they pass to the liver, where they are partially broken down and combined with other substances. Some of these by-products are then dumped into the large bowel, to await disposal. The bacteria which live in the large bowel are however capable of reconverting the oestrogen products into a useful form, and this is then reabsorbed into the blood and used. The bacteria are therefore raising the blood levels of oestrogen by their action. However, this recycling does not happen to progestogens, so the bacteria cannot influence the blood levels of progestogen in the body.

Antibiotics are designed to destroy bacteria, and if you take certain ones, particularly the so-called 'broad spectrum' ones like penicillin and tetracyclines, you may find that the bacteria in the gut have temporarily disappeared, and with them has gone your extra source of oestrogen. Since some women's blood levels of oestrogen may be only just high enough with the help of the bacteria, there is a danger that their taking antibiotics may reduce the oestrogen to a level at which they might become pregnant. This is why additional precautions are advised if you take such antibiotics while you are on the combined pill. However, since the bacteria have no effect on progestogen, their presence or absence is immaterial when you are on the POP. It is thus quite unnecessary to take additional contraceptive precautions if you are given a course of antibiotics for conditions such as cystitis, acne, or a sore throat.

Two antibiotics do exist, however, which *will* affect the POP. These are called Rifampicin and Griseofulvin, and they work on the liver itself, increasing and speeding up the actual destruction of the progestogen by the liver enzymes. Rifampicin is used to treat tuberculosis, and Griseofulvin is used for fungal infections of the skin and nails.

The POP and other medicines

The effectiveness of the POP can be affected by any medicine which may speed up the work of the liver enzymes, as this increases the speed at which the progestogen is destroyed. This includes many of the medications used in the treatment of epilepsy (except sodium valproate or Epilim and the newer anti-epileptics marketed in the last six years), Rifampicin (as mentioned above), and some medicines used in the treatment of mental disorders. A complete list of these can be found on p. 84, since both the combined pill and the POP are affected by them. Because the POP is such a very low dose, it is probably best to avoid using it if you are taking one of these medications. If you are very keen to use it, you may wish to try taking two tablets a day, but whether this will be enough is not known.

Who should consider using the POP?

'I was devastated. Only 35 and too old for the pill! I can't give up smoking, I've tried before. I looked at a cap and thought, 'you must be joking'. And then, I certainly don't want to be pregnant for another couple of years.'

'The doctor said my blood pressure was too high to stay on the pill. I don't want to risk my health, either. When I changed to the progestogen-only pill, it went down within a few months, pretty well to normal.'

'I'm diabetic, and they could never get my insulin right while I was on the other pill. Now I just take this one with my evening injection, so it's easy to remember. My periods aren't so regular, but you can't have everything.'

It should be clear from this chapter that almost everyone can safely take the POP. It is probably most suitable for women over the age of 30, and for women who for some reason cannot or do not want to take oestrogen. It is also the best hormonal contraceptive to use while breastfeeding. Its principal disadvantage is the difficulty of remembering to take the pills to a strict timetable, but most women learn to manage this in the end. Unfortunately it is still a little-known option, but this is beginning to improve.

CHAPTER 7

Injectable Progestogens and Implants

Injectable progestogens consist of the hormone progestogen given in the form of an injection. Because no oestrogen is contained in them people often believe that they must work and behave like the progestogen-only pill (POP); however, although some similarities exist, there are also some very significant differences.

How do injectable progestogens work?

The method is exactly the same as that of the combined pill; they stop ovulation. You may find this surprising, since the POP is, after all, also a progestogen-only method, but depends more heavily on thickening the cervical mucus so that it becomes impenetrable to sperm, and on making the lining of the womb thin, so that the fertilized egg cannot implant itself. Injectable progestogens perform both these functions, but since they work primarily by preventing ovulation, they are far more effective, having a failure rate of only 0.1 per hundred woman-years. This means that if 1,000 women used this method for a year, only one would be expected to become pregnant.

What then makes the injectable progestogens differ from the POP? In fact the POP has a far lower dose of progestogen; in Fig. 7.1 you can compare the blood levels of an injectable and a POP over a period of three months. The dose of progestogen contained in an injectable begins at a high level and gradually decreases, but it never falls below the level needed to prevent ovulation. Before this level is reached a further injection will have been given. This is in contrast to the POP, which has much lower blood levels; furthermore these rise and fall every day and thus cannot be relied upon to prevent ovulation.

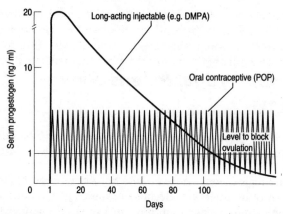

Figure 7.1 Comparison of the blood serum levels of progestogen in users of oral and injectable progestogens

(*Source*: Modified from Population Reports BS, Population Information Program, Johns Hopkins University, Baltimore, USA)

A pill, or any other substance which needs to be taken by mouth, is of course liable to be destroyed by the stomach acids and enzymes, or may be lost due to vomiting or diarrhoea. In addition, it is then immediately subjected to further attack by enzymes in the liver. On the other hand, a hormone given by injection, or by any route which does not involve the stomach, is not subject to these pitfalls. For the same reasons medicines such as antibiotics, which can interfere both at the stomach and liver stages, are less likely to be able to affect it. Finally, there is no need for the woman to make the effort to remember to take a pill. Overall, therefore, injectables are likely to be more foolproof and easier to use than pills.

What types of injectable are available?

At present there are two types on the market: depomedroxyprogesterone acetate and norethisterone oenanthate. Their corresponding brand names are Depo Provera and Noristerat, which are much simpler. Both are intramuscular injections, and can be given either into the bottom or into the upper arm. They differ principally in that it is necessary to give Depo Provera every twelve weeks, and Noristerat every eight weeks. Noristerat, which is oil based, and therefore thicker, is also a more painful injection, and is less popular than Depo Provera. To simplify this account, since they are otherwise very much alike, we will use the name Depo Provera to refer to them both, unless it is necessary to highlight a specific difference.

Some advantages of injectable progestogens

'It's great, all I have to do is keep a note in my diary of my next appointment. No more worries about 'have I taken my pill?'

The fact that a woman need no longer trouble to remember to take her pill contributes largely to the effectiveness of Depo Provera as a method of contraception. In addition, of course, there is the advantage that it is unnecessary to take any particular precautions before intercourse. Furthermore, as with the POP, there are, naturally, no oestrogen-related side-effects or health risks, so that it is a safe method for women who cannot take oestrogen, such as, in particular, smokers over 35, and women with a history of problems linked to oestrogen.

Specific health advantages include the fact that it is protective against pelvic inflammatory disease (salpingitis, or infection of the Fallopian tubes), because of the reaction of the cervical mucus: that is, since the sperm cannot penetrate the barrier, many bacteria will be in the same position. Like the combined pill (although in contrast to the POP), it greatly lowers the risk of an ectopic pregnancy (a pregnancy in one of the tubes). This is also due to its prevention of ovulation: if a woman does not ovulate, there is no egg in the tube for the sperm to meet. Depo Provera also resembles the Combined Pill in that it reduces the risk of an ovarian cyst. (This too is because it stops ovulation, since the ovaries thereby become inactive.)

Injectables have also proved safe and reliable in conjunction with various forms of medication, and for women suffering from diseases which make other methods of contraception inadvisable. They are now recommended as the best form of contraception for those women who suffer from sickle cell disease since it has been shown that users have fewer relapses, or 'crises', and their blood shows an improvement compared with non-users. In addition, women who need to take long-term medication of a nature which can interfere with both the combined and progestogen-only pills, such as medication for the treatment of epilepsy or tuberculosis, can still safely use Depo Provera. The only difference is that such women should preferably receive the repeat injections two weeks earlier than usual. If you are given other antibiotics which interfere with either or both of the pills, they will not interfere with Depo Provera, so you will have no need to take special precautions.

Using injectables during breastfeeding

There is no reason why Depo Provera should not be used during breastfeeding, as it does not stop or reduce the production of milk. As with the POP, a small dose of hormone passes into the breast milk, but no ill effects have ever been noted. In this respect, however, and provided you can remember to take it, the POP may be preferable: it contains a smaller dose of progestogen, so even less will pass into the milk, and when it is combined with full breastfeeding it is as effective as Depo Provera. (There is no evidence that the amount of hormone transmitted to the baby is at all damaging, but many women feel uneasy about even small amounts of hormone passing into their milk.) It is recommended that breastfeeding women wait for between four and six weeks after delivery to start either the POP or Depo Provera. This is because bleeding irregularities seem to be more common if you start earlier. Reassuringly, no woman has ever been reported as having conceived within four weeks of having a baby, so this appears perfectly safe from the contraceptive point of view.

Return of fertility after using injectables

'I've heard that in some countries they won't give you Depo Provera if you haven't had children. Does that mean it can make you infertile?'

There is no permanent effect on fertility after using Depo Provera, although there is often a delay in becoming pregnant. Since for most women pregnancy will occur between six months and a year after stopping, it is advisable to plan a pregnancy about a year in advance; if you know you will want to become pregnant fairly soon, you should choose a different method. This delaying effect will be just the same whether you have had one injection or fifty: that is, there is no evidence that long-term use will produce greater problems.

Some general disadvantages of injectables

You should bear in mind that Depo Provera is a long-acting injection; once you have received it you will be compelled to put up with any side-effects for as long as it lasts (three months for Depo Provera, two for Noristerat), so you should think carefully before making the initial decision. There is also the fact that it may take a year for you to become pregnant after you stop; again, if you will not find it convenient to take such long-distance decisions about your life, it would be better to use an alternative method of contraception.

It has been known for women to put on a few pounds in weight when they begin using this method, but this should settle down fairly soon. A very small minority put on more weight, but unfortunately it does not seem possible to predict who they will be. Interestingly, women who are already overweight seem less likely to gain weight than women who are slim. Another effect attributed in some cases to Depo Provera is depression; but reports relate only to women who are already prone to this, and there is no evidence of it emerging in women who are not normally depressed. This type of side-effect is very difficult to study, because depression is such a complicated problem and fluctuates over time.

Surprisingly uncommon side-effects are acne, greasy hair, and loss of interest in sex, despite the fact that Depo Provera contains a relatively high-dose of progestogen given without any oestrogen. Their rarity may well be due to the fact that Depo Provera has a different chemical derivation from most of the other progestogens in use.

What happens to periods?

While you are using Depo Provera you should, with any luck, stop having periods, or have them only infrequently. Since on Depo Provera you should not need to be anxious about pregnancy, there is no reason why the absence of periods should trouble you. In many cultures where women experience frequent pregnancies, periods are a rarity, since they do not occur during pregnancy and only occasionally during breastfeeding. These women can therefore pass from one pregnancy to another without ever seeing a period. It has also been noted that some types of cancer, for example breast cancer, cancer of the womb, and cancer of the ovary, occur more frequently among women who have had many periods (that is, women who have begun to have periods at a very young age, who have experienced a late menopause (change of life), and who have had no children). This has been mentioned before, in connection with the combined pill (see p. 36), and it is just as applicable here. It has indeed been suggested that any process which prevents ovulation (and therefore periods) will probably also protect against cancer of the womb and ovary, and under certain circumstances perhaps also against breast cancer, so the avoidance of periods seems to be positively beneficial. It should also be made clear that periods are not necessary in themselves in order to cleanse the womb. If they do not occur the reason is that the lining of the womb has become thin and contains few blood vessels, so there is nothing which needs to come away. (This is an effect of progestogen, which also helps prevent implantation.)

Not only are periods unnecessary for a healthy life, they can also be a dreadful nuisance, causing pain and discomfort, worries about travelling, and the expense and annoyance of buying, carrying about, and wearing towels and tampons. Some women also experience an improvement in the symptoms of pre-menstrual syndrome on Depo Provera, and obviously, if they are not having periods at all, these will improve still further. Although you may start off with irregular periods, many women find that their periods dwindle and stop completely by the end of the first year. The textbooks state that only 40 per cent of women have no periods at all by the end of a year, but the figure is probably much higher. In research terms, even one day's bleeding in six months probably means that a women cannot be said to have 'no periods', and this will naturally lower the figures.

> '*The doctor didn't tell me I could bleed all the time: I thought my periods would just stop immediately, like my friend's did. So I had the injection when I went travelling round the Far East for three months with my boyfriend. It was terrible, I think I had about two dry weeks in the whole time.*'

Despite these potential advantages, the effect of Depo Provera on periods is not always good. As we have said, many women will have infrequent periods, or stop altogether; but before this happens (and for some women it never happens) there is a chance that you may get very irregular, unpredictable, possibly frequent bleeding or spotting. You should be prepared for this eventuality before you make a decision to try Depo Provera, as its effects cannot be predicted. If it is no feasible for you to put up with it, at least for a few months, for example because you are planning a long period of travel, or because your religion would mean that your activities, both social and sexual, would have to be restricted, then you should not try this method.

However, if you wish to continue with Depo Provera but find your periods are a problem, there are several ways of improving them. If you are able to take oestrogen, a short course of it may well dispose of the problem (often just one packet of the combined pill is sufficient, but more can be given if necessary); or the next injection may be given a couple of weeks early. Furthermore, the longer you have been receiving injections, the better are your chances of getting infrequent or no periods. Things will probably improve if you persevere; but you should consider carefully whether you are prepared to wait for this or whether another method might suit you better.

Injectables and risks of cardiovascular disease

There is no evidence that Depo Provera has any effect on blood-clotting, so even if you have had a thrombosis in a vein it is quite safe to use this method. It also has no effect on blood pressure. However, there is some controversy about its effect on HDL cholesterol levels. In the chapters dealing with the combined pill we described the effects of HDL cholesterol in detail; but to put it briefly, HDL (high density lipoprotein) cholesterol is thought to be good for your arteries, while other kinds of cholesterol are bad. There are relatively few studies of the effects of injectables on lipids, and even fewer reliable ones using modern technology. Bearing those limitations in mind, it does appear that Depo Provera may cause a slight lowering of HDL cholesterol, of about 15 per cent. In this case, there does appear to be a difference between the two types, with a couple of studies suggesting that Noristerat causes a greater reduction, of up to 30 per cent. What effect this actually has in practice is not known. It does, however, suggest that it would be advisable to discuss your case with a specialist, and probably have your blood levels of lipids checked before making a decision, if for any reason you are already at very high risk of arterial disease (for example, if you have a family history of lipid disorders or you are a very heavy smoker).

Injectables and diabetes

Like the combined pill, injectables can slightly alter the body's response to insulin, the hormone in charge of controlling blood sugar. This is not likely to affect a non-diabetic person, but, if you are diabetic, your insulin requirements may change when you start Depo Provera, and may need monitoring more closely, especially as the blood levels of progestogen do not stay constant. In addition, the slight lowering of HDL cholesterol raises the question of whether the risk of arterial disease (already higher in a diabetic) might be increased. The progestogen-only pill or the Mirena is usually a better choice for diabetic women.

Depo Provera and cancer

Very few women in this country use Depo Provera, although we have seen that it is an effective, easy to use, relatively safe method of contraception. Most women have a vague impression of the method being unsafe, that it should be avoided. To see why, we must look at the history of Depo Provera from the beginning. Depo Provera was first used in the mid-1950s, when very high-doses of it were given to women both for the prevention of recurrent miscarriage, and also for the gynaecological condition endometriosis. That is, women were receiving massive doses during pregnancy, and yet no ill effects were observed, and the United States Food and Drug Administration (FDA) did not hesitate to approve it for general use in these conditions. Then, by the early 1960s, it had become apparent that women who had received these large doses of Depo Provera during pregnancy were not conceiving for more than a year after they had their child, even though they were using no contraception. This evidence, linked to the fact that Depo Provera had already proved to be safe, even in huge doses, suggested that it might be a good idea to use it as a contraceptive, and when this turned out to be successful an application was made to have it licensed for this use in the United States.

However, at this point the matter was obscured by some unfortunate publicity. The results of some studies in beagle dogs were published, which suggested that if enormous doses of Depo Provera were given to beagle bitches for several years they would create a high risk of breast cancer. Breast cancer is a very emotive subject and naturally these findings received a great deal of publicity. Shortly afterwards, however, it was proved that, in fact, beagle bitches are naturally prone to develop breast cancer, with or without Depo Provera, so the original conclusions were not reliable. Nevertheless, a powerful hate campaign against Depo Provera developed in the time between the first scare and its refutation, and such an impression was made on public opinion that scientific evidence was disregarded.

This 'Ban the Jab' movement was brought about not only by anxiety over health risks of Depo Provera, but also because it was known to be used primarily in developing countries. It was believed that it was being tested on Third World women, and that they were being kept in ignorance of the risks so that they could be used as guinea pigs for the West. One important point about the relative nature of risk should be made here. The vast majority of contraceptive methods are indeed tested first in countries where there is a high risk of death (both for mother and child) as a result of pregnancy. A woman who has already borne ten children and is aware that her next (unplanned and unwanted) pregnancy would put her life at risk would be more likely to be willing to try an effective contraceptive whose possible side-effects are not yet fully known. However, in Western countries death due to pregnancy is very rare, so the acceptable level of health risks (or uncertainty about the risks) from contraceptive methods is lower. The balance of risks versus benefits is quite different in these two situations.

In fact, the image of Depo Provera as confined to developing countries is inaccurate; although it was (and still is) extremely popular in countries such as Thailand and Indonesia, it was also widely used in a number of developed countries, such as New Zealand and Australia. Accusations were made of misuse in certain countries, injections being forced on women as a form of selective population control: some of these may well have been true. However, it should be remembered that the fault lay with the providers rather than with the method itself.

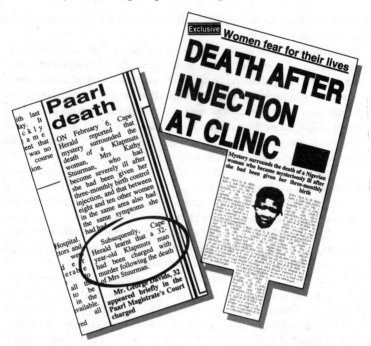

Figure 7.2 Press scare about injectables from South Africa. It was later discovered that the woman had been murdered.

Evidence against Depo Provera was extremely sketchy, but none the less the campaign became increasingly heated. As a result, although the medical experts advising the United States FDA recommended the licensing of Depo Provera, it was compelled by political, rather than scientific, pressures to withdraw its approval. A licence from the FDA is regarded as a touchstone by all other countries, and if such approval is not forthcoming they become nervous of sanctioning the medication themselves. It took until 1984 before Depo Provera was licensed for use as a contraceptive in this country, and even then the bad publicity lingered around it, since scares and scandals are far more newsworthy than positive information.

When the original licence was granted in this country its use was limited to women who had had rubella vaccine, to those whose husbands had had a vasectomy and were awaiting clearance, and to those who for some reason were unable to use any other method of contraception. That is, it was regarded as a last resort, a second-class medication, intended for women who could not manage to use any other method, such as people with learning difficulties, the socially deprived, and ethnic groups. These opinions have never been thoroughly dispelled, since most doctors are far too busy to keep themselves absolutely up to date with areas outside their own speciality. As a result, there are still a good many doctors in this country who have reservations about prescribing Depo Provera.

In 1991 the results of an important study carried out by the World Health Organization (WHO) became available, clarifying the cancer situation considerably. Reassuringly, the study showed no overall increase in the risk of any cancer studied. Indeed, the study showed that Depo Provera had a fivefold *protective* effect against cancer of the endometrium (lining of the womb), and that the effect persisted for at least eight years after stopping the method.

There was no effect on ovarian cancer, which is in some ways surprising. Depo Provera and the combined pill both work by stopping ovulation, and, as already mentioned, the risks of endometrial and ovarian cancer seem to be higher in women who have ovulated many times. The pill lowers the risks of both cancers quite considerably, and as we have seen Depo Provera was shown to have a protective effect against endometrial cancer. So why was there not also a protective effect against ovarian cancer? The answer may lie in the type of women who were in the study: they had all had children and most would have breastfed (when you also often stop ovulating), so they were actually a fairly low-risk group. If the 'background' risk of cancer is low, then either the effect of a product has to be extremely strong, or the number of women studied must be very large, before it is possible to detect that effect. Perhaps in women who are at higher risk a protective effect against ovarian cancer may still be found. There was no increase in the risk of cervical cancer, which is also good news.

With regard to breast cancer, there was no overall increase in risk. However, there was a slight increase for women who had used Depo Provera for less than four years: in practice, this meant the users were under the age of 35. However, if this was a true increase, it should be greater the longer a woman has used the method. In this study, the opposite was the case: women were at greatest risk of having breast cancer detected within three months of their first injection, and the risk diminished with time, so that long-term users actually experienced a very slight protective effect. This suggests that what was happening was that women who chose to use Depo Provera were being examined for breast lumps, either by themselves or by the medical staff: after all, many would be aware of the controversy regarding breast cancer in the past. Thus, cancers which were already present were being found: it is biologically quite implausible that a cancer should develop from nothing to a palpable lump within three months.

Interestingly, another study (published in 1989) from New Zealand, although it showed no overall increase in the risk of breast cancer, did produce evidence of a very slight increase in risk among those women who had used the method for more than six years under the age of 25. The number of women in this category was of course extremely small (less than ten), so it is hardly possible to draw definitive conclusions. Once again, while Depo Provera appeared to increase the risk slightly in very young women, it also appeared to be slightly protective in older women. Attention has been drawn to the fact that, in both these studies and the studies on the combined pill and breast cancer, the age of 25 is a significant factor. The common element may perhaps be the protective effect against benign breast lumps of both treatments. Young women normally have lumpy breasts, so that it is difficult to diagnose cancerous lumps, more particularly since cancer is so rare in the lower age group. When these benign lumps are smoothed out by some hormonal treatment the cancerous one will suddenly become more obvious. Thus, it may not be a question of cancers developing earlier, but simply that, with this choice of contraception, a cancer which would have developed anyway can be diagnosed earlier.

The bottom line with regard to breast cancer is that there certainly does not appear to be any overall increase in the risk. The issue of whether the risk is slightly raised in young women is still unresolved. However, because breast cancer is rare in young women, even if there does eventually prove to be a slight increase in risk, it will not make much difference to the actual number (that is, an increase in a very small number is still a very small number). We have discussed this before in relation to the combined pill (see Chapter 3).

The good news provided by the World Health Organization studies no doubt influenced the United States FDA in its decision finally to grant Depo Provera a licence. The announcement was made in October 1992, thirty years after Depo Provera had been first introduced for contraception. This was an important landmark in its history, since Depo Provera will therefore have greater acceptance worldwide. And indeed, in 1995, Depo Provera was at last granted a full licence in the UK, officially allowing its use as a 'first-choice' rather than 'last-resort' method.

Depo Provera and osteoporosis

Does Depo Provera affect your bones? This question was raised by a study from New Zealand in 1991, but, unfortunately, no conclusive answer was provided. The study compared a small group of women who were long-term users of Depo Provera (at least five years) with two groups not using Depo Provera: one group was using other forms of contraception, while the second consisted of women who had gone through the menopause (change of life). (You may already be aware that, when women go through the menopause, they stop producing oestrogen and this leads to a thinning of the bones, known as osteoporosis.) The study suggested that the women using Depo Provera, while better off than those who had gone through the menopause, had a lower bone density than women using other methods of contraception. A low bone density implies 'thinning of the bones' which may result in fractures. The Depo Provera users did not have enough 'thinning' to place them at risk of a fracture, but, obviously, any lowering would be worrying, especially as a woman approaches the menopause.

Unfortunately, what the researchers had not taken into account was that there were big differences between their Depo Provera user group and the comparison groups. The Depo Provera users were much more likely to smoke, and to smoke more heavily, than the non-users. This in itself might account for much of the difference, since smoking also causes a reduction in bone density. The Depo Provera users also tended to have less healthy diets and be generally socially less privileged than the non-users: remember that, until recently, this was a method viewed with suspicion, especially by women who were politically and socially 'aware'.

The differences between the women would not have mattered if measurements of bone density had been made before women started using Depo Provera. A repeat measurement five years later in the same women would show whether an individual's bone density had changed following (and therefore perhaps as a result of) Depo Provera use. Unfortunately, this was not done, so it is quite possible that the Depo Provera users simply had 'thinner' bones to start with, and did not change at all.

Theoretically, since Depo Provera does stop ovulation, it is plausible that there could be less oestrogen circulating in the body, and that this would lead to a reduced bone density in the long term. However, it is equally possible that there might be enough oestrogen to make the effect minimal, or absent. We do not know for certain. However, recently, a copy of the New Zealand study was performed in the UK, this time making sure that there were no such enormous differences in social and smoking habits between the Depo Provera users and other method users. This study showed no difference in bone density between the two groups of women, which is reassuring. Over the next few years, we should have more evidence, and particularly from studies which have looked at the same women over a five- or ten-year period, as mentioned above. Those studies should finally resolve the issue.

What should you do meanwhile? Even in the New Zealand study, there was no evidence that any effect on bones occurred within the first five years of use, so if you plan to use, or have been using, Depo Provera for less than five years, there is no cause for concern. (Most of the women in the study had in fact been using Depo Provera for around ten years.) If you are a long-term Depo Provera user, especially if you are in your forties, it may be an idea to have a bone density scan, just to check that your bones are all right. A bone density scan is completely painless, takes five minutes, and involves an X-ray dose which is one-hundredth of that of a chest X-ray. However, it is expensive and not always easily available. It may be easier, though not as accurate, to have the oestrogen level in your blood checked: this test is not always reliable for various technical reasons, but can sometimes be helpful in making a decision. If the bone density scan shows thinning of the bones or the blood test suggests a much lower than normal level of oestrogen, you should discuss the situation with your doctor. One solution would be to take a low dose of natural oestrogen as a supplement while continuing to use Depo Provera.

This would be similar to using hormone replacement therapy (HRT), with the Depo Provera providing both contraception and the progestogen which is required to counterbalance oestrogen in HRT.

Starting and continuing injectables

The correct time to give both Depo Provera and Noristerat is within the first three days of a period. No further precautions will then be required, even during stomach upsets and with the majority of antibiotics, as these do not affect injectables. Future injections should be given at twelve-weekly intervals for Depo Provera, and eight-weekly intervals for Noristerat. However, if medication which speeds up liver enzymes is being taken, the injection interval should be shortened by two weeks. It is very important that you do not miss appointments for repeat injections, as being late can cause a lot of problems trying to establish that you could not be pregnant before the next injection is given. If the timing of your appointment is inconvenient, always go earlier, rather than later. Giving the next injection early is no problem, but if you are more than a few days late, you may find yourself taking the emergency pill and having pregnancy tests. You may think this is ridiculous, when we have seen that, if anything, it is likely to take several months to become pregnant after stopping Depo Provera; however, in an individual case, it is not possible to predict how long it might take, and pregnancies have occasionally occurred within a couple of weeks of stopping the method.

As mentioned earlier, women wishing to use this method after having a baby should preferably have their first injection between four and six weeks after delivery, in order to avoid problems with irregular bleeding.

Who should consider using injectables?

'I had been using the pill, but was becoming fed up with it. My work involves a lot of travelling, abroad as well as at home. Trying to remember pills when you are always in different hotels in different places is awful. Then, if I did a long-haul flight, there was the problem of time-zone changes. I frequently forgot pills and then I would get breakthrough bleeding, not to mention having to use the sheath as well. . . . eventually, my doctor

*suggested Depo Provera. I was horrified at first, as I had heard
all sorts of bad things about it, you wouldn't be able to have
children, you could get cancer—but she explained that wasn't
true and gave me some leaflets to read. I decided to try it. The first
few months were tricky, as I had quite a lot of bleeding, but then
I had been getting that anyway when I forgot my pills. After the
second injection, I stopped having periods altogether, and
haven't had any since. Now I think it's great: I don't worry about
travelling. I don't have to remember pills, no more packets on
public display during the handbag search! I feel fine.'*

Clearly many women would find the particular advantages of Depo
Provera beneficial, although anyone who would find a disruption of
her periods unacceptable should avoid it, and it is also unsuitable for
women who are likely to want to become pregnant fairly shortly.

The suspicion and fear with which it has been viewed in the past
are now beginning to fade, and more and more doctors have
accepted that it is actually a remarkably safe and effective method. It
is no longer regarded merely as a very last resort, and women are
increasingly becoming aware that it is a source of effective, trouble-
free contraception. Professional women in particular may find it useful, especially if they are frequently obliged to travel and are faced
with both hectic schedules and time-zone changes. Such women
find the dual freedoms from pill taking and periods a blessing.

Although you should never make any decisions about contraceptive methods without being in full possession of the facts, this is even
more important in relation to injectable progestogens, since a single
injection will last for two or three months, and you may be forced to
put up with any undesirable effects until it wears off. Another long-
lasting consequence can be irregular periods, which may also prove
most inconvenient if you are not prepared for the problem.

We have attempted to supply all the necessary information in this
chapter, but only you can weigh up the potential benefits and disadvantages for yourself to see whether this method will suit you.

Norplant

Norplant is another way of giving a long-acting progestogen, but this
time as an implant which is inserted under the skin and slowly

releases a low-dose of hormone. Norplant is already available for normal use in many countries, including Finland, Sweden, and the United States, and was introduced into the UK in the autumn of 1993.

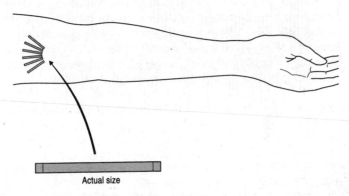

Actual size

Figure 7.3 Norplant capsules implanted in the arm

Norplant consists of six soft silastic capsules containing levonorgestrel, each of which is 3.4 centimetres long and 2.4 millimetres thick. To insert them a very small incision (which will not require stitches) is made in the inner side of the upper arm and they are placed under the skin. There they initially release between 50 and 80 micrograms of levonorgestrel every day and then the level slowly drops to 38 micrograms (a similar dose to the progestogen-only pill). Norplant is effective from day one if inserted on the first day of your period and lasts for five years. After this period the capsules have to be removed through the original incision.

'I always had trouble remembering to take pills, especially since I travel so much for work. But I also want a very effective method— I want to choose when I'm going to have a baby, not have it sprung on me unexpectedly. Admittedly, having the capsules put in was a bit of a performance, but it was over quite quickly. It's so good to know I don't have to worry about contraception for five years—but also that I can have them out any time I want.'

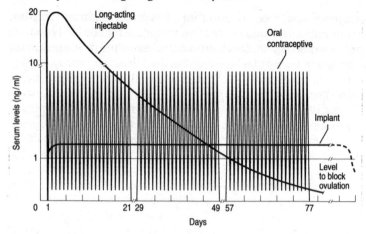

Figure 7.4 Comparison of blood serum levels of progestogen in users of progestogen-only pills, injectable progestogens, and implants
Source: Szarewski, *Hormonal Contraception* (Macdonald Optima, 1991)

Norplant has a couple of advantages over the POP which make it overall more successful. In the first place its blood levels—although lower than those of injectables like Depo Provera (see Figure 7.4)—are steadier and much more constant than those of the POP, and, secondly, it does not have the POP's strict timetable for pill taking. The failure rate is between 0.2 and 1.6 per hundred woman-years; this is on a level with injectables and the combined pill, although using an early version it was shown that failure rates were higher in women who were considerably overweight. However, the manufacturers have now produced a version using a different polymer: this type is very effective and it seems that even heavier women do not have a significantly higher failure rate. This is the version which is currently on the market in the UK.

Although Norplant functions in a similar way to the POP, research suggests that fewer women using Norplant will continue to ovulate. However, like the POP, it backs up this contraceptive effect by thickening the cervical mucus, so that sperm will find it hard to penetrate as far as the womb, and by making the lining of the womb thin, so that implantation of any fertilized egg will probably be unable to take place. Because it contains no oestrogen, women who use it will not suffer any oestrogen-related side-effects or health risks. In addition, Norplant contains only a very small dose of hormone, so its effect on blood fats and sugars is also small. Like both injectables and the POP, the worst of its side-effects is irregular bleeding, but this is likely to improve during the first year or so. Occasionally infection has been known to occur at the insertion site: great care should be taken to ensure that a sterile technique is used, and the risk of infection can be reduced by keeping the insertion site dry for three days. This is a disadvantage of Norplant, in that it does need to be inserted by a trained person, and preferably in a clinic where sterile equipment is available. Against this there is the advantage that, although Norplant can remain in place for five years, it can be removed at any time before that. Again a trained person is needed to remove it, and you may have heard reports in the media about problems with removals. It is certainly true that if the Norplant was inserted incorrectly, it may be difficult to remove later. However, the number of cases where there are real problems with the removal is small, but, of course, those are the ones you hear about. Despite its long duration of action, there is no effect on fertility.

One disadvantage of Norplant is the sheer number of capsules required. Six is a large number to insert and remove, and since the capsules are inserted immediately under the skin, they can be felt and sometimes seen. To meet this problem a newer version of Norplant, called Norplant 2, uses only two capsules, making it less obvious. Norplant 2 is at an earlier stage of development so it will be quite a while yet before it reaches the market, especially since it was delayed for some years by a problem with one of the polymers used in the silastic part of the capsules. It will not be as long-lasting as the original Norplant (about three years only), but it will have the advantage of being much easier to insert and remove.

Implanon

Another exciting possibility for the near future is a single-rod desogestrel implant. Desogestrel is one of the new, specific progestogens, so it should be better for those women who get acne or other progestogenic side-effects even with the small amount in Norplant. This implant (called Implanon) is very much easier to insert and remove and lasts for three years. Barring any unforeseen problems, it could be on the market within the next year or so.

CHAPTER 8

Intrauterine Devices

The intrauterine device, or IUD, is thought to have been used first by North African Arabs, who placed a stone in the womb or vagina of female camels in order to try and stop them becoming pregnant on long desert journeys. However, it was Hippocrates, over 2,500 years ago, who thought of applying the method to women. Once the idea took hold, all sorts of materials were used: wood, glass, ivory, gold, and even platinum studded with diamonds! Some of these were in fact probably used illegally to achieve abortions rather than contraception.

The first of the more modern types of IUD was made in 1909 by a German doctor: it consisted of a ring made out of silkworm gut. In 1930 the next step forward occurred, when another German doctor, Ernst Grafenberg, added silver wire to the silkworm gut, creating the Grafenberg ring, which was still around in some countries until quite recently. At around the same time a Japanese doctor designed a gold and silver ring, the Ota ring. (It was the ring shape which gave rise to the other commonly used name for the IUD, the coil.) These rings had to go into the womb just as they were, so the insertion must have been very unpleasant, even though the only candidates in those days were women who had already had children. Although there was considerable initial interest, problems with infection started to appear and the devices lost their popularity.

Nothing much happened until the 1950s, when plastics became widely available. The advantage of plastic was that it could be made to spring back into its original shape after being stretched for a short time, and this meant that the devices could be made thinner for insertion and would then assume their proper shape once inside the womb. The earliest of these newer devices were the Lippes Loop and the Marguiles spiral. The Lippes Loop was the first IUD to have a tail, which made it easier to remove, and also allowed confirmation of its presence after it had been fitted. Of the IUDs in Figure 8.1, the Lippes Loop stayed in use the longest, and indeed was still around in this country until the end of the 1980s, so some women may still be using them.

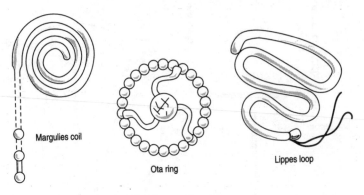

Margulies coil

Ota ring

Lippes loop

Figure 8.1 Three types of coil no longer in use

The main problem with these IUDs was that their effectiveness was directly proportional to their size. Unfortunately, the bigger they were, the more side-effects they caused, in particular cramping pains and heavy bleeding. The uterus responds to the idea of an impostor by trying to eject it, and the bigger the foreign body, the harder it tries. So the target was to try to create an IUD which would be small and yet effective. Eventually, it was found that copper wire wound round a plastic base was the answer. These copper-bearing IUDs are the ones we use today. Some extra refinements have been introduced, such as using a silver wire as well as the copper, in order to make the copper wire last longer. Adding copper wire to the arms, as well as to the stem, of the IUD also appears to improve efficacy. T-shapes are now the most favoured, since they are more 'womb-shaped' and it seems that the womb finds them harder to expel.

The latest concept is to add a reservoir of hormone to the basic IUD, so that it slowly releases the hormone over a long period of time. The first IUD of this type, the Progestasert, was not a success, but the newer type, the levonorgestrel-releasing intrauterine system (the

Mirena), is very exciting. This has now become available and is discussed at the end of the chapter.

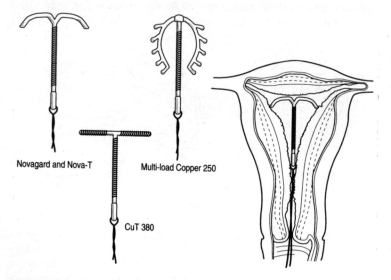

Novagard and Nova-T

Multi-load Copper 250

CuT 380

Figure 8.2 Examples of modern IUDs

How do IUDs work?

There has been considerable debate and controversy over this question for some time. Many mechanisms have been proposed and found wanting, partly because IUDs seem to work differently in animals and humans. Currently it is thought that there are several components, all acting together. In the first instance, the presence of a foreign body in the womb sets up an inflammatory response. You can think of this as being rather similar to what happens when a piece of grit gets into your eye: lots of tears are produced, and you blink furiously, trying to wash it away. In the womb, large numbers of white blood cells rush to the scene: these are normally called in to fight infection, but also to fight anything which the body does not recognize as 'itself'. Thus white cells are also part of the allergy mechanism.

The white cells stay around constantly while the IUD is present.

Because their function is to fight and 'swallow' bacteria and viruses, they also swallow and destroy sperm, which, after all, are just as foreign. Given half a chance they will also swallow the egg when it makes its way into the womb from the ovary. So IUDs in part work by causing the destruction of the sperm and/or the egg.

White cell

White cell changes shape and develops 'fingers'

Sperm being engulfed by white cell

Figure 8.3 White cell engulfing sperm

The presence of the white cells also has an effect on the lining of the womb, the endometrium. The endometrium builds up each month in preparation for a possible pregnancy. It provides the nest for the fertilized egg to lie in and receive nourishment while it is growing. The 'bedding down' of the fertilized egg in the endometrium is called implantation, and takes place about five days after the egg and sperm have joined together (fertilization). The effect of the white cells is to disrupt the endometrium, so that it no longer offers a comfortable shelter. Thus even if an egg is fertilized it cannot implant, and so a pregnancy cannot occur.

It is this effect on implantation which has caused much controversy. Some religious groups claim that a viable pregnancy begins the moment an egg and sperm join together, that is, as soon as fertilization has taken place. However, scientifically, a pregnancy is considered to be viable only after implantation has occurred, because the fertilized egg cannot survive if it does not implant, and many are naturally lost in this way—they simply get washed out in the next menstrual bleed. Legally, an abortion is also defined as occurring only after implantation has taken place. Thus the scientific and legal view is that the IUD is a contraceptive, because it acts before implantation, but some religions nevertheless maintain that anything after fertilization is an abortion. Of course, as we have seen usually the IUD will in fact prevent fertilization, by destroying the egg or the sperm. This is now believed to be the main effect, but you cannot be sure which way it is working at any given time.

Another effect of the IUD is that its presence seems to stimulate the production of substances called prostaglandins in the womb. These are responsible for causing the muscle of the womb to contract, and also to bleed, which may explain partly why IUD users may have heavier and more painful periods.

IUDs without copper have to rely on their larger size to have enough 'irritating' effect. However, copper itself seems to be an irritant, and therefore the IUD can be smaller (causing fewer side-effects), while still maintaining efficacy.

How effective are IUDs?

IUDs are a very effective method of contraception, with failure rates of about 0.3 to 2 per hundred woman-years (that is, if 200 women used the method for a year, between one and four would have an accidental pregnancy). Currently the most effective IUD is the Copper T 380, with a failure rate of 0.3 per hundred woman years. Younger women (under 30 years old) have failure rates towards the higher end of the range (because they ovulate more frequently and are therefore more fertile), while women over 30 have the lower failure rates, which are as good as the combined pill. They also get better the longer the device is used, typically dropping to 0–0.3 failures per hundred women per year beyond the fourth year of use. The majority of problems with IUDs, such as expulsion, perforation of the womb, and infection, are most likely to occur within the first year. Thus, those women who continue to use the method after that are the ones who are least likely to have experienced problems or an accidental pregnancy early on. Of course, there is very little that a woman can actually do wrong once she has had the IUD fitted, and this is one of the reasons for its high efficacy.

How long do IUDs last?

If there are no problems, plastic IUDs never need to be changed, but copper-containing ones do need to be replaced at intervals. Just how long these intervals should be has been a subject of much debate in recent years. At first, it was thought the IUDs would 'wear out' after three years (because the copper would dissolve), but gradually it was realized that this did not seem to be happening nearly as quickly, and it is now agreed that all the copper IUDs can stay in for five years, even if the manufacturer's instructions suggest a shorter time. Some of the newest IUDs (especially the most effective one, known as the Copper T 380) are effective for even longer. The Copper T 380 is now licensed for eight years' use in the UK and ten years in the United States.

There are positive benefits in making the fittings less frequent: many of the problems with IUDs (such as infection and heavy periods) are much more likely soon after insertion, and become less and less frequent as time goes by. So it would seem obvious to try to avoid unnecessary changes, especially when the devices do not appear to become less effective for at least five years. In addition, it has now been agreed that an IUD fitted when a woman is over 40 years old can stay in until the menopause. By this age, a woman's fertility is much reduced, and even if the IUD were a little less effective it would still be perfectly adequate.

Advantages of the IUD

'It's great. Once I had got over the fitting, no more worries about contraception for five years! All I have to do is to check that it's still there every now and again. No taking pills, no mess, no carrying supplies around, no hassle. It makes me feel secure.'

The IUD is an extremely effective, long-lasting, and very easy method of contraception. It is used by the woman, but is not obviously visible. It requires no memory, no action at the time of intercourse, and only a check-up once a year. It can be used while breastfeeding and has no effect on the milk. It has never been shown to have any effect on any kind of cancer. If it suits you it really is a method you can virtually forget about. Despite the problems discussed below, which can be minimized, it deserves to be used by far more than the 5 or 6 per cent of women who currently have one. However, it is best if you have had at least one child first (see below).

Having an IUD fitted

'Nobody warned me how painful the fitting was going to be: I nearly passed out. And then I got cramps for hours afterwards.'

Having an IUD fitted is not one of the world's most enjoyable experiences, especially if you have not had children (a fact which for other reasons as well normally means it would be better to use another method). The problem is that the entrance to the womb, the cervical canal, is very sensitive to being stretched, and that is exactly what has to happen for the IUD to be able to get inside. Once you have had children the canal is wider anyway, so the fitting is easier.

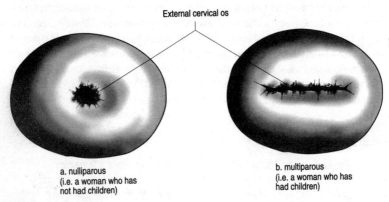

External cervical os

a. nulliparous
(i.e. a woman who has
not had children)

b. multiparous
(i.e. a woman who has
had children)

Figure 8.4 The appearance of the cervix before and after having children

You should think about who is going to fit your IUD and where it will be done. Studies have shown that if an IUD is fitted by an experienced doctor, in the right conditions, problems are very much less likely. So try to find out if the doctor fits IUDs regularly (for example, does he or she run a regular family planning/IUD clinic?), and is a member of the Faculty of Family Planning. Unfortunately, there is no legal requirement for doctors to be properly trained in family planning or IUD fitting: theoretically, anyone can fit an IUD. But, at least, if they have the letters MFFP, they have undergone supervised training. Some of those with the Diploma (DFFP) have also done the advanced course in IUD fitting: they should tell you if this is the case.

It is helpful to be given a pain-killer half an hour before the procedure. The type usually used is called mefenamic acid or Ponstan and helps prevent crampy pains after the fitting. If you have not had children, are very nervous, or have had trouble with IUD fittings before, it is worth considering having a local anaesthetic. This is injected around the cervix itself, making the area numb. However, you have to balance the discomfort of the injection against the discomfort of the actual fitting. It is just like going to the dentist: sometimes the pain of the injection is worse than having the filling without it. For this reason, and because most IUD users have had a child, in practice most fittings are done without anaesthetic.

You will be asked to lie on a couch and the doctor will first do an internal examination to make sure there is no tenderness and also to check whether the womb is tilted backwards or forwards. Then an instrument called a speculum will be placed in your vagina, just as if you were having a cervical smear. The cervix is cleaned and gripped with a special pair of forceps. Many women find this part of the procedure uncomfortable, but it is necessary for correct fitting. The IUD has to be pushed through the cervical canal and, even if it has been folded to make it thinner, the stretching sensation as it goes through is usually the most uncomfortable part of the procedure. Afterwards, you are likely to have a little bleeding and some cramping pain, though this can be minimized by having taken a pain-killer beforehand. It actually only lasts a couple of minutes, with the more uncomfortable parts lasting seconds at a time. And when you think about it, you are getting, hopefully, five to ten years of trouble-free contraception, depending on which device is chosen.

The IUD has threads, which need to be shortened by the doctor after the fitting. However, it is important that they are not made too short or they can stick out of the cervical canal like a bristle. You will not notice anything, but your partner is likely to give an agonized howl! You will be taught to feel for the threads yourself, so that you can check that the IUD is still in place. Ideally, you should do this after every period, because it is during periods that it is most likely to fall out.

Modern practice is that you should be seen one to two weeks after the fitting and certainly you should return by then if you have excessive pain, discharge or fever (see below) as this could mean you have an infection. After that you will be checked about six weeks after the fitting, to ensure all is well and that the IUD has not slipped out of its best position.

What are the problems during and after IUD fittings?

During the fitting itself, the womb can be perforated. This is very rare, but is less unlikely just after a pregnancy, whether you had a baby or a termination (because the womb is softer than usual), or during breastfeeding. Unfortunately the device will not work in the wrong place, but, although there may be increased pain at the time, often neither you nor the doctor will notice. However, an early warning can be if the threads disappear: this always means you should use another contraceptive method as well until the problem is diagnosed.

The other major, and more common, problem is infection. This is discussed below, but if it is going to happen it is more likely in the three weeks after the fitting. Your vagina and cervix are not sterile areas, and bacteria from there can be pushed into the womb and then infect the tubes. For this reason, nowadays it is usually advised that you have a swab taken for chlamydia before IUD fitting. Chlamydia is a sexually transmitted organism which causes infection of the Fallopian tubes (salpingitis, or pelvic inflammatory disease). However, it can just remain in the cervix for long periods of time without causing any symptoms at all. Salpingitis is a nasty condition which can lead to infertility, so it is important to try to prevent it starting. Although it is inconvenient to have to make two trips, the first for the swab and the second, after the result is known, for the fitting, it is well worth the protection in the long run. You should always go back to the clinic if you notice pain or discharge soon after you have had an IUD fitted. Do not dismiss it as just a side-effect of the fitting: it may be an infection.

Follow-up

Once you have had your six-week check, if all remains well, an examination once or twice a year is all you will need. However, you should yourself continue to feel for the threads.

When should an IUD be fitted?

There is a very common myth that IUDs can only be fitted during a period. This is absolutely untrue. An IUD can be fitted at any time in the first half of the cycle, as long as you could not already be pregnant. As we mentioned before, a pregnancy is not said to have occurred until the fertilized egg has bedded down, or implanted, in the lining of the womb. This happens about five days after ovulation (since the egg only lives for about 24 hours). So if you have a regular 28-day cycle, an IUD can be fitted up to day 19 (ovulation will take place on day 14, and you add five days). This is also the basis for the use of the IUD as a method of emergency contraception (see Chapter 11).

When should an IUD be removed?

Unlike insertion, removal really is best done during a period, because IUDs often work by preventing implantation rather than fertilization. If a device is inadvertently removed when fertilization has occurred or is still possible, then the woman may become pregnant that month because the IUD was not there to stop implantation. If removal during a period is not possible or is very inconvenient, then you should use another form of contraception for the preceding seven days to avoid the risk of pregnancy. Sometimes an IUD has to be removed in an emergency, for example due to infection. In such a case, if you have had sex in the previous few days it may be advisable take the emergency contraceptive pill (see Chapter 11).

> *'I was very nervous, remembering the fitting. But the doctor insisted it would be easy. I lay on the couch and he put in the usual metal instrument, like for the fitting and for smears. I felt a slight tugging and that was it. I couldn't believe it was all over.'*

Having an IUD removed is a very simple, quick procedure, so you do not need to get nervous about having it done.

Problems with IUDs

> *'I had heavy, painful periods before, but that was nothing compared to this. I'm going through tampons every couple of hours and wearing pads as well. And as for the pain ...'*

'My periods used to last four days. Now I dribble for three days, bleed properly for five days, and spot for another couple of days.

Then I sometimes get some spotting mid-cycle as well. It's ridiculous. I just always seem to be bleeding.'

Whatever your periods were like before the IUD, they will be longer and at least a bit heavier afterwards. This means you really should not have one fitted if your periods are already at the margins of bearability. Women who have not had children do least well. IUDs are best suited to women who have light, relatively pain-free periods. It is worth persevering for at least a few months, though, since the first few after insertion are the worst, and things may settle down.

'I thought my last period was a bit funny, lighter than usual and nearly a week late. Then suddenly I got this awful pain in my left side and I felt really faint. My mother took one look at me and called the doctor. He sent me to the hospital straight away. They said I had a pregnancy in my left tube and I had to have an operation. I was lucky it hadn't burst the tube or I could have died.'

Although IUDs are effective at preventing pregnancies in the womb, they are less effective at stopping them in the Fallopian tubes (an ectopic pregnancy). There has been much controversy over the magnitude of the risk of ectopic pregnancies in IUD users, and it does appear that the problem has been made out to be greater than it really is. IUD users are in fact not at higher risk of an ectopic pregnancy than users of no contraception, in terms of absolute numbers. However, although the actual number of all pregnancies is much reduced in IUD users (because they are so effective), the proportion which are ectopic is up to ten times higher. Also, since other contraceptive methods, such as the pill and injectables, actually reduce the risk, IUD users can seem much worse off by comparison.

There is another factor which may increase the risk of ectopic pregnancy in IUD users. Infection of the Fallopian tubes can lead to their being permanently damaged, even if they are not actually blocked. The egg will take longer to travel down a damaged tube (like trying to drive along a road full of pot-holes and roadworks) so the sperm has a greater chance of meeting it while it is still in the tube. IUD users are at higher risk of infection (see below) and this in turn can therefore result in a higher risk of ectopic pregnancy.

> *'My boyfriend had been away working abroad and I was really looking forward to seeing him again. I took a couple of days off and we had a wonderful time. A few days later I noticed I was getting a discharge, but things were so hectic I didn't really have time to think about it. Then sex started to be painful. I began to feel a bit fluish and decided I'd see the doctor. When she did an internal I thought I'd die of the pain. She said I had salpingitis, that my tubes were infected. I had to take a huge course of antibiotics or I might be infertile.'*

Pelvic infection is the biggest problem with IUDs. The most notorious was the Dalkon Shield, whose tail literally acted as a rope ladder for bacteria. The Dalkon Shield was a popular IUD in the 1960s, but gradually reports came in of massive infections in women who

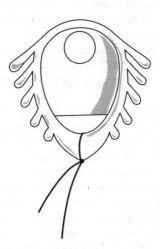

Figure 8.5 The Dalkon Shield IUD

became pregnant while using them. They would have a fairly late miscarriage, followed by a sudden and serious infection which sometimes even caused their death. Not surprisingly, there was a huge outcry and the manufacturer went out of business as a result of all the lawsuits. Since then it has been shown that even a non-pregnant Dalkon-Shield-user can suddenly develop a massive pelvic infection, and so it is advised that all women who had them fitted should have them removed as soon as possible.

Unfortunately, the Dalkon Shield saga affected all IUDs and their popularity plummeted. This was not justified, since the tail of the Dalkon Shield was quite unique to that device and the risk with other IUDs is far smaller. As we mentioned before, since many other contraceptive methods, including the pill, injectables, the POP, and barriers, actually offer protection against PID (pelvic inflammatory disease), it is not valid to compare IUD users with women employing these methods. Importantly, it has also been shown that the risk of PID is directly related to the risk of acquiring a sexually transmitted disease in the first place. Actually, when you think about it, this is pretty obvious: after all, infections do not come out of thin air. It has been shown that if a couple is truly monogamous, that is, neither of them has other partners, the woman's risk of PID, even if she is an IUD user, is very small. However, the risk increases in direct proportion to the number of her or her partner's sexual contacts. The big problem with this is that a woman deciding whether or not to use an IUD can be reasonably sure about her own sexual behaviour, but has no actual control over that of her partner: there are plenty of women who are faithful to their partners, but whose partners are not faithful to them.

Why are we so concerned about PID? There are two reasons. First, it is a nasty condition. It often starts with some vague pelvic pain and discharge, then pain during sex, and sometimes bleeding between periods. The periods themselves may suddenly become heavier and more painful. If not treated, it can progress to a more generalized infection, during which you will feel feverish and indeed may run a fever. Finally things may get so bad that you have to be admitted to hospital and given intravenous antibiotics. During PID all the internal organs become very inflamed and can stick together. These adhesions, as they are called, do not always go away even after the infection has been treated. So a woman can end up with her womb partly stuck to her tubes, her bowel, her bladder, and so on. This can result in long-term pain, often during sex, during periods, and so on, because the organs are pulling on each other. Flare-ups of PID can occur even without a new infection, often when you are run down. So you can end up with a problem for life, for which there is no real cure.

The second concern about PID is its effect on fertility. When the tubes become inflamed, their sides stick together. They may not always come apart again when the infection is treated, so they can be permanently blocked. This means the egg cannot reach the womb and therefore has no chance of meeting a sperm. Or, if the tube is partially blocked, the egg may take so long travelling down it that the risk of it meeting a sperm actually within the tube, and therefore the risk of an ectopic pregnancy, is increased. This dangerous condition was described in the last section.

It has been shown that the risk of infertility goes up with each episode of PID. After only one attack the risk of infertility due to blocked tubes is about one in eight. After two attacks the risk rises to one in three, and after three to one in two—or worse. This is why doctors try to dissuade women who have not yet had children from using an IUD. If you have already had children, not being able to have more is unlikely to be as devastating as being told you are infertile when you are childless.

What should you do if you notice any pain or discharge? Any woman, but especially an IUD user, should never ignore these symptoms. The best place to go is in fact a sexually transmitted disease clinic (these are also called departments of genitourinary medicine), since there they will be able to do swab tests to check what type of infection is present. (You do not need a letter of referral from your GP; you can just make your own appointment.) It is also important that your partner is checked, even though it may be embarrassing and difficult to explain, especially if another man is involved. (In the end, it is in your interests to think of some way to tell him, as it is your health at stake and maybe his as well.) If you cannot get to one of these clinics, go to a family planning clinic or your GP. If an internal examination strongly suggests PID, you will need a two-week course of antibiotics, usually oxytetracycline or erythromycin at 500 milligrams four times a day. Amoxycillin is not the right antibiotic in this case (nor indeed is any of the penicillin group), since it is not effective against chlamydia, the most likely organism to be involved. You should also take five days of another antibiotic called metronidazole, or Flagyl, at 400 milligrams twice daily. Metronidazole has a very nasty reaction with alcohol, so avoid alcohol during the course. Tetracycline should not be taken with dairy products, and eryth-romycin can cause bad stomach cramps. Make sure your partner is treated as well and do not have sex with him again until he has finished his antibiotics, or you will be reinfected and go through the whole thing again. If you do not start to feel better within 48 hours, the IUD should be removed, if that was not done earlier, since it can act as a focus of infection and impair recovery. If this is the case you should not have another IUD fitted for six months, if at all. Even after a mild bout you would be best advised to think about alternative methods in the long term.

> *'I was feeling fine, but my cervical smear apparently came back showing a funny infection. I didn't have to have any antibiotics, but my doctor suggested I have a new IUD.'*

There is a very rare but very serious type of PID which is caused by a bacterium called Actinomyces. In practice, it hardly ever occurs, but what does happen is that IUD users can have a cervical smear which shows the presence of 'Actinomyces-like organisms' (ALOs). This is not a definitive statement, but a suggestion that there just might be some Actinomyces present. In such cases, you should first be examined to make sure there are no signs that you need treatment. If not, you could just watch and wait, having annual cervical smears, given that the number of cases of PID due to this organism is so small. You would have to be particularly careful to seek advice if you had even the slightest twinge of pain or discharge. Many women cannot tolerate this kind of uncertainty and choose the other option, which is the one we normally recommend for users of copper IUDs: this is to have the current IUD removed and replaced immediately with another one. If this is done a cervical smear six months later is almost always clear of the ALOs. If you have a Mirena (IUS) fitted, the usual policy is to watch and wait rather than change the device, since the risk is felt to be extremely small.

What happens if you become pregnant while you still have an IUD?

First of all, it must be established that the pregnancy is not ectopic: although accidental pregnancies are uncommon in IUD users, those that occur are more likely to be ectopic. However, if the pregnancy is confirmed to be inside the womb, the course of action will partly depend on whether you want to continue with the pregnancy or not. Obviously, since you still had the IUD in, the chances are that the pregnancy was unintended. If you have an abortion the IUD may as well be taken out at the same time. You might think that if you continue with the pregnancy it would be better to do nothing, in case tampering provokes a miscarriage. However, it has been shown that miscarriage is actually much more likely if the IUD is left inside. Over half the women whose devices are left in will miscarry. There is also the risk of infection and also an increased risk of a premature baby. Usually, therefore, the doctor will very gently try to remove the device. Sometimes the IUD moves upwards and the threads disappear. In such cases there is often no choice but to leave things alone. Reassuringly, there is no evidence that babies born snuggled up to an IUD are more likely to be abnormal.

> *'I hadn't checked my threads for ages, so I was already feeling a bit guilty when I went for my routine visit to the clinic. The doctor did an internal and looked worried. She couldn't feel the threads. When had I last felt them? I felt awful. Had I had a normal period? I couldn't remember. I started to feel sick—could I be pregnant?'*

Lost threads are quite a common problem. After insertion, the IUD often moves up further into the womb: if the threads are on the short side, they may just slide up inside the cervical canal and disappear from view. Unfortunately, if they can be neither seen nor felt an alternative possibility is that the IUD has fallen out or, rarely, perforated the wall of the womb. So first and foremost you should assume that you cannot rely on it for contraception until it has been proved to be present and correct.

After ensuring that you are not pregnant, your doctor should try to see if the threads or the end of the IUD can be found by checking the cervical canal with a pair of forceps. It may be possible to bring the threads down by using a special instrument. If this fails, the chances are that you will be sent for an ultrasound scan, where a special machine is just passed over your abdomen: it is not an X-ray, but is very good at showing whether the IUD is in the right place. Unfortunately, you have to drink a lot of water beforehand, which can make it a little uncomfortable.

If the IUD is in the right place that is fine, provided you want to keep it. Then you can just have regular scans to make sure it is still there (once a year is fine). If you want to have it removed things are a little more complicated. You may need to have a local anaesthetic injection into the cervix so that the device can be searched for more thoroughly. If done by an experienced operator this is usually successful. A general anaesthetic is rarely necessary.

If it is shown that the IUD has in fact gone through the wall of the womb (an uncommon event), then you will need an operation to have it removed. IUDs, and in particular the copper ones, are irritant and can cause the formation of adhesions, as discussed in the section on infection. So, although it is not usually an emergency, any IUD which has gone through the wall of the womb should be removed.

'My doctor said I shouldn't have an IUD because the first one I tried fell out.'

It is certainly true that if a woman loses an IUD there is a higher chance that another will also be expelled. Maybe her womb is trying to tell her something! However, it is also possible that the first one fell out because it was not fitted correctly, so if you are very keen to use an IUD, it is worth another try. It may be helpful to have an ultrasound scan done, in order to check that there is no problem inside the womb itself, for example a fibroid (see page 42).

'I had so many problems with my first IUD. I bled all the time and got cramping pains. In the end I thought having it changed to a different kind would help, so I did. The same thing happened. Then one day I was going out and borrowed a friend's ear-rings, just cheap ones, but they looked nice. I got the most awful swelling and itching of my ears. That was when I remembered

*why I wear gold. And then I thought, could I be allergic to my IUD
as well?'*

Modern IUDs contain copper and sometimes silver as well. In fact
true allergies to pure copper and silver are very rare. Most of the allergies to cheap jewellery are due to nickel, and, although nickel belongs
to the same chemical 'family' as copper, it has not been proved that
women with nickel allergy are more likely to have problems with
copper IUDs. Nevertheless, it does sometimes seem to be the case
that a woman has constant problems with her IUD and no other
explanation is found: when the IUD is removed, her problems stop.

'My doctor said I can't use an IUD because I'm diabetic.'

There has been a suggestion that IUDs are less effective in diabetics,
but recent research has not confirmed this. Also there is concern
about the potential for infection, which would be likely to be worse in
a diabetic. However, if nothing else suits you, then it can certainly be
tried, with careful supervision. A better option, while still using an
intrauterine method, would be the intrauterine system, or Mirena, as
this does not increase the risk of infection.

'I was born with a heart defect: can I use an IUD?'

If there is any increased risk of an infection of the heart valves, called
endocarditis, then it is not a good idea to use an IUD. If this is the
case, you have probably also been advised to take antibiotics when
you have dental treatment. There is always the risk of infection with
an IUD, both during insertion and in the long term, which could be
very dangerous if it spreads to the heart. If for some reason absolutely
no other method is possible, and if your cardiologist approves your
having one, the fitting should be done by an expert under antibiotic
cover, and you would have to be exceptionally careful to avoid any
infection thereafter.

What type of woman is well suited to use an IUD?

Despite the catalogue of potential problems, an IUD is an excellent
choice for many women. Ideally, you would already have a couple of

children, so insertion would be easier, periods are better, and the risk of infertility is not such a problem. You would have light, relatively pain-free periods. You are in a stable relationship where both you and your partner are faithful to each other. You would be over 30, so the failure rate is around one per hundred woman-years, or even lower with the new Copper T 380 device.

Who should think twice about using an IUD?

In particular, young women who have not had children and who are not in a stable relationship. Add to this very heavy, painful periods, a past history of pelvic infection, or an ectopic pregnancy, and you have a recipe for disaster.

The way forward

There is a new IUD on the horizon which will overturn all our current thinking about IUDs. It is even more effective than ordinary IUDs, causes lighter, less painful periods, and does not increase the risk of pelvic infection or ectopic pregnancy. In fact, suddenly almost all the problems we have discussed disappear. This is a hormone-releasing device, the levonorgestrel-releasing IUD.

The levonorgestrel-releasing intrauterine system (Mirena)

Hormone-releasing IUDs are not an entirely new idea. The first released natural progesterone and was called the Progestasert. Unfortunately, this caused a lot of trouble with irregular bleeding, and had a high ectopic pregnancy rate, and needed replacing every year. The Mirena is quite different. It releases a very low-dose of the progestogen levonorgestrel, which has been used in other contraceptives, such as the combined pill and the progestogen-only pill. Because the progestogen does not have to pass through the stomach and liver an extremely low dose can be used, minimizing both health risks and side-effects. The hormone is stored in a special capsule on the stem of the device and is slowly released at a rate of 20 micrograms per 24 hours. There is enough in store to last at least seven years.

How does the Mirena work?

The mechanism of action is actually rather similar to that of the progestogen-only pill. The hormone has three effects. First, it makes

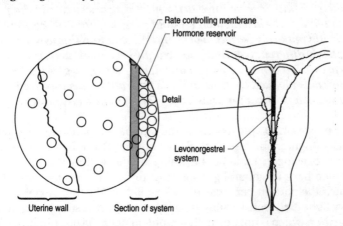

Figure 8.6 The levonorgestrel-releasing intrauterine system (Mirena)

cervical mucus much thicker and less likely to let sperm through. Secondly, it makes the lining of the womb, the endometrium, thinner and less likely to allow implantation to occur (the effect is even stronger than with ordinary IUDs). Lastly, it does have some effect on ovulation. Approximately three-quarters of women who use it ovulate, but one-quarter do not.

Efficacy

Studies have shown that the failure rate is about 0.1 per hundred woman-years (one failure per thousand users per year), even in young women. This is even lower than the rate among users of the best copper IUDs.

Ectopic pregnancy

The Mirena has a very low ectopic pregnancy rate, lower than any of the non-hormonal IUDs, and, indeed, because its overall efficacy is so high, it is actually protective against ectopic pregnancy.

Bleeding patterns

> *'I was amazed when the doctor suggested that an IUD would help my heavy periods. I had always thought IUDs were dangerous and had never wanted to try one. I'd also been told in the past that it was the last method I should consider, precisely because it would make my periods worse. But she said that this was a completely different type and had actually been used successfully in cases just like mine. I was sceptical, but decided to give it a try. I've never looked back. My periods have almost disappeared. I'm not a prisoner for a week out of every month any more.'*

The most remarkable feature of the Mirena is that it actually makes periods lighter and less painful than normal. This is a direct result of the progestogen making the lining of the womb thinner. Most women have irregular, light spotting for the first few months, after which the pattern becomes more regular but the bleeding remains very light. Between 10 and 20 per cent of women stop bleeding altogether, which is not normally a problem (for a full discussion of this subject see Chapter 7 on injectables). The majority of women have a marked reduction in period pain and many say they have less of a problem with pre-menstrual symptoms.

These period-related benefits are so great that the device is being suggested as a solution for women who normally suffer very heavy, painful periods and have decided to have a hysterectomy for this reason. Having the Mirena fitted can often spare such women a major operation.

Pelvic inflammatory disease (PID)

Unlike ordinary IUDs, the Mirena may actually offer protection against PID. The cervical mucus effect is important in this context: if sperm cannot get through, neither can bacteria. As a result, the Mirena is more suitable than copper IUDs for women who are young and childless.

Reversibility

There appears to be no problem with infertility and there is a rapid reversal of the hormonal effects, just as with the progestogen-only pill.

Side-effects

As mentioned above, there can be some irregular spotting, but few women find this a problem. There are no problems with weight gain, blood pressure, or levels of blood fats or sugars. Occasionally acne has been reported, probably because levonorgestrel is still one of the 'older' progestogens (see Chapter 4). Let us hope that a device releasing one of the new progestogens will become available.

Insertion

Here there is a problem for women who have not had children. Because of the hormone-containing reservoir, the Mirena is thicker than most ordinary IUDs (though about the same thickness as the Copper T 380). It is therefore slightly more difficult to insert, particularly in women who have not had children. A local anaesthetic for the fitting is often a good idea (see page 131).

Using the Mirena as part of hormone replacement therapy

This will also be discussed in Chapter 12. Since the device releases a constant, low-dose of progestogen, it is ideal for use in the years approaching the menopause. Between the ages of 40 and 50 many women are starting to have problems with hot flushes, mood swings, vaginal dryness, and so on, and would therefore benefit from hormone replacement therapy (HRT). However, they also need contraception, which is not provided by conventional HRT. The Mirena provides the contraception and also the progestogen which is a necessary part of HRT, to protect the lining of the womb (endometrium) from developing cancer. So all that needs to be done is for the woman to take oestrogen, either as tablets or patches. This is likely to be a major use of the device in the future.

The Gynefix

Many of the problems associated with IUDs are caused by their size, which makes the uterus respond by contracting, causing bleeding and pain. An ingenious idea is to get rid of the plastic frame altogether and get down to basics—nothing but the copper tubing and a thread. This is the Gynefix, developed in Belgium. It consists of six copper tubing segments attached to a nylon thread. There is a knot at the top end which attaches it to the fundus (roof) of the womb when it is inserted (insertion and removal being otherwise very similar to conventional IUDs). Trials have been very successful, with low expulsion rates, high efficacy, and a reduction of side-effects—especially of painful periods.

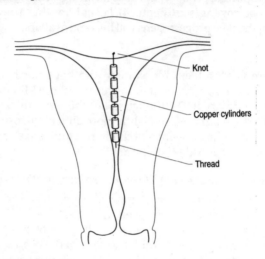

Figure 8.7 The Gynefix IUD

CHAPTER 9

Barrier Methods: Caps and Condoms

The condom (sheath, rubber, French letter)

Condoms are probably the oldest contraceptive methods recorded. They were already known in ancient Egypt, since tomb paintings show men wearing brightly coloured linen sheaths. Fashion certainly changes: it is thought these were in fact used to increase male attractiveness rather than for contraception. The word 'condom' is popularly held to stem from Dr Condom, a physician at the court of Charles II, who is said to have advised the King that use of condoms would prevent illegitimate children and venereal disease. However, it is not certain that any Dr Condom existed and it is rather more likely that the word originated from the Latin 'condus', which means 'receptacle'.

Casanova was a famous user of condoms, to protect himself from venereal disease during his many sexual encounters. However, the first published description was by an Italian doctor, Gabriel Fallopio (who also lent his name to the Fallopian tubes), in 1564. He recommended a linen sheath moistened with lotion as a protection against infection. Linen sheaths, although thick and unwieldy, became widely used in the eighteenth century, again to protect against sexually transmitted disease. James Boswell, Dr Johnson's biographer, recorded the use of condoms in his Journal, referring to them as his 'armour', a term which no doubt reflected their comfort and sensitivity.

In many ways, it was the close connection between condoms and infection which harmed their reputation, since they became generally regarded as something only to be used during illicit sex. Marie Stopes, who campaigned vigorously for contraception in the 1920s, condemned condoms in her book *Contraception*, saying, 'The condom for both emotional and physical reasons is not advisable for use in ordinary healthy coitus. It has its use in connection with disease and danger, and for other special circumstances.' She was firmly of the opinion that contact with semen was somehow beneficial to women and that any method (including coitus interruptus) which prevented this was detrimental to them.

Of course, in the last few years the protective effect of condoms against HIV infection has once again become an important, even life-saving, aspect of their use, and we shall look at this in detail later.

How effective are condoms?

'The leaflet said the failure rate was very low, almost as good as the pill. Yes, it did say that was if you always used it correctly, but you don't start out intending to make a mess of things.'

Condoms can be very effective in older couples who are already experienced in their use. Unfortunately, it is often not made clear that they tend to have a much higher failure rate in young couples, and also among people of any age during the first year of use (that is, there is a learning curve). So, although failure rates of around two per hundred woman-years may be quoted for older, experienced users, for younger couples failure rates of fifteen per hundred woman-years have been shown. In general, it is reasonable to estimate the failure rate for women under the age of 25 as around ten per hundred woman-years (that is, if 100 women used condoms for a year, ten would become pregnant in that time).

What this means is that for young women, in practice, condoms are not nearly as effective as hormonal methods like the combined pill, the progestogen-only pill, and injectables. For this reason it is recommended that, if you are young and wanting very effective contraception and protection against sexually transmitted disease, you should consider using the condom in addition to another, more effective method of contraception.

Why do they fail? Well, mostly because there is just too much human error involved. You can get carried away and your partner does not put one on. He can put it on too late, after genital contact has already happened. He can be in such a hurry he catches it on a finger nail and does not notice the hole till later. He attempts penetration too soon and you are not lubricated enough: the friction makes it break. You add some cream to help the lubrication: it is a cream which damages the rubber. He forgot to hold the teat while putting it on, so the semen leaked out at the base. He can let it slip off during sex. He can let it slip off just after sex. It can leak just a little on the way out of the vagina. After he has taken it off, there are likely to be sperm on the penis, and he makes genital contact again before putting on another one ... By now you may be thinking that the real question is not why they fail, but how do they ever work?

All this explains why more failures happen to couples who are recent users of the method, or who use it only infrequently: basically, practice makes perfect. The problem is getting through the practice period without an accidental pregnancy. It is often recommended that spermicide should be used in addition to the condom, but it has never actually been proved that this improves efficacy because a study would be so difficult to do. However, it makes sense theoretically that addition of a spermicide will act as a back-up if the condom does break or come off. Some condoms are themselves lubricated with a spermicide, or the spermicide can be used separately, as a pessary or cream inserted into the vagina.

It is a pity that more users of barrier methods in general do not realize the availability and importance of emergency contraception (see Chapter 11). The so-called 'morning after pill' can be used up to 72 hours after unprotected sex, whether this was as a result of forgetting to use the condom or because of an accident. Many unplanned pregnancies could be prevented if condom users got themselves to a clinic or their GP for this type of back-up. Another problem is the all-too-frequent assumption that, unless the accident was mid-cycle, there is little risk of pregnancy. Unfortunately, sperm have been known to survive for nearly a week, so an accident shortly after a period can still result in pregnancy.

If you are a condom user, or are planning to use condoms, please read through the section on emergency contraception and, just as importantly, find out how you could get hold of it, particularly at weekends, if you did have an accident. Family planning clinics provide this service, but your local one may not be open at weekends or on certain days of the week. However, your GP should always be able to prescribe emergency contraception (what used to be called the 'morning after pill'), though he or she will not thank you if you call them out at night for it. If all else fails and time is running out, your local casualty department ought to be able to help (after all, you can argue that this is both an accident and an emergency).

So how does the condom work?

Quite simply, by providing a physical barrier which stops sperm from getting into the vagina. The following are ways in which you can try to ensure that this barrier is indeed in place. Use a condom every time you have sex. Never assume it is 'safe'. The condom should be put on as soon as the penis is hard, but before any genital contact has taken place. Minute, invisible amounts of semen can leak out of the penis at any time, but even minute amounts contain thousands of sperm. Pinch the end to expel air, and then roll the condom all the way down to the base of the penis. Take care not to catch the rubber on a fingernail.

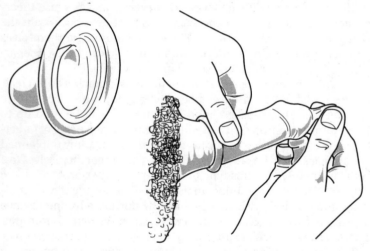

Figure 9.1 Putting on a condom

Do not use any oil-based lubricants as they can rot the rubber within fifteen minutes. If in doubt, do not use any preparations before checking with the manufacturer whether they are oil or water based: if they are oil based they are likely to be unsafe. Here is a list of common substances which should *not* be used with condoms (or diaphragms).

✗ Baby oil
✗ Vaseline
✗ Petroleum jelly (KY jelly is water based and therefore safe)
✗ Gyno-Daktarin cream and pessaries;
✗ Gyno-Pevaryl cream and pessaries (but Pevaryl is safe)
✗ Nystan cream (but pessaries are safe)
✗ Monistat cream
✗ Ecostatin cream and pessaries
✗ Sultrin cream
✗ Butter or margarine, or any kind of oil
✗ Skin lotions
✗ Sun-tan lotions
✗ Face cream
✗ Oestrogen creams, such as those used in hormone replacement therapy (e.g. Premarin, Orthodienoestrol)
✗ Cyclogest (sometimes used for treatment of pre-menstrual syndrome)

The following substances are thought to be safe for use with condoms or diaphragms.

✓ lubricating jellies: e.g. KY jelly or Senselle
✓ Spermicidal creams and pessaries
✓ Aci-jel
✓ Betadine
✓ Canestan cream and pessaries
✓ Pevaryl cream
✓ glycerine

Make sure you withdraw while holding the rim of the condom firmly in place against the base of the penis. Check for tears before you throw it away. If you do notice a tear, get emergency contraception at the earliest opportunity.

Use each condom only once. Make sure that genital contact does not occur again without a new condom in place. Store condoms in a cool, dry place, not exposed to direct sunlight. Heat, humidity, and strong light will all damage rubber. Check the expiry date: condoms should keep for about five years in temperate climates, but only for about three years in the tropics. Also, always make sure that you are using a condom which bears the British Standards Institution Kitemark.

Figure 9.2 The British Standards Kite Mark

How condoms are made and tested

Condoms are produced by dipping glass moulds into latex. They are then dried in an oven, dusted with powder and rolled off the moulds using brushes. A number of tests should be carried out to check their safety. Holes are found by testing for electrical resistance: rubber should not conduct electricity (which is why it is often used as an insulating material). If any electric current manages to go through from one end to the other, there must be a hole. Condoms are also tested for water leakage, by filling them with water until they stretch and seeing if they leak. Their strength is tested by blowing them up like balloons and seeing when they break: a condom should be able to hold 25 litres of air without bursting. Of course, if would be impractical for every single condom to be tested in all these ways. All condoms are tested for electrical conductivity. But, as regards other tests, a few from each batch will be checked: if they fail, the whole batch is rejected, but if they pass, so do the untested ones. However, the number of faulty condoms that slip through is thought to be very small.

All this only applies if the manufacturer has indeed tested the product properly. Different countries have different regulations, so it is wise to check the packet. If it carries the British Standard Kitemark, it has been properly tested. There is also a new International Organization for Standardization (ISO), whose aim is to try to make standards in different countries comparable. Thus an ISO mark is also an indication of a good quality condom.

Different types of condoms

Condoms come in all sorts of thicknesses, materials, colours, and textures, but usually in only one size. This appears to be based on the principle that all penises are the same size when erect, and probably to avoid acute embarrassment at the pharmacy. Indeed, in the USA, when the idea of differing condom sizes was brought up, it was suggested that they would have to be called 'jumbo', 'colossal', and 'supercolossal'.

In the past, condoms were made of linen, then from animal intestines. In fact, lamb intestine condoms are still available, at a price, claiming to be luxury items which provide the best sensation. However, for the last hundred years most condoms have been made of rubber. In order to make them thinner, stretchier, and lubricated, various chemicals are added. Although they are unlikely to cause allergies, it does occasionally happen. If so, you will have to dress expensively in lamb intestines (which are not actually Kitemarked).

Nowadays, condoms come in different colours, even mint flavoured (among others), and with various bumps and ridges, designed to enhance sensation for both partners. Always remember to check, however, that these more exotic types carry the Kitemark.

Where can you get condoms?

The ridiculous thing is that there are very few GP's surgeries that supply condoms. However, family planning clinics will provide free condoms, and they will see men as well as women. Condoms can also be bought from chemists and vending machines: indeed, one of the advantages of the method is that you can get supplies without any form of medical intervention. It is interesting that in Japan, where 75 per cent of couples use condoms, they are sold in supermarkets alongside tampons and sanitary towels. Britain still has a long way to go in terms of marketing.

What are the advantages of condoms?

Of the barrier methods, condoms are probably the most reliable in terms of contraceptive efficacy. They have no health risks and the only real side-effect is that of allergy, to either the rubber or the spermicide.

Once the concept has been understood, condoms are relatively easy to use and do not require visits to the doctor or clinic. This is time saving and provides confidentiality. They are small and easy to carry, as well as being relatively inexpensive (or free from clinics). For some couples, the fact that the semen remains contained within the condom may be an advantage, for example if the woman dislikes the messiness or smell, or if secrecy is important (no stains on the sheets).

'I stopped taking the pill some time ago because I got migraine attacks. Since then I've used a cap, but my boyfriend uses condoms sometimes—he says I should have a rest occasionally!'

Some couples like the man to take responsibility for contraception, or at least to do so some of the time, so that the burden is shared. Also, of course, a condom is visible, providing concrete evidence that contraception is being used. Some men find that the slight tightness helps them maintain an erection, or that the slight reduction in sensual stimulation actually helps prolong intercourse. Condoms may also be a good option for couples needing short-term contraception, for example while waiting to start the pill, or for those who have sex only infrequently.

'I trust my boyfriend, but you can't be too careful nowadays. I'm still on the pill, but I've insisted we still use condoms, at least for a while.'

Condoms provide protection against sexually transmitted diseases, including AIDS (Acquired Immunodeficiency Syndrome). Indeed, the condom is the only contraceptive method which protects against HIV (Human Immunodeficiency Virus) infection. Use of additional spermicide, or spermicidally lubricated condoms, may increase the degree of protection, since the commonly used spermicide, nonoxynol 9, has been shown to have some anti-virus activity in laboratory conditions. It should not be forgotten that the condom also protects against infections which are more common than HIV, such as trichomonas, gonorrhoea, and pelvic inflammatory disease. Cervical cancer is thought to be at least partly caused by a sexually transmitted agent, and, in line with this, long-term condom users appear to have less risk of developing the disease than non-users.

What are the disadvantages?

Probably the greatest disadvantage is the degree to which condoms interfere with intercourse. This may have the effect of cooling the atmosphere, but is also a major reason for non-use or incorrect use, since couples get carried away and forget or make mistakes. Leading on from this is their relatively high failure rate when used by the average couple, compared to non-barrier methods. Some people think of condoms only in relation to illicit sex and feel it would be somehow 'dirty' to use them. This image problem has hindered the more widespread acceptance of condoms for many years, though the advent of AIDS—with all the positive publicity about condom use—has suddenly made them more respectable.

Condoms, of course, require co-operation on the part of the man, which may not be forthcoming. Some men find the loss of sensation unacceptable, which contributes to their reluctance to use them, though ultra-thin condoms may help in this respect. On the other hand, condoms may help some men who have premature ejaculation by reducing the sensitivity of the glans during intercourse. Some couples dislike the lack of genital contact. Allergy to either the rubber, or more commonly the spermicide, may also be a problem. Non-rubber condoms are available, if expensive, and the spermicide problem may sometimes be overcome by using a non-lubricated condom and a separate spermicide, other than nonoxynol 9.

You have to get rid of condoms afterwards: rather than flushing them down the toilet, it is more 'environmentally friendly' just to wrap them in paper and put them in a dustbin, where they will simply be destroyed rather than entering the sewage system.

Why don't more people use condoms?

About 20 per cent of couples in the UK use the condom. Usage varies enormously world-wide, with, for example, 75 per cent of couples in Japan using the method, while Africa, the Middle East, and Latin America together account for only 4 per cent of world-wide use. Usage figures directly reflect the image the condom has in a given country. Where they are positively promoted, usage is higher. Where contraception is a subject only discussed in hushed tones and with embarrassment, usage is lower. In the UK, although advertisements have been seen on television warning about the dangers of AIDS, it is still illegal to advertise condoms on TV before 9.00 p.m. Britain, supposedly liberated and progressive, still has much to learn.

Diaphragms and caps

The terms diaphragm and cap are often used interchangeably, though strictly speaking 'cap' should only refer to cervical caps, which will be discussed later. The idea of a female barrier, like the condom, dates back to early times. The ancient Egyptians (who seem to have been remarkably interested in contraception) promoted the use not only of coloured sheaths, but also of vaginal pessaries made from a combination of honey and crocodile dung. The Talmud in AD 230 recommends the use of a moistened sponge, while a Greek physician in the sixth century AD described pessaries made from the pulp of pomegranates or figs. Prostitutes in ancient Japan and China used pieces of oiled bamboo tissue placed over the cervix. However, the first 'modern' cervical cap was not developed until 1838, by a German gynaecologist. He took a wax impression of the woman's cervix and tailor-made a rubber cap for her (his idea was resurrected more recently, but unfortunately did not prove successful).

The first diaphragm was also developed by a German doctor, who was so worried about his reputation that he used a pseudonym when he published his paper in 1880. Diaphragms quickly became popular in Germany and Holland, to such an extent that they were popularly known as 'Dutch caps' in the UK. Marie Stopes, who advocated cervical caps, but was not so keen on diaphragms, wrote: 'It is widely used in Holland, but from what I know of Dutch women they are somewhat different from the English in build.' What she thought these differences were may be inferred from her comments that it 'must essentially lead to an unwholesome stretching [of the vagina] in the average woman' and that the Dutch cap 'is really useful for slightly abnormal cases, such as very fat women'.

During the first half of this century diaphragms were extremely popular. This is understandable, given the enormous need for contraception and the lack of methods available. The diaphragm at last gave women some control over their fertility, with the advantage over the sheath that it was under the woman's control. However, with the advent of oral contraceptives and IUDs, usage of diaphragms declined, and now only about 2 per cent of contraceptive users rely on this method.

Types of diaphragm

Diaphragms come in a variety of shapes and sizes, as you can see from Figure 9.3. Most common are the flat spring diaphragms, which are generally simple to fit and use. The coil spring variety is useful for women who find the pressure of the rim of the flat spring too great:

this can result in discomfort or symptoms of cystitis. (However, if cystitis is still a problem, changing to a smaller size or using a cervical cap may be useful.)

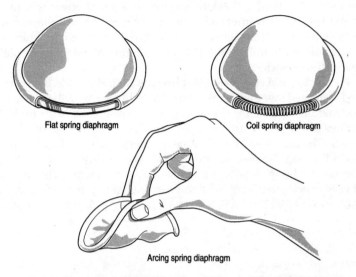

Flat spring diaphragm

Coil spring diaphragm

Arcing spring diaphragm

Figure 9.3 Different types of diaphragm, with part of the rim cut away to show the flat spring and coil spring

Arcing spring diaphragms are often more difficult to insert, but they have a definite advantage. They are of most use to women who find it difficult to be sure that the cervix is covered, particularly women who tend, because of their particular anatomy, to slide their diaphragm in front of, rather than covering, the cervix. This may be especially helpful for women with a retroverted uterus. The womb can lean either forwards (anteverted) or backwards (retroverted): this is as trivial as being right- or left-handed. However, just as left-handed people often find their lives made a little more difficult by everything being geared to right-handers, so women with a retro-verted uterus can find diaphragm fitting takes a little more care and effort. This is really because it is that much easier to slide the diaphragm in front of, rather than covering, the cervix.

This is quite difficult to visualize: the only way to understand how a diaphragm is fitted is to be shown by an experienced doctor or nurse. However, Figure 9.4 gives a rough idea. Care must be taken to ensure that you do not simply hit the side of the cervix, assume that it is the back wall of the vagina, and thus leave the cervix completely exposed. This is why checking with your finger afterwards is to so important. Most women will find it easier to insert a diaphragm either when squatting right down, or with one leg raised (for example on a chair or the toilet seat). Having an empty bladder also usually makes things easier.

Flat spring and coil spring diaphragms should be held by the rim and squeezed together. It often helps to hold the rim with the thumb and middle finger, using the index finger as an 'anchor' in the middle. It does not matter whether the diaphragm is 'dome up' or 'dome down'. The diaphragm should then be inserted into the vagina rather like a tampon, downward and inward. The rim should tuck neatly behind the bony ridge at the entrance to the vagina. You should always check afterwards that you can feel your cervix through the rubber of the diaphragm. A cervix feels rather like the tip of your nose,

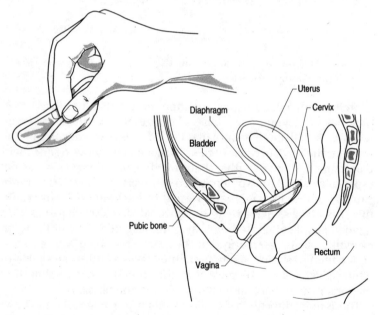

Figure 9.4 Inserting a diaphragm

and will move away if you give it a gentle push. The arcing spring diaphragm has to be 'dome up' to be inserted, but otherwise the principle is the same.

It is important to realize that you cannot harm yourself inserting a diaphragm (or at least, we cannot think of a way in which this is possible). The vagina is very strong and very elastic (how else could it put up with the mechanics of sex—and having babies?), so pushing a piece of rubber around is not going to damage or perforate it. To take it out you need to hook your index finger behind the rim at the front, thus dislodging it from its bony ledge. Then you just pull outward with it grasped between your index and middle fingers.

What about spermicide?

'There I was, in the bathroom, trying to get this thing in. We were about to go for dinner, and at the last minute, I thought, 'I'll be really well organized, I'll put my cap in now.' I slapped the cream on, grabbed the rim—and the stupid thing shot out of my hands and straight out of the window!'

It has never actually been proven that using spermicide with diaphragms improves efficacy, but it makes sense theoretically that it should. The spermicide can make the procedure rather messy, putting couples off. However, you do not need to put an enormous amount on: two strips on the side which will be facing the cervix are probably enough.

When should you put the diaphragm in?

The answer to this is 'any time'. The beauty of the diaphragm is that it does not have to interfere with love-making, in contrast to the sheath. You can put it in before going out for the evening: some women put it in every day and just take it out once for washing. You may think this makes sex premeditated, but in fact it is just like taking a contraceptive pill every day. If you do not have sex, it does not matter; if you do, you are protected.

If you do put your diaphragm in more than three hours before making love, you may need to add more spermicide. You should also add more spermicide each time if you make love more than once. Pessaries are often a quick and convenient way of doing this, or you can add jelly or cream with an applicator.

How long should the diaphragm stay in?

It must not be removed within six hours of the last time you had sex. This is because there are likely to be some hardy sperm floating around the vagina for a few hours, despite the spermicide.

When should I have a new one?

A diaphragm should last around two years, but it is wise to check it regularly in case holes have appeared. Again, like condoms, they last longer in a cool, dry climate than in the tropics.

What about the size?

Diaphragms come in several sizes, from 55 millimetres to 100 millimetres in diameter. In the past, it was thought that exact fitting was crucial: however, since the vagina changes both size and shape during intercourse, this is obviously not the case. (It is also another argument for the use of spermicide, since the physical barrier itself is not sperm-tight.) Nevertheless, if a diaphragm is much too small it is going to be easier to insert incorrectly and to dislodge. If it is too big, it will cause discomfort. So fitting is important, and the size should be checked if you lose or gain more than three kilos (7 lbs.) in weight.

How effective is the diaphragm?

Like the condom, a lot depends on age and experience. In an older (over 35), experienced user, the failure rate can be as low as three per hundred woman-years. However, in new users and younger women failure rates as high as twenty-five per hundred woman-years are often found. In general, in this country it is reasonable to assume a failure rate in younger women of between ten and fifteen per hundred woman-years in practice (meaning that if 100 women used the diaphragm for a year, between ten and fifteen would have an accidental pregnancy).

Failure rates for the diaphragm in particular are often quoted incorrectly, giving the impression to a new user that the method is more effective than it is. Unfortunately, most women are not in a position to know how studies are carried out, and therefore cannot judge the results on this basis. For example, a British study frequently quoted is the Oxford/FPA study, carried out in collaboration with the Family Planning Association. There was nothing wrong with the study, which was carried out as meticulously as one would expect. However, it is important to look at their entry criteria before making decisions based on the results. In this study, which started in the 1960s, all the women were married, white, and with a minimum age at entry of 25 years. Women up to the age of 39 were accepted, regardless of whether they had ever been pregnant. Therefore this was a predominantly middle-class, older group who were well-motivated and careful users, and probably included women who were not highly fertile. But the most important entry criterion was that all the women were already established, successful diaphragm users: they must have used the method successfully for at least five months before entry in the study. This effectively excluded anyone who had fallen pregnant soon after using the method, or who was not sure they were happy with it. As we have discussed before, the failure rate for many methods is highest in new users, especially within the first year of use. Most of such women would have been excluded from this study. Not surprisingly, the failure rates in this group were remarkably good, at six per hundred woman-years in women between the ages of 25 and 34, and two per hundred woman-years in women over 35. Unfortunately, the literature you see often quotes these figures without making it clear that they apply only after the first six months in users over the age of 25.

A study at the Margaret Pyke Centre in London, published in 1984, which included women under 25 (though most were over 20 years old) and new users showed a failure rate for the diaphragm of eleven per hundred woman-years.

Are there any side-effects?

> *'Ever since we started using the diaphragm, I've noticed that I get itching and soreness afterwards. At first I thought I was getting thrush, but I've been checked many times and the tests always come back negative.'*

Allergy to the rubber or to the spermicide can sometimes occur, causing itching. Unfortunately, all diaphragms are made of rubber, but different types of spermicide can be tried (see below). Diaphragm users are at greater risk of cystitis than users of other methods. This is thought to be partly due to the pressure of the rim on the bladder neck (see Figure 9.4) and also because the diaphragm 'traps' secretions and bacteria, causing them to be in the vagina longer than they would be otherwise. Using a coil spring diaphragm may help, and also using a smaller size. However, if the problem persists, the only final solution is to use a different method. Cervical caps are a suitable alternative, and are discussed later in this chapter. If the diaphragm is too big, sustained pressure on the vaginal walls can cause soreness or even abrasions. Once again, changing to a coil spring diaphragm and reducing the size should help.

Advantages of the diaphragm

'It's great. At last I really feel in control: I always somehow felt 'different' when I was taking the pill, now I'm back to my old self. I can still make love whenever I want, I put the cap in every morning, just like I took the pill.'

The main advantage is almost certainly the lack of side-effects and health risks. There is really no way a diaphragm can pose an appreciable risk to your health—unless it would be dangerous for you to become pregnant. Indeed, diaphragms may have some health benefits, in that they appear to offer some protection against pelvic inflammatory disease (salpingitis or infection of the Fallopian tubes). Also, diaphragm users appear to be at slightly less risk of developing cervical cancer. It is possible that these protective effects are at least partly due to the concurrent use of spermicide.

Use of the diaphragm is under the woman's control, and in addition it can be inserted at any time before intercourse. Both of these considerations often make it preferable to the condom. Once it has been fitted and the technique mastered, the user is relatively independent of medical or nursing attention.

Disadvantages of the diaphragm

'I thought we were going back to my place before we went out, but he'd cooked dinner and drove me straight to his flat after work as a surprise. He'd gone to so much effort and it was all so romantic. I kept thinking, 'I haven't got my diaphragm, I'll have to tell him.' But it got more and more difficult.'

The most important disadvantage is its relatively high failure rate. Human error is probably a major factor. Too often, diaphragms are sitting idle in their boxes when they should be inside their owners! They may be inserted incorrectly, especially if this is done in a rush just before sex. They may be dislodged during sex, without anyone noticing. They may be removed too soon, or the spermicide may be forgotten. They may have developed a hole which has gone unnoticed. All diaphragm users should be aware of the existence of emergency contraception (see Chapter 11) for occasions when they realize things have gone wrong.

Some couples find use of the diaphragm interferes with love-making, though this can be overcome by earlier insertion. Men sometimes complain they can feel it, which may be a sign that it is not correctly positioned. Allergy, usually to the spermicide, can occur in either partner, but can often be helped by changing the brand. The spermicide is often perceived as being messy: again changing the type may help. Use of a diaphragm inevitably involves the woman in touching and manipulation of her genital area. While some women like 'getting to know more about themselves', others find the whole idea very off-putting.

Who should consider using a diaphragm?

'I was fed up with taking the pill, it was all right before we were married, but now being pregnant wouldn't be a problem. I'd rather it didn't happen for another six months or so, but it wouldn't be a disaster if it did.'

'Alice was born three months ago and I'm breastfeeding her. I want to have my children close together, so that they can play with each other. I suppose we'll try for another baby when Alice is about eighteen months old. Matt is using a sheath at the moment, but we're getting fed up with it.'

These two women are excellent candidates for using a diaphragm. They both want a pregnancy fairly soon, and are not too worried when it happens. Breastfeeding in itself gives some contraceptive protection, so this will improve the efficacy of the diaphragm. Basically, the diaphragm is suitable for any woman who does not need a high degree of protection against pregnancy. This also includes older women, in their forties, who are less fertile. You will not know if you like using it until you actually try one. Often women are surprised at how easy they find it, though others realize it is not for them.

Cervical caps

There are three main types of cervical cap, the Prentif cavity-rim, the Vimule, and the Dumas. The main advantages of all these caps is that they are small, cannot be felt during sex, and can be left in place for more than 24 hours if desired. They are particularly suitable for women who have poor vaginal muscles and cannot keep a diaphragm in place, or who have had trouble with cystitis when using a diaphragm. Marie Stopes was a great advocate of cervical caps, which she felt were the least intrusive form of contraception. Indeed, she is said to have suggested that half a lemon squeezed and placed over the cervix was better than nothing in an emergency!

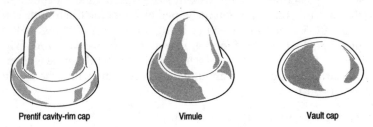

Prentif cavity-rim cap   Vimule   Vault cap

Figure 9.5 Cervical caps

The Prentif cavity-rim cap is thimble shaped and fits over the cervix, where it is held by suction. To be able to use one of these, you must have a reasonably long, straight-sided, symmetrical cervix and must also be able to reach it properly: short fingers and a long vagina are not a good combination here. Prentif caps are available in three sizes and must be fitted by an expert or they just slip off. The cap should be about one-third full of spermicide and is then fitted by locating the cervix and pushing the cap into place, pinching it first to create the suction pressure. It is very important to check that the cap is sitting firmly against the cervix, as dislodgement is the most common problem with this method. To remove the cap, you have to break the suction seal by tipping the cap with your finger, hook your finger over the rim and then pull.

The Dumas cap is shallow, bowl-shaped, and useful for women with poor muscle tone whose cervix is not suitable for the cavity-rim cap, for example women who have a short, wide cervix. It works by suction to the vaginal wall. The Vimule is a sort of combination of the cavity-rim and the Dumas caps, in that it has a high, narrow dome, but is wide and fat at the sides, allowing for suction to the vaginal wall. It is useful for women who have an irregularly shaped cervix.

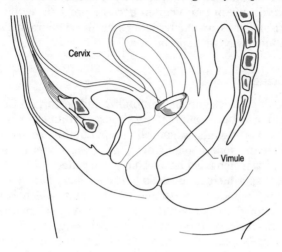

Figure 9.6 Cervical cap in place

Learning to use one of these caps usually takes longer than learning to use a diaphragm, and not all women are suitable. The efficacy appears to be similar to that of the diaphragm, though fewer studies have been done. As with the diaphragm, more spermicide should be added each time you have sex, and the cap should be left on for at least six hours afterwards. Indeed, some women wear these caps for several days without removing them at all, and this does not cause problems. However, it is preferable to remove them after 30 hours because of the small risk of toxic shock syndrome.

What about the honey cap?

The idea behind the honey cap was that a small diaphragm was soaked in honey before use, in the hope that the honey would allow it to be left in the vagina continuously for a week without vaginal infections or odour. It was originally designed by an American gynaecologist, who claimed good results. Unfortunately, no one has yet managed to duplicate them, but trying to do so has in fact provided indirect evidence that diaphragms work better with spermicide than without: a British study of a similar diaphragm showed a failure rate of twenty-five per hundred woman-years (in other words one in four women become pregnant within the first year of use). This is obviously higher than for a diaphragm used in the conventional way, with spermicide.

Spermicides

Spermicides are designed to immobilize and destroy sperm. Women appear to have been willing to try almost anything: crocodile dung, honey, rock salt, vinegar, carbolic soap, quinine, cocoa-butter, fig paste, mercury, lemon juice, Coca Cola . . . Since sperm dislike acidity, anything which is acidic may have some effect.

Modern spermicides consist of an active ingredient and a carrier. The active ingredient is usually a surfactant, which is short for 'surface-acting', meaning it destroys the sperm cell membrane (its 'skin'). The carrier is simply the way in which you get the active ingredient into the vagina. They come in several different types: jellies, creams, foams, foaming tablets, pessaries, and film. Jellies and creams come with an applicator if you want to insert them directly into the vagina. They can also be smeared on to a diaphragm or cap. Foams are manufactured as an aerosol spray, which is also inserted into the vagina by means of an applicator. Foaming tablets are not available in the UK at present, but are widely used in other countries. (A feature of the foaming tablet is that it creates a feeling of warmth in the vagina: although this put couples off at first, it is now being used as a positive marketing feature: 'Neo Sampoon—for that warm sensation'.) C-Film is a square which can be directly applied to the cervix, wrapped around the tip of the penis, or used on the inside surface of a diaphragm. Pessaries are bullet shaped and look like suppositories. They are simply inserted high into the vagina with the fingers.

The most commonly used active ingredient is nonoxynol 9. This is to be found in creams, jellies, spermicidally lubricated sheaths, and foam. Indeed, if in doubt, you can assume you are using nonoxynol 9. Table 9.1 gives a list of common brands and the spermicide they contain.

TABLE 9.1 Common types of spermicide

Brand name	Name of ingredient
Foams	
Delfen Foam	Nonoxynol 9 (12.5%)
Creams	
Delfen cream	Nonoxynol 9 (5%)
Duracreme	Nonoxynol 9 (2%)
Orthocreme	Nonoxynol 9 (2%)
Jellies	
Duragel	Nonoxynol 9 (2%)
Orthogynol	Di-isobutylphenoxypolyethoxyethanol (1%)
Gynol II	Nonoxynol 9 (2%)
Staycept	Octoxynol (1%)
Pessaries	
Double Check	Nonoxynol 9 (6%)
Orthoforms	Nonoxynol 9 (5%)
Staycept	Nonoxynol 9 (6%)

Note: All spermicidally lubricated sheaths use nonoxynol 9.

As you can see, the list is pretty monotonous: nonoxynol 9, virtually throughout. This is bad news if you happen to have an allergy to nonoxynol 9. In this case your choice becomes restricted to Staycept jelly (not the pessaries) and Orthogynol jelly.

When used alone, spermicides have failure rates ranging from eleven to thirty per hundred woman-years. They are therefore better used in conjunction with other methods, such as diaphragms or sheaths. Pessaries should be inserted into the vagina about ten to fifteen minutes before intercourse, which some couples find a nuisance. Jellies, foams, and creams are effective immediately. Inevitably, there is some discharge when they dissolve, which makes the method rather messy.

Laboratory testing suggests that nonoxynol 9 does not only kill sperm, but can affect some sexually transmitted infections, such as gonorrhoea and chlamydia. For this reason spermicides are sometimes recommended for use in conjunction with IUDs, to help prevent the acquisition of infection. It has even been suggested that nonoxynol may destroy HIV, the virus which causes AIDS, but it should be stressed that this occurred in a test tube, not in a woman. Against this is a study which showed that repeated daily use of nonoxynol could cause abrasions of the vaginal wall, which might make HIV transmission easier. Normal use does not seem to cause this problem.

At one time there was concern about the possible effects of spermicides on babies born when the method failed. It was suggested that there might be a higher risk of congenital abnormalities: however, studies have so far failed to confirm any link whatever.

The female condom (Femidom)

The Femidom has been available in this country since 1992, with the idea that it combines the features of a condom and a diaphragm. Like a diaphragm it is used by women and can be inserted well before intercourse (the inner ring aids insertion, which is similar to that of a diaphragm, though you do not need to check that the cervix is covered). Like a male condom, it prevents genital contact and also contact with semen, but does this by lining the vagina, rather than covering the penis.

In theory, like the male condom, the Femidom should protect against sexually transmitted diseases, including AIDS; however, there are as yet no studies actually showing this. Although the original version was lubricated with the spermicide nonoxynol 9, recent worries about possible over-use of this spermicide (see earlier) led to the manufacturers changing to a silicone (non-spermicidal) lubricant.

Like the male condom, it is available over the counter and comes with an illustrated leaflet. Another advantage is that, because it is made of polyurethane, rather than latex rubber, it is about ten times less likely than the male condom to break during use. In addition it is completely resistant to damage by the chemicals affecting male (latex) condoms, which are listed on page 151.

There have been few studies on the efficacy of the Femidom, but, in general, it appears to have a failure rate of around twelve to fifteen per hundred woman-years, comparable to other barrier methods.

Reports about its acceptability are mixed, and a sense of humour certainly helps. A particular advantage for some couples is that it does not require the penis to be fully erect before actual (and protected) intercourse can commence. However, problems have included the possibility of the penis 'missing' the correct position, and entering the vagina down the outside of the condom—which means, of course, that you aren't protected at all. In a research study of volunteer cohabiting couples, there were also complaints that it was aesthetically unattractive, since the outer rim remains outside the vagina, easily visible to both parties. Over half of these couples dropped out of the trial within the first three months because they did not like the method. However, roughly a third did find the method satisfactory and said they would carry on using it. Some couples alternate with male condoms—'his night' then 'her night'! The acceptability of the Femidom in more casual relationships, where the partners do not know each other so well, has not been studied. No method suits everyone, so every development that widens choice is welcome, especially when the method is under the woman's control.

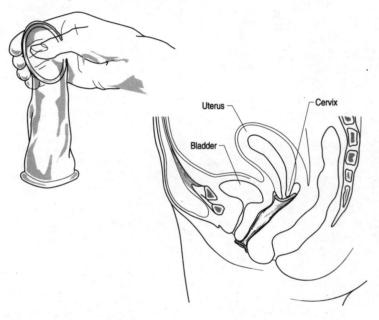

Figure 9.7 The female condom

In summary

Barrier methods are a useful option, though they are not as effective as the more 'medical' methods. They are relatively free of side-effects and health risks and, once initially mastered, simple to use. An important aspect of their use is protection against sexually transmitted disease. Condoms can prevent the transmission of HIV, and thus are advocated for safer sex along with another method providing a higher degree of protection against pregnancy. Research is continuing to design simpler, more effective and acceptable barriers and spermicides, which do not interrupt love-making. Some of these ideas are discussed in Chapter 15.

CHAPTER 10

Natural Family Planning

'John and I felt very strongly that we didn't want to tamper with nature, but we did want to limit the size of our family. Using this method has made us feel closer, because both of us have to be involved all the time. John can't just leave me to it and say, "It's your problem, dear." He came to all the teaching sessions and learnt about the methods. Now he's the one who hands me my thermometer as he goes to make our morning tea. I think we have a better, more understanding relationship because of it.'

Natural family planning is what most people think of as the 'rhythm method', although this is a bad name because in fact it involves much more than just counting days. It has tended to have a poor image, partly because it involves relatively long periods of abstinence, and also because (since these are often not actually observed) it can have a high failure rate. However, in highly motivated, properly taught couples, the failure rate in use can be comparable to that of barrier methods.

Many people dabble in the rhythm method: what woman has not at one time tried to calculate whether last night was 'safe' or not? However, this is precisely the worst way to go about it. If you are serious about using natural family planning, then it becomes a combination of an art and a science, with a proper training period. Indeed, it is quite impossible to learn this technique from a book, since practical guidance and learning on yourself are of paramount importance. At the back of this book you will find the addresses of organizations which offer teaching: most of the people involved in this are not in fact doctors, but lay people who are long-term users themselves and want to pass on their knowledge, experience, and enthusiasm to others.

There are a few crucial facts that all potential users must know.

First, the egg is released from the ovary between twelve and sixteen days before the next period begins, so you cannot be sure of the timing until afterwards. Once released, the egg can live only about 24 hours, so after that pregnancy is impossible. However, and this is where most people come unstuck, sperm can laze around in the cervix, womb, and tubes for up to seven days just waiting for an egg to come along. So, in a short cycle, even having sex straight after a period could cause pregnancy.

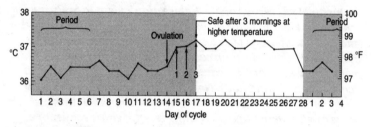

Figure 10.1 An example of a temperature chart, showing the rise which occurs after ovulation

So how do you calculate the 'safe period'? Well, if you just use the calendar method, it goes like this. First you must keep a diary of the length of your cycles for at least six months. Work out what your longest and shortest cycles are. The earliest you could ovulate would be sixteen days before the end of your shortest cycle (for example if this was twenty-five days long, you could ovulate on day 9). Now deduct another seven days to allow for sperm survival. That brings you to day 2. The latest you could ovulate would be twelve days before the end of your longest cycle, so if that was thirty days, you could ovulate on day 18. Now add 48 hours for egg survival, to be on the safe side. That brings you to day 20. Using this method, you can see that you cannot safely have sex from the second day of your period until the twentieth day of your cycle. (Some natural family planning teachers may allow you more days but this increases the risk of failure because of the lengthy survival of sperm.) In effect, you will have between five and ten days each month when sex is 'safe'. It is just bad luck if your partner is away then, or you have a cold.

Recording your body temperature

Because the calendar method used alone is so restrictive, other methods are usually added to try and work out the timing more accurately. One way is to measure your temperature every morning before getting up or having a drink. When you ovulate, the ovary alters its production of hormones, and starts to produce more progesterone and less oestrogen. Progesterone makes your temperature go up (have you ever noticed that you feel warmer the week before your period?), although it is by less than 1° Celsius. To measure your temperature to such a degree of accuracy it helps to have a special thermometer, either a bigger-scale mercury thermometer, or an electronic one. It is also very important that you measure your temperature in the same place each time, either under the tongue, or in the vagina or rectum, and that you leave the thermometer in for the full time (five minutes under the tongue, three minutes in the vagina or rectum).

To use this technique properly, you need to take your temperature every day and plot it on a chart. When you have noticed a consistent rise (over three days) of between 0.2° and 0.6° Celsius, you can assume that ovulation has occurred. The temperature usually drops again just before menstruation, so when the rise is sustained this method can also be used as an indicator of pregnancy. Unfortunately, if you have a cold or other illness your temperature may go up, so you have to be careful that you have the 'correct' rise. For this reason it is good also to have a calendar worked out, so that you know how plausible it would be for ovulation to have taken place at a given time.

Cervical mucus changes

This is often called the 'Billings method' because it was pioneered by an Australian husband and wife team called Billings. They showed that the mucus produced by glands in the cervix changes at different times in the cycle in response to the hormones released by the ovaries. Early in the cycle there is very little mucus, and it is thick and sticky. However, as ovulation approaches and more oestrogen is produced by the ovaries, the mucus becomes more and more watery. It also becomes elastic, so that it will stretch for several centimetres, and is sometimes described as being like raw egg white. This is called 'spinnbarkeit', which is just the German for 'stretchiness'. After ovulation has taken place the mucus once again goes back to being thicker, sticky, and sparse, as it was at the beginning of the cycle.

A woman can be taught to recognize these changes in her mucus, but a lot of teaching and practice are involved, not to mention a willing attitude! She has to observe her mucus every day, noting how copious it is and how far it can be stretched. The mucus gets stretchier and stretchier and then one day it suddenly changes back to the dry, sticky type. Ovulation is assumed to have happened on the day before, that is, the last day of the stretchy mucus. Four days are allowed for safety before it is considered that there is no risk of pregnancy.

Many things can interfere with the cervical mucus. Sex, for a start, as the semen will produce a discharge which, to an inexperienced woman, can seem similar to the watery type of mucus. For this reason couples using the method are often advised only to have sex on alternate days during the first half of the cycle. If you have any kind of vaginal infection, such as thrush (candida) or trichomonas, there may be a discharge which may mask the mucus. Or, if you decide occasionally to use a barrier method, the spermicidal cream or pessary will produce a discharge.

Changes in the cervix itself

At the beginning of the cycle the cervix tends to lie low in the vagina, near the entrance, and feels dry and firm. As ovulation approaches, it gradually moves upward, making it harder to reach. It also feels softer and wet, because of the mucus which its glands are producing. If you feel its centre, the hole which was tightly closed is now likely to admit a finger. After ovulation the cervix once again starts to move downwards towards the entrance of the vagina and also becomes firm and dry, as at the beginning of the cycle.

Ovulation pain

'Every month, in the middle of the month, I get a sudden sharp pain on one side. It is really quite bad and lasts a day. After that, just as suddenly as it came on, it disappears. Although I used to

be worried by it, once I realized that it meant that I was ovulat-ing, it's actually quite useful. I don't have to keep charts or do anything, I just wait for my pain and a couple of days later I know I'm safe.'

A minority of women can actually feel themselves ovulate. They get a sudden sharp pain on one side, which is thought to be caused by the covering of the ovary being stretched prior to the release of the egg. Again, this has a German name, 'mittelschmerz', which just means 'mid-cycle pain'. The egg is actually released about 24–48 hours after the pain, so, allowing three days for its life span, you can assume it is safe to have sex five days after the pain occurs. However, waiting until the fourth day after the peak mucus symptom would be more reli-able if there is ever any discrepancy with the calculation based on this pain.

Being taught

Teaching natural family planning is a highly skilled process. It involves imparting basic information about the menstrual cycle and how to detect the changes in temperature, mucus, and so on, but also being able to support the couple emotionally if they have difficulty coming to terms with the method. The World Health Organization has recognized the special qualities required of teachers in this field and has produced guidelines for the training of people who want to teach the method. You should always make sure that you are being taught by someone with proper training, since your success will depend greatly on their expertise. Most teachers will want to teach the couple together, rather than just the woman herself, so you should discuss beforehand whether this is going to be acceptable and feasible. This is a very individual form of teaching, which will be tailored to suit you as a couple.

Combining the different techniques

In order to try to increase the chances of success, most couples are advised to use a combination of the techniques described above. The particular 'mix' will depend on individual preference and possibil-ities. However, as you may have noticed, these methods may not give you sufficient warning of when ovulation is going to occur. This is why all of them will fail more often if you have sex before ovulation, and there are sperm around just when you do not need them. Natural family planning can have a low failure rate, but generally this requires you to restrict penetrative sex to the post-ovulatory part of the cycle.

Combining natural family planning with other methods

'I prefer to be in charge of my body, not put chemicals into it, so we use a combination of the temperature chart and changes in my mucus. We tried doing it really strictly at first, with no sex until after the temperature had gone up for three days, and the mucus had gone dry, but sometimes it was just too much of a strain. So I used my diaphragm in the second week of my cycle, when it might be more risky. The trouble with that was that the jelly really messed up the cervical mucus and I couldn't rely on it. So now Richard uses the condom instead, which is much better, as the mucus changes aren't affected.'

Some couples find that they can use natural methods part of the time and a barrier for the more risky times in the first half of the cycle. This gives greater freedom in terms of the timing of love-making and may therefore prove more acceptable in the long term. However, you have to remember that if you do this, you are accepting the failure rate which comes with the use of barrier methods, so, in fact, the overall efficacy may not be as good as if you did indeed keep strictly to the post-ovulatory time.

Special circumstances when natural family planning is not reliable

- Immediately after stopping the pill. Since you have not been having normal cycles, you cannot know what your pattern of bleeding will be, nor can you be used to the changes in cervical mucus throughout the month. You may not have a period for several months, so you may wait endlessly for the right mucus pattern and for your temperature to rise. You can start trying to use the natural family planning approach after you have had a 'proper' period, unconnected with the pill (but users of the Persona are advised to wait three months after stopping the pill).

- While breastfeeding. Breastfeeding can in itself be slightly contraceptive (see below), depending on how fully you are doing it, but it may not combine very well with natural family planning. The hormonal changes which occur during breastfeeding can make both the cervical mucus and temperature methods give confusing results, and may lead to both false reassurance and false alarms (see Chapter 12).

- Immediately after a baby (when not breastfeeding), a miscarriage, or an abortion. Again, your cycles may take a while to get back to normal and hormonal changes may confuse the picture.

- In the years approaching the menopause. Periods often become erratic and unpredictable at this time, making the calendar unreliable. There are also hormonal fluctuations as the ovaries gradually wind down production, which again will affect the temperature and mucus methods.

Advantages of natural family planning

The major reason for use of this method is undoubtedly when religious or cultural teaching prohibits anything else. However, it is also a valid choice for those couples who like the feeling of having control of their fertility without outside interference. It certainly teaches you about the natural cycle and is actually a very good way of learning the optimum times for achieving pregnancy when you want to.

Once learnt, the method costs nothing and involves no visits to clinics or doctors. It is also always available, unlike pills or diaphragms, which may be in the wrong place at the wrong time. The method requires a great deal of co-operation and involvement on the part of the male partner, which may be viewed as a welcome sharing of responsibility. It involves no health risks for the woman, which is often an important consideration for those choosing to use it.

Disadvantages of natural family planning

'The "safe period" may be used by individuals who find that their own type is such that the 'safe period' is suitable, but it should never be recommended in general. Even for those whom it appears to suit, I think the method a cold, calculating, pseudo-restraint which tends to debase the true sex relation and reacts unfavourably on the character of both participating parties, and is, moreover, quite unnatural.' (Marie Stopes, 1923.) Marie Stopes had strong views on natural family planning, as she did on most subjects! Indeed, she went on to say, 'No natural female animal allows the male entry when she is not "on heat". It is also unnatural because it prescribes the times at which a man is to approach his wife without any relation whatever to his feelings, to her natural disposition and rhythm, or to incidental and quite right stimuli such as anniversaries, romantic remembrances etc.' She added, concerning the type of woman whom it might suit, 'I have noticed these women, however, are of the type which I should call "ascetic" or intellectual, with the sex activity rather below than above normal, although their emotional and affectional activity is strong and romantically felt.'

Certainly, the restrictions placed on the timing of sex can defeat many couples. On the other hand, those who continue often say that their relationship is stronger in other ways as a result. This is something that individuals have to work out for themselves, and inevitably leads to a process of self-selection of those couples who feel they can cope.

Very few statistics are available on couples practising natural family planning, because they do not attend clinics or come to their doctors' attention.

Although natural family planning can be quite effective if adhered to strictly, in practice it often has a high failure rate, precisely because couples 'cheat' on days which are not safe. So, unless you have a will of iron, it is probably not an ideal method if you need very effective contraception.

There has been some suggestion, still unproved, that when the method fails the resulting pregnancy may be more likely to have a congenital abnormality or to miscarry. This is because it is more likely that, when a failure occurs, an ageing sperm will meet up with an ageing egg, which may produce a higher chance of congenital abnormality. Spontaneous early miscarriages are common, and are thought to be the body's way of dealing with an obviously abnormal foetus. However, although such a risk has been shown in animals and in two human studies, other good studies have not supported it. If there is a problem then it is certainly very small.

Breastfeeding

You may be surprised to find breastfeeding listed as a method of natural family planning, but it is nature's way of trying to protect a mother from having another pregnancy too soon. When a baby suckles, it makes the pituitary gland in the brain produce a hormone called prolactin. The main action of prolactin is to stimulate the breast tissue to produce more milk. However, it also has a secondary effect, that of stopping the release of hormones which act on the ovary and lead it to produce eggs. If high levels of prolactin are maintained consistently, ovulation will not occur. This is why women who fully breastfeed often do not see a period for some months.

However, in this country it would not be wise to assume that breastfeeding on its own gives a reliable degree of protection against pregnancy. In some cultures, where the mother demand-feeds for up to three years, it is certainly an effective way of preventing pregnancy, but very few mothers in the West are going to feed in this way, which really does mean feeding the baby very frequently, and not timing or spacing out the feeds at all—even at night. Unfortunately, if you do not do this, the production of prolactin becomes reduced and will not be enough to prevent ovulation, so getting the baby to sleep through the night, or introducing occasional bottle feeds, will reduce the contraceptive effect. Nevertheless, normally less effective contraceptive methods are often quite suitable for use while breastfeeding because the combination of the two results in an efficacy which is better than that of either used alone (see Chapter 12).

New technology

Ironically, the advances which are being made in this area are mostly the products of the ever-increasing and lucrative field of infertility treatment. One such is the Persona.

This is a small computer, not much bigger than a computerized personal organizer, but also incorporating your very own mini laboratory! It measures two hormones, Luteinizing Hormone (see Chapter 1) and a product of oestrogen in your urine. By doing this, it can work out in advance when ovulation is likely to occur, and give ample warning to allow for sperm survival. It also monitors the actual ovulation time, so that it can tell you when it is definitely safe again.

Basically, it is a very sophisticated way of avoiding all those temperature measurements, mucus assessments and calculations.

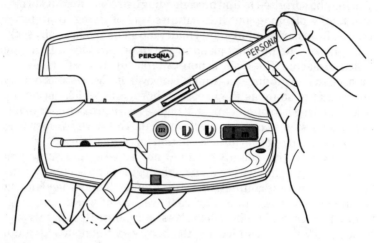

Figure 10.2 The Persona monitor and test stick

How does it work in practice? First of all, the computer has to get to
know your individual, unique cycle. In order to do this, you need to
give it information for three months, in the form of urine tests. It
comes with dipsticks for the urine samples; these are inserted into
the device and measure the levels of the two hormones. In the first
month, sixteen urine tests are necessary, reducing to eight as the
computer 'gets to know you'. It communicates with you by a
sequence of coloured lights: a red light tells you it is definitely not safe
to have sex, a green light says 'all clear' and a yellow light means it
needs more information and therefore you should do a urine test.

As the measurements are very accurate, there should only be
about eight days in the month when the device gives a red light. However, you should expect more 'red days' during the first three
months, while the computer is still collecting information. Early
studies have suggested that only between five and seven women in a
hundred would get pregnant in a year, if they use the device correctly,
and abstain during the 'red phase'. However, remember that if you
choose to use a condom or diaphragm during the 'unsafe' days, you

will then be subject to the failure rates of those methods. On the other hand the failure rate can be reduced by, for example, using a condom during the first green phase (from the first day of your period until the red light shows, which is always less safe), abstaining when the red light shows, and then using nothing during the second green phase.

Naturally, the Persona cannot work if you are using a hormonal method of contraception (or have done within the last three months). However, it may not be so obvious that the emergency pill is a problem. If you do have unprotected sex during the red phase, either using nothing or because a barrier method fails, you might think 'Oh, I'll nip down to the clinic and get the emergency pill to be on the safe side.' However, if you do indeed take it, you will have to reset your Persona all over again, as though starting anew—and not rely on it for three months. So, potentially, if you have an accident four times a year, and take the emergency pill, you may be unable to rely on your Persona at all!

The manufacturers advise that the device should only be used by women who have cycles that are between 23 and 35 days in length. In addition, it should not be used while breastfeeding or if you are starting to go through the menopause (because in both cases, hormone levels may fluctuate too greatly). Persona is not available on the NHS, but can be obtained from chemists. (The price (currently) is £49.95 for the device itself and monthly supplies of test sticks cost £9.95.)

CHAPTER 11

Emergency Contraception: Not Only for the Morning After

The idea of trying to shut the stable door after the horse has gone has been around since ancient times. Various methods have been suggested, including jumping several times immediately after sex, in an attempt to dislodge the sperm, and douching with various mixtures, some quite extraordinary: American students in the 1960s are even said to have used Coca Cola. However, since sperm reach the womb within seconds of ejaculation, none of these methods can prevent pregnancy.

> *'We were having such a lovely evening, and I realized he really was a great guy. I had planned to wait at least a few more months, to be sure, but I was sure already. I hoped he would use something, but he didn't.'*
>
> *'Half-way through dinner I suddenly had a mental picture of my cap—sitting at home in the bathroom cabinet. How could I have been so stupid? And he'd gone to so much effort, planning the evening. I couldn't ruin it now. It was only a few days after my period—I'd take a chance.'*
>
> *'He said he'd used Durex before, but I could see he didn't really know what to do with it. The trouble is, neither did I. I wasn't that surprised when it came off.'*

For various reasons it is clearly necessary that there should be some effective way of preventing pregnancy after sex rather than before. Many young women, when having sex for the first time, fail either to use any contraception themselves or to ask their boyfriends to do so. Problems can also arise with barrier methods of contraception, such as the diaphragm or the sheath: sheaths may break or slip off, diaphragms can be dislodged, or on some occasions they may be forgotten altogether. It is also very important to be able to prevent a pregnancy after the event in the case of rape.

Nowadays, there are two main methods of post-coital or emergency contraception: the emergency pill and the IUD.

The emergency pill

The old name for this, the 'morning-after pill' is now out of date, because it is so misleading. Its name implies that you have to leap out of bed and rush to your doctor that same day: in fact, the most commonly used type can be given up to 72 hours after the event. Although a number of different methods have been used, most of these involved high-doses of oestrogens for several days, and they consequently produced too many side-effects. Instead, the modern emergency pill consists of two high-dose combined pills, with another two to be taken twelve hours later. It is common for women to experience nausea after taking the pill, and some 20 per cent will vomit at some time during the 24 hours. It is often helpful to take the tablets with food, as taking them on an empty stomach seems to make both nausea and vomiting more likely. If you should vomit within three hours of taking any of the tablets there is a possibility that they may not have been absorbed, so it is important that you return to the doctor and get some more. If you think you may have trouble in this way discuss it with your doctor or nurse. One option is to take an anti-emetic tablet (like a travel sickness tablet such as Kwells or Joy-rides) about an hour before the pills to prevent vomiting. However, anti-emetics themselves can have side-effects; also their use makes the pill-taking procedure more complicated.

From this it must be obvious that emergency pills are by no means a perfect solution to the problem, and it is not recommended that anyone should rely on them frequently. However, they are better than nothing, and many women are content to feel sick for a day if this is the price of escaping an unwanted pregnancy.

'I thought I'd better come because we didn't use anything last night. I'm mid-cycle now, so I guess I could become pregnant.'

It is only possible to take the emergency pill after the first time unprotected sex has occurred since your last period. There is no truth in the idea that having sex without contraception is quite safe early on in the cycle, provided that you remember to get an emergency pill after sex on day 14. It is, on the contrary, perfectly possible to become pregnant as a result of sex taking place as early as day 5: since, as we have said, sperm are capable of surviving in the uterus for up to seven days, they can be lying in wait for the egg when it appears. However, there are alternatives. Those women who have let more than 72 hours pass since having unprotected sex, or who have had sex several times, may be able to be fitted with an IUD, which is very effective in this situation and is discussed later in the chapter.

How does the emergency pill work?

The way in which the emergency pill works depends on where you are in your cycle at the time. If ovulation (releasing an egg) has not yet taken place, then the pill can delay it. In this case the hope is that the sperm will have died by the time you ovulate. However, since another, later arrival of sperm could still cause pregnancy, you should take care to remember to use the sheath or diaphragm for any sex after the treatment.

If, on the other hand, you have already ovulated, then the emergency pill will prevent the embedding of the fertilized egg in the womb (implantation). This has been described as an abortion, but is does not fulfil the legal definition of the term. Both scientifically and legally, abortion is said to take place after implantation has already occurred; any prevention of pregnancy before implantation is described as contraception. In fact, if this could be defined as abortion, the same definition would apply to the progestogen-only pill (POP) and the intrauterine device (IUD), since they are capable of working that way at least sometimes.

Will my next period come on time after the emergency pill?

There is no easy answer to this, as it is impossible to predict what is likely to happen in any individual case. If you take the pill before you have ovulated, and ovulation is therefore delayed, your period is likely to be late. If, however, you take it after ovulation then you may well find that your period is on time, or even early. The evidence of research in this case is that most women have their next period roughly on time, while about 20 per cent have an early period and 10 per cent a late one.

How effective is the emergency pill?

In the first place, one must bear in mind that not every woman who takes the emergency pill would have become pregnant anyway: it has been estimated that a woman who has sex just once in the middle of her cycle has about a 30 per cent chance of becoming pregnant. The failure rate of the pill can only be quoted in terms of a single cycle, since that is what it is designed for. Taking account of this, the failure rate of the emergency pill has been calculated at between 1 and 5 per cent, the higher figure applying to mid-cycle (highest risk) use. Taking into account those women who would not have become pregnant anyway, it has been estimated that the emergency pill prevents 75 per cent of the pregnancies that would otherwise have happened. The IUD is more effective, so if it is essential for you not to become pregnant, it would be more suitable for you to have an IUD fitted (see below).

There is no evidence that taking the emergency pill within 24 hours after having sex can give a higher level of protection against pregnancy: the rates apply to use at any time within 72 hours. Because there is no need for special haste, and you need not take the first dose as soon as you receive it, it would be sensible to organize your taking of the pill so that, for example, you do not find that you need to take the second dose in the middle of the night.

Why can't I just take the emergency pill every month?

For a start, it is simply not effective enough if you start using it regularly. Remember that the failure rate refers to each month only. So, even if you assume the lower rate of 2 per cent, if you were to take it twelve times a year the failure rate would be twenty-four per hundred woman-years. This means that, out of 100 women using it in this way for a year, a quarter would become pregnant. Furthermore, if you start using it a lot, you might as well take the combined pill regularly—the dose in the emergency pill regimen is roughly equivalent to a week of normal pill taking—and you would not have to suffer the side-effects.

Can the emergency pill be used by women who cannot take the combined pill?

In most cases there is no reason why such women should not take the emergency pill, since they are, after all, taking only a single dose of oestrogen, and should not therefore be exposed to any of the long-term health risks posed by the combined pill. Age and smoking would not debar you, but if you have already had a thrombosis (blood clot) then you should not take an oestrogen-containing emergency pill. In addition, if you suffer from the type of migraine known as focal migraine (see page 63) you should not use the emergency pill if you actually have a focal migraine at the time of the emergency. It would of course still be feasible for you to use an IUD; if for some reason this is unacceptable, a progestogen-only pill can be used, as described later.

Are there any other health risks?

Since there is a very small possibility of an ectopic pregnancy (a pregnancy in the Fallopian tube), you will be asked by the doctor to come back for a check-up if your period is overdue or you have pain. (It is thought that any such cases are caused by a previously damaged tube and so could happen even without the treatment.)

If the method fails

Emergency contraception will normally be used by women who have a strong desire to avoid pregnancy; consequently many of these women will opt for termination if the pill fails. Not all women find abortion an acceptable option, however, and they may be worried about whether the hormones will have had any effect on the baby . It should be said that if you know a termination would be out of the question, you would be better advised to use an intrauterine device (because it is much more effective) rather than the pill method. Reassuringly, there has been absolutely no increase in the rate of abnormality above the general rate which happens anyway, but even without the treatment no one can ever be promised a baby free from all abnormality.

When should the emergency pill be considered?

You should consult your doctor about using the emergency pill in the following situations.

- If you have not used any method of contraception even if you think your risk of pregnancy is low.
- If a barrier method, such as a sheath or diaphragm, has failed in some way.
- In cases of rape. Counselling, and a check-up for infection, are also advisable.
- If you have forgotten to restart a packet of the combined pill. Remember that it is particularly dangerous to miss the pills at the beginning of the packet. Later in the cycle, when you have been taking pills for seven days or more, your ovaries are dormant, and it will take some days for them to become seriously active; however, after your pill-free week, they have had seven days already without any pills, and may well be showing signs of activity. When you forget to take the first two (or more) pills at the beginning of the next packet (or more than two at any time in the first week), your ovaries experience a dangerously long time without any control; their activity can rise to hazardous levels. Indeed, when the control you maintain over them is suddenly removed, they can sometimes be extra active, and ovulation could suddenly occur. If you have had sex without other precautions then you are at risk of pregnancy, and you should definitely consult your doctor and get the emergency pill. Afterwards you can just continue with your packet as usual. If, on the other hand, you should forget pills at the end of a packet, run straight on to the next packet after the current one ends. Alternatively, just restart the next packet seven days after the first pill you missed: in other words, treat it as part of your pill-free week.

The emergency pill is not required unless you miss four or more pills in the middle of a packet because the ovaries need longer than that amount of time to 'wake up' again.

- If one or two progestogen only pills (POPs) have been missed, and you have had sex already without using additional precautions while the mucus might not have been blocking sperm (see Chapter 6). The emergency pill should be taken and then you should continue with your POP packet as usual, using additional precautions (such as condoms) for another seven days.

- If an IUD has to be removed suddenly, for example because of a severe pelvic infection. If you are in this situation and have had sex within the last few days, you could become pregnant because the IUD might be working by blocking implantation (see Chapter 8).

What happens if you are breastfeeding? Does it affect the baby?

The older, high-dose oestrogen-containing emergency pill regimens did cause problems in breastfeeding women, as oestrogen can suppress breastfeeding. However, the lower doses now used in modern emergency pills do not appear to have any appreciable effect, so the method can be used while breastfeeding. There is still the issue of the small amount of hormone which passes into the breast milk: this is not thought to cause any harm, but if you are very worried about it, you can express milk for 24 hours and throw it away. Of course, this does mean you would need to bottle-feed your baby during this time.

There are also alternative methods of emergency contraception which can be used while breastfeeding: the progestogen-only pill and the IUD (see below).

How can you get the emergency pill?

Since so many contraceptive accidents occur at weekends, it can be difficult to know where to turn. Remember that you do have up to 72 hours to take the first dose, and you may therefore find that you have time to visit your doctor in a clinic, even if it means waiting in the 'no appointments' queue. There is often a special emergency procedure in family planning clinics, by which women can come in without an appointment for this treatment. You may be able to find a clinic which is open on Saturdays, although such clinics are usually private ones: you will often find their services advertised in women's magazines. If you cannot find any way of getting hold of the pill, then do get in touch with your GP: it is, after all, an emergency, and the potential consequences (pregnancy) are serious. If you cannot reach your GP it is possible that, as a last resort, the local hospital casualty department may be able to help, but make sure that you then have a follow-up visit back at a clinic or with your GP.

It is important that, before you are given the emergency pill, your doctor should make sure that there is no reason why it might be inappropriate for you, and should discuss with you which of the various alternatives will suit you best. If you have not been using any contraception, you should consider taking this opportunity to discuss the matter, ask any questions, and arrange contraception for the future. The doctor will probably check your blood pressure, and may do an internal vaginal examination (not always necessary) to ensure that there is no abnormality present already. This is so that, if your period does not come, or if an ectopic pregnancy is suspected, the doctor will know of any circumstances apart from pregnancy which may be responsible. You will be asked to return if you do not have a normal period, if you develop pain or have any problem you are worried about.

If you decide to start either the combined pill or the progestogen-only pill with your next period, you should start whenever you are sure it is a normal period. This may mean waiting beyond the first day. As we explained on page 78 we consider that you will still be protected if you start at any time up to and including the third day. Do make sure that you use some form of contraception until then, as you could still become pregnant as a result of unprotected sex after you have taken the emergency pill (see above).

Emergency contraception without oestrogen

If there is a reason why you cannot take the usual post-coital pill, there are two progestogen-only options. The first really can be described as a 'morning-after pill' since it has to be taken almost immediately. You have to take twenty tablets of the progestogen-only pill Microval, all within twelve hours of the unprotected sex. The second is a little kinder, as it can be started within 48 hours of unprotected sex. This time you have to take 25 Microval tablets, with the dose repeated twelve hours later.

The failure rate of both methods appears to be about 3 per cent. A few women feel nauseated, but there are generally few side-effects. They can be useful options for women who are breastfeeding, to avoid problems with the milk due to oestrogen (see Chapter 12).

The intrauterine device (IUD) as a method of emergency contraception

The IUD is a very effective method of emergency contraception, with very few failures ever recorded. It is therefore the best choice if you want extremely high protection against pregnancy, for example if both having a baby and having an abortion are out of the question. Since the IUD can also be used as a long-term method of contraception, you may wish to have one fitted as an emergency method, but continue with it afterwards. In this case you should consider all the pros and cons of an IUD in your particular situation. There is a full discussion of these in Chapter 8.

What are the advantages of the IUD over the emergency pill?

The main advantage is its efficacy, as described above. In addition, an IUD can be fitted much longer after the accident has occurred and also if you have taken risks several times. This is because IUDs are able to work by preventing implantation, the bedding-down of the fertilized egg in the lining of the womb. Implantation takes place about five days after fertilization. In turn, fertilization can be assumed to take place within 24 hours of ovulation, since the egg only lives that long. So, if one calculates the earliest possible time in the cycle when ovulation could take place, the IUD can be fitted up to five days after that. For example, in a woman who has regular 28-day cycles, and therefore ovulates around day 14, an IUD may legally be fitted up to day 19.

This makes the IUD a much more flexible method of emergency contraception than the emergency pill. It does not matter how many times or when you had sex, as long as you can make sure you have the IUD fitted before implantation could take place. And, if you like, you can keep it as a long-term method thereafter. However, if it is not a good long-term choice (for example, because you have not had children) it can be removed after your next period.

Disadvantages of the IUD

These mainly relate to the fitting and the risk of infection. Having an IUD fitted involves a vaginal examination˙and a not entirely pleasant procedure. In addition, if the fitting is being done when time is running out, it may not be possible to wait for the results of an infection swab, to try to reduce the risk of introducing infection into the womb and the tubes. These problems are discussed fully in Chapter 8, and should be carefully considered before you choose to have an IUD fitted.

Are there any situations when an emergency IUD may not be a good idea?

An IUD will not be advisable if there is a particularly high risk of infection. Women who have been raped are at high risk of having caught an infection and having an IUD could make matters much worse. If an IUD needs to be fitted under such circumstances, swabs should be taken for infection and antibiotics started immediately, even before the results are known, as a precaution. Similar precautions could be considered if a woman has a past history of pelvic inflammatory disease (salpingitis). If a woman has had an ectopic pregnancy (a pregnancy in the tube) in the past, an IUD is not ideal because it may increase the risk of another one. However, even without the IUD there is a risk of another ectopic, so the use of an IUD is not ruled out—though it may be better to remove it after the next period.

A possibility for the near future

Mifepristone, or RU486, is already available in this country as the 'abortion pill'. However, a recent study has suggested that it could also be used as an emergency contraceptive. A single dose given within 72 hours of unprotected sex, just like the emergency pill, was very effective. Indeed, in that study, no pregnancies occurred, compared to a failure rate of 2 per cent for the normal emergency pill. Although Mifepristone can be used to induce an abortion if given later in the cycle, if given post-coitally it works by preventing implantation. Apart from being very effective, the other advantage shown in this study was that side-effects such as nausea were much less common than with the normal emergency pill. So this may be a better option, once it becomes available.

CHAPTER 12

Contraception at Special Times

Contraception while breastfeeding

Breastfeeding in itself has a contraceptive effect, because the hormone which stimulates the production of milk also has the effect of inhibiting the ovaries. However, this is only consistently the case in full 'demand' breastfeeding, when the baby is fed very frequently both day and night. If you start to add water, other feeds, or train the baby to feed at regular, spaced intervals the contraceptive effect is greatly reduced. This is because the milk-stimulating hormone prolactin is only released when it is required, which is when feeding takes place. It does not remain in the bloodstream for very long, so as soon as you stop feeding its levels go down, and so does the effect on the ovaries.

> *'I was determined to breastfeed as fully as possible and hadn't seen a period in ages—it was already nine months since Jamie was born. I wondered whether it was still safe to use the cap or whether I should use something else. But the doctor said it was fine for the time being.'*

Women who are fully breastfeeding and are not seeing any periods are thought to have only about a 2 per cent chance of becoming pregnant for the first six months after delivery (see Figure 12.1).

Even if you are not in this well-protected category, this does mean that contraceptive methods are generally more effective during breastfeeding because fertility is at least slightly reduced. Although this does not make much difference if a method is already very effective (for example, Depo Provera), it can make normally less effective methods temporarily a better proposition.

Obviously, a major concern is that neither the milk nor the baby

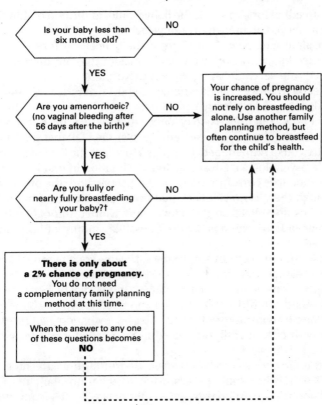

Is your baby less than
six months old?

NO

YES

Are you amenorrhoeic?
(no vaginal bleeding after
56 days after the birth)*

NO

Your chance of pregnancy
is increased. You should
not rely on breastfeeding
alone. Use another family
planning method, but
often continue to breastfeed
for the child's health.

YES

Are you fully or
nearly fully breastfeeding
your baby?†

NO

YES

**There is only about
a 2% chance of pregnancy.**
You do not need
a complementary family planning
method at this time.

When the answer to any one
of these questions becomes
NO

Figure 12.1 Breastfeeding as a method of contraception

should be adversely affected by the contraceptive used. The combined pill is therefore unsuitable for use during breastfeeding because the oestrogen in it may work to stop the production of milk. There is however no reason why any of the progestogen-only methods should not be used. The progestogen-only pill (POP), as we saw in Chapter 6, combines well with breastfeeding, since the slight contraceptive action of the latter increases the pill's efficacy to almost 100 per cent. In addition, it contains a very low dose of progestogen, so correspondingly little can pass into the breast milk and affect the baby. Even if you were to take the POP every day while breastfeeding for two years, the baby would, at the end of that time, have absorbed no more than a single tablet.

Norplant (see page 120) is not actually licensed for use during breastfeeding. However, we would consider that our discussion of the POP, above, would apply equally to Norplant.

Injectable progestogens, such as Depo Provera (see Chapter 7), can also be used while breastfeeding. They do not stop the production of milk, and there is no evidence that there is any effect on the baby. Injectables have the advantage over the POP that they do not require you to remember to take pills. However, the POP may have at least a psychological advantage in this situation in that it is a lower dose, therefore correspondingly less must pass into the breast milk. Although there is no evidence that the higher amount from injectables has any effect on the baby, many women undoubtedly feel happier to know there is the least possible amount of hormone in the milk.

With both the POP and injectables it seems you are more likely to have irregular bleeding if you start soon after delivery. The FPA leaflets recommend starting on day 21, but it may be better to wait until about the fifth week. There is no need to worry about other methods of contraception until then, as ovulation has not been known to occur in a fully breastfeeding woman before the forty-third day after delivery.

Intrauterine devices (IUDs) can be used during breastfeeding. Like the POP and injectable progestogens they are normally not fitted until about the fifth or sixth week after delivery. This is not due to concern over bleeding problems: IUDs fitted earlier have a higher chance of being expelled. If you have had a Caesarean section, you may be asked to wait until the eighth week, to allow complete healing of the scar (remember the womb, not just your abdomen, had to be cut open). Fitting an IUD soon (even 8 weeks) after any form of pregnancy is best done by an experienced doctor, since the womb is still soft and easier to perforate.

An IUD (other than the hormone-releasing type) cannot affect the breast milk or the baby. Obviously, before you choose an IUD in these circumstances you should think about all the pros and cons, just as any other potential user should. These are discussed fully in Chapter 8.

Barrier methods such as diaphragms and sheaths are all suitable for use during breastfeeding. Their failure rate is reduced in these circumstances, though they will still not be as effective as the methods described above. Diaphragm and cervical cap users should wait until about six weeks after delivery and then have their cap size checked: both the cervix and the vagina can alter in size after a pregnancy.

A disadvantage for barrier-method users in particular is that use of the emergency pill is slightly more problematic while breastfeeding, making it more difficult to compensate for 'accidents' (see page 188). Another possibility is the use of the progestogen-only versions of the emergency pill. The first of these has to be taken within 12 hours of the unprotected sex. However, the second can be started within 48 hours of unprotected sex. The failure rate of both methods appears to be about 3 per cent, but, as we have said, like all forms of contraception it may well be more effective during breastfeeding. The IUD, on the other hand, can be fitted up to five days after the calculated date of ovulation.

In our opinion the temperature and mucus methods are not advisable during breastfeeding. Periods can be irregular or even absent, making use of the rhythm method very unreliable. Breastfeeding also affects the cervical mucus, making its assessment difficult.

It is generally considered unwise to decide on sterilization of either partner immediately after having a baby (see Chapter 14). For a start, although you may be sure you have now completed your family, babies can die while still very young. Equally, the months following childbirth can be very stressful, with the baby disrupting your lives, keeping you up all night, and so on. It is very tempting to say 'never again'. But when you see your child a couple of years later, walking, starting to talk, and no longer waking you up, you could feel quite differently. So unless you are already very sure and have had counselling before the baby was born, it is best to postpone the decision for a while.

Contraception for the older woman

Unfortunately, in gynaecological terms 'older' means any woman of 35 or above. It is a significant age in relation to contraception, since, if you are 35 and smoke, you will have to stop using the combined pill.

Although fertility gradually declines after the age of 35, contraception is still necessary. In addition, particularly in the over-forties, the psychological and physical consequences of an unwanted pregnancy can be unpleasant. As you can see from Figures 12.2 and 12.3, the lives of both the mother and the baby are at greater risk when women in their late thirties and forties become pregnant. Most women are also aware that the risk of having a baby with Down's Syndrome goes up over the age of 40. So, although the danger of pregnancy is reduced, the consequences of an accidental pregnancy may actually be more serious than at a younger age. A woman who already has a family she loves and who could theoretically bring up another child often finds the dilemma of a late, unwanted pregnancy agonizing. To avoid this, many women want to be doubly sure that their method of contraception will be effective.

'I thought I was going mad. I felt so dreadful, so tired, so moody. I would burst into tears for no reason. Peter was very good, but he didn't understand what was going on either. In the end, he made me go to the doctor. She said it might be the beginning of my change. But I'm only 45.'

The other factor which enters the equation at this time in a woman's life is her approaching menopause. Symptoms of this, such as mood swings, depression, vaginal dryness, and so on, may occur. The ovaries start to slow down, and periods become irregular. At first they may be heavier and more frequent, and only much later will the frequency decline. This 'imminent menopause' stage may continue for a number of years and can be very distressing. Thus, not only do women need contraception, many would benefit from relief from all these symptoms as well.

There is an increasing trend towards acceptance of hormone replacement therapy (HRT) even for women whose periods have not yet stopped, but who are beginning to suffer 'menopausal' problems. There are many advantages to HRT in terms of protection against thinning of the bones (osteoporosis) and against heart disease, quite apart from relief from hot flushes, mood swings, and so on. The hormone which actually needs to be replaced is oestrogen, normally produced by the ovaries.

The obvious solution to all these problems is to stay on the combined pill for as long as possible. The combined pill, which contains oestrogen, provides perfectly good hormone replacement therapy as

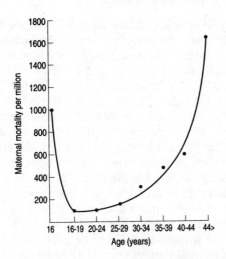

Figure 12.2 Maternal mortality per million births against maternal age
(*Source*: Beard, in Roberts and Chester, *Changing Patterns of Conception and Fertility*, Academic Press, 1981)

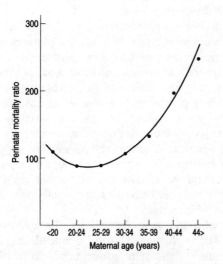

Figure 12.3 Perinatal mortality ratio plotted against maternal age
(*Source*: Beard, 1981)

well as very effective, simple contraception, so if it is possible for you to stay on the pill, this is the perfect solution. Fortunately, research has shown that, provided you have good general health and do not smoke, there is no reason why you should not stay on the combined pill up to the age of 50. One of the reasons for this is that pregnancy itself is a dangerous condition at this age, and the pill may well present fewer risks (at least to a non-smoker). Not only are there physical dangers inherent in pregnancy for both mother and baby but also an unwanted pregnancy at this time can have serious psychological effects. Even in the United States, which is traditionally very conservative in its medical practices, the Food and Drug Administration's Fertility and Maternal Health Drugs Advisory Committee recommended in October 1989 that healthy non-smoking women should not be restricted by any upper age limit in their use of the pill.

Of course, not all women over 45 will be candidates for the pill: various elements in each woman's medical and family history must be taken into account. For example, if a woman's family history contains serious lipid (blood fat) related problems she will be advised to have a blood test to ensure that her blood fats are normal before the pill will be prescribed. Similarly, caution needs to be exercised if you suffer significantly from migraines.

Pills given to older women should in any case contain the lowest possible dose of hormones, and preferably one of the new progestogens, so that no problems with blood fats and sugars need arise if possible (see Chapter 3). At present the most suitable brand is probably Mercilon, since it contains only 20 micrograms of oestrogen combined with a new progestogen. However, as has been said, any pill containing the new progestogens would be perfectly acceptable (although now the issue of venous thrombosis risk needs to be taken into account, see Chapter 3), and not all women are happy with the same brand. Furthermore, blood levels of the pill vary so much in different women, as has been shown above, that the small difference in dose is probably not very important, especially since all the pills contain a very low dose anyway.

Those women who do not smoke may thus be able to remain on the combined pill up to the age of 50 and escape all the problems of the 'pre-menopausal' years. The conventional form of hormone replacement therapy will be available when they reach 50. At that stage it may be possible for your doctor to assess whether your ovaries are still functioning: if they are not then you will no longer require contraception. If, however, it emerges that you may still be ovulating your fertility will certainly be much lower than that of younger women, and a very simple method will usually offer enough protection. Spermicides (e.g. foam) alone, although they have an unacceptably high failure rate in young women, are perfectly adequate at this stage.

Women who smoke, or who for some reason are unable to use oestrogen-based pills after the age of 35, can turn to progestogen-only methods. The progestogen-only pill (see Chapter 6), injectable progestogens, implants (see Chapter 7) or particularly the progestogen-releasing intrauterine system (Mirena, see Chapter 8) are safe even for smokers (though heavy smokers over 45 should note the comments about injectables, see page 107). Injectables have a high success rate at all ages, and the POP is in fact more effective for older women: by the age of 35 its failure rate is about 1 per cent and by 40 it is 0.5 per cent. Older women may also find it easier to adhere to the strict timetable demanded by the POP, since on average their life-styles will be more settled.

> *'I was shocked when the doctor said I would have to have a D & C I thought irregular periods were just a sign of the change, and perhaps because of the progestogen-only pill. But he said we couldn't just assume that.'*

The disadvantage of these methods is that they can cause irregular bleeding which may lead to unnecessary concern. As you get older, the chances of cancer of the lining of the womb (endometrium) increase, even though it is still uncommon. Since one of the signs is irregular bleeding, one cannot safely just dismiss this as being due to your contraceptive. This can mean having various investigations for something which will almost always turn out to be a false alarm; however, nowadays it would be better not to do a D & C (dilatation and curettage) because there are simpler methods available (for example, a biopsy of the lining of the womb).

Intrauterine devices (IUDs) can be a good choice for older women. Not only are they more effective in the over-thirty-fives, but the health risks with which they are associated decrease with age. The majority of such women are likely to have had a child, making the insertion easier. Periods are often less heavy and painful after having a child, again an advantage for a prospective IUD user. (If you do suffer from heavy, painful periods, the Mirena would be a good option, whether or not you smoke (see Chapter 8).) Relationships are generally more stable, reducing the likelihood of infection. Best of all, it has been agreed that any IUD fitted after the age of 40 can stay in until the menopause. Thus, if all goes well, with one fitting a woman over 40 can look forward to ten years of effective, uncomplicated contraception.

Barrier methods are quite suitable at this age as their failure rate is lower in older women. Couples who have used them before are often quite happy to continue. However, those who have not sometimes find it quite a shock after the ease and spontaneity of the pill. Older men may find it harder to maintain an erection when using the sheath. For women who have lax vaginal walls because of childbirth keeping a diaphragm in can be difficult. The arcing spring diaphragm (see Chapter 9) or a cervical cap may be the answer. The sponge is not really suitable until the years actually around the menopause. By the age of 49 or 50 fertility is so low that the method is acceptably effective.

Natural family planning is often not suitable in the years approaching the menopause. Your hormones can be all over the place, your periods erratic, far too much so for the rhythm method. For the same reason, cervical mucus and even temperature charts become unreliable. Coitus interruptus, or withdrawal, may be more effective in older couples, especially if the man is experienced in its use. However, the failure rate is likely to remain high until the woman is at least 45 years old.

Emergency contraception should not be forgotten. Even though a woman may not be able to take the combined pill on a long-term basis, there is usually no danger in taking the emergency pill. So you can take it even if you are over 40 and smoke or are overweight. However, if you have had a blood clot in a vein (thrombosis) you should not use this kind of emergency treatment, although the intrauterine device (IUD) is still an option (see Chapter 11).

Sterilization of one of the partners seems an obvious choice for older couples who are sure their family is complete. Indeed, in the UK, this is the most popular form of contraception for couples over the age of 35. However, it is important that the woman has a gynaecological examination, even if it is her partner who is considering a vasectomy. She may have a gynaecological problem for which she should consider a hysterectomy, rendering any sterilization unnecessary. The Mirena may offer a very viable option to hysterectomy if a woman has gynaecological problems, such as heavy periods or fibroids. Indeed, it may be worth considering anyway as an alternative to sterilization because of its benefits in this area, coupled with the possibility of using it as part of hormone replacement therapy.

Even in older couples the decision to be sterilized should not be taken lightly. Divorce and remarriage are now very common and a new relationship may lead to a desire for a child with the new partner. This is especially likely to be the case if one partner has no children from the previous marriage. You also need to think carefully about which of you should be sterilized. From this point of view a woman over 40 who already has a child may be a better candidate for sterilization: she is unlikely to want, or for that matter be able, to have further children even is she has a new relationship. Meanwhile, a man continues to be fertile into his seventies, and may well enter a relationship with a younger woman who has not yet had children.

> *'I'm only 43, but my mother had an early change too. I've been getting hot flushes every couple of days. It's so embarrassing, I suddenly start to literally drip with sweat. I was trying to cut down, but if anything I'm smoking more because I feel so stressed. Sex is a problem as I'm so dry. We use jelly, but I know he thinks it must be partly that I'm not interested any more. But I get my period every month, not exactly to the day as it used to be, but I don't miss any.'*

Those women who cannot take the combined pill, but who are getting menopausal symptoms in their forties, have a problem. They need hormone replacement, but must also find a means of contraception. This can produce deeply unsatisfactory results, since they may end up taking more progestogen in hormone replacement than they would have received if they had been taking the combined pill. Since no hormone replacements using the new progestogens are as yet in existence, the replacement therapy may also have a greater effect on their blood fats and sugars than one of the new-generation combined pills.

The obvious question here is why is it necessary to take progestogen at all, when what the body needs is oestrogen? When hormone replacement therapy was first introduced, it did in fact contain only oestrogen; on its own this protects menopausal women from heart disease, and is usually well tolerated. Hot flushes and other symptoms of the menopause are eased by it, and it also protects the bones against osteoporosis (a process in which bone tissue is actually lost, and the bones become weaker and therefore more likely to break). In the long term, however, it became clear that women taking oestrogen alone were at greater risk of cancer of the endometrium. The solution to this was to add progestogen, and it is now accepted that for at least twelve days in every month progestogen should be taken to neutralize the added risk of uterine cancer. (The number of days for which it is taken appears to be even more important than the actual dose used.)

> *'I thought that at least I'd stop having periods once I went through the menopause. Sometimes I don't know what was worse, the flushes or having the periods back again.'*

Progestogen itself was by no means a perfect answer, since above all it will probably cause the woman to bleed every month, and most women will be heartily sick of periods by this stage. Other side-effects may include headaches or a kind of premenstrual syndrome.

The problem of providing both replacement and contraception simultaneously (if you cannot take the combined pill) has been solved in various ways. The principle is that natural oestrogen (which affects clotting less than the synthetic type) should be combined with a progestogen. It is possible to supply the oestrogen (which is usually oestradiol) by mouth, by patch, or as an implant (a sort of glorified injection), which lasts three or six months. Alongside this the woman may take the progestogen-only pill all the time, or for twelve days out of every twenty-eight she must take a progestogen. Neither of these latter choices is ideal, since taking the POP may cause irregular bleeding, while, whereas taking a (usually rather higher-dose) progestogen for twelve days each month will give a more regular bleed, there is a strong possibility of side-effects such as depression and headaches (and it may not be reliably contraceptive).

Another alternative is to use the injectable progestogen Depo

Provera as the contraceptive while taking natural oestrogen. Depo Provera is a very effective contraceptive and is easy to use, since it just involves an injection every three months. And as we saw in Chapter 7, it is actually protective against cancer of the endometrium. An exciting new option which will hopefully be licensed officially in the near future, is the levonorgestrel-releasing intrauterine system (Mirena). This would again provide both contraception and the progestogen necessary to protect the endometrium. It appears that there is very little bleeding, which most women would consider an advantage. Natural oestrogen could then be taken as pills, patches, or implants as before.

In general, if you need this type of treatment, it is best to find a gynaecologist who has had experience in dealing with it, as he or she can advise you on what is likely to be most successful in your case. If your reason for not being able to take the combined pill and having to go through all this trouble is smoking, wouldn't it be reasonable to consider the option of giving up cigarettes?

CHAPTER 13

What about Men?

The most obvious male method of contraception is of course the condom, which has already been discussed in Chapter 9. This chapter will look at other reversible methods which can or could be used by men.

Coitus interruptus (withdrawal)

And Judah said unto Onan, 'Go in unto thy brother's wife, and marry her, and raise up seed to thy brother.' And Onan knew that the seed should not be his; and it came to pass, when he went in unto his brother's wife, that he spilled it on the ground, lest that he should give seed to his brother. And the thing which he did displeased the Lord: wherefore he slew him also. (Genesis 38: 8–10)

Coitus interruptus, or spilling the seed, is probably the earliest form of contraception practised. The description in Genesis has been used to condemn the method as sinful, but there is in fact some debate as to whether it was the actual form of contraception which was sinful, or the fact that Onan did not obey the command to produce heirs for his brother. Whichever is the case, coitus interruptus is sometimes referred to as 'onanism' as a result of the story.

The method depends on withdrawal of the penis from the vagina before ejaculation takes place and therefore requires considerable control on the part of the man. Marie Stopes had very firm views on this aspect of coitus interruptus:

The effect on the man's nervous system is that, at the moment when the power of thought and central control is or should be in abeyance . . . he is called upon to exercise careful watchfulness and critical control from the central nervous system. The strain is very great even if successfully accomplished . . . The evil effect on individual men is sometimes so great as to destroy the general health and make them thoroughly nervous and rundown, or even to induce more explicit symptoms of neurasthenia and even functional disorders.

The woman subjected to this process is also deprived of the possibility, after the union has been completed, of the beneficial absorption from the seminal and prostatic fluids . . . when pressed for a description of her feelings after the act, replied that the only way she knew how to express it was that 'she felt like she wanted to sneeze and couldn't'.

Some doctors agreed with her:

I was much struck by your opinion that the health of a married woman depends to some extent upon her experiencing the sexual orgasm and some absorption of the male ejaculate. I have long held this view. I have found that the physical signs of age are most noticeable in married women whose husbands practise withdrawal and who themselves never fully complete the sexual act. (*Contraception*, 1928)

Marie Stopes believed that any method which prevented a woman coming into contact with 'the beneficial effects' of semen was detrimental, since she thought wrongly that semen was in some way a stimulant.

Unfortunately, even one drop of semen contains millions of sperm, which is why failures occur. It is very difficult to prevent the loss of even one drop and this can also happen well before ejaculation. Young men often find it difficult to achieve such a level of control and therefore young couples using the method are likely to have a high failure rate. (Incidentally, re-entry without first washing the penis can also cause failures, as there may still be sperm around.) However, if the user is experienced (and usually older), failure rates of about ten per hundred woman-years have been recorded (that is, if 100 couples used the method for a year, ten women would become pregnant). So, although the method is not as effective as some others, it should not be disregarded, and is certainly better than nothing in an 'emergency'.

The method has other advantages which may make it attractive to some couples. It is entirely free of interference by the medical profession or indeed anyone else. Thus it is possible to keep one's activity a secret, aided by the fact that there are no supplies to keep hidden.

There is no expense involved and it cannot be left behind when going on holiday. It has no side-effects or health risks, other than those of an unwanted pregnancy.

> *'I think it shows he cares, he's taking responsibility: after all, it's a sacrifice for him, too.'*

> *'I couldn't bear the constant worrying about whether he would manage it or not. A couple of times he hadn't, but we'd been lucky. For me sex just became too stressful.'*

Although some couples adapt well to the method, women who want a high degree of protection against pregnancy often find that the risk element is too great. One way of improving efficacy may be to use the sponge or another spermicide as well. This might cope with the 'lost' drop of semen.

Coitus reservatus

This is one of the few methods of contraception officially permitted by the Catholic Church. It involves the man reaching the point just before ejaculation would normally happen, but not letting himself ejaculate. The disadvantage of this, of course, is that he does not reach orgasm, and if he does not quite succeed the method can become coitus interruptus instead. Again, leakage of sperm is possible even though full ejaculation has not occurred. Nowadays the technique is sometimes promoted, not as a method of contraception, but as a way of prolonging intercourse.

Where is the male pill?

This question has been asked for many years, but despite a great deal of debate a 'male pill' seems unlikely to emerge in the near future. Why should this be so?

> *'Me, trust him to take a pill? You must be out of your mind. Well, it's not him who's going to get pregnant, is it?'*

> *'Would you really trust a man who said, 'it's all right darling, I'm on the pill.?'*

These comments reflect a genuine problem. After all, many women have difficulty in remembering to take the pill regularly even though they may well suffer the consequences of their forgetfulness in the form of pregnancy. It is hardly to be expected that men, with less at stake, would be more successful. Furthermore, some women might not be prepared to rely on their partner's memory, or even on their honesty: nothing can change the basic fact that it is the woman who will pay for the failure of contraception. This point is made rather well by a poster which has been used to try to increase men's involvement in contraception.

Despite all this, there is no doubt that a male contraceptive would be very useful. Its principal use would probably be in stable, long-term relationships, where it would enable couples to share the responsibility for contraception. That this desire to share responsibility does exist can be seen in the increasing number of men who have vasectomies.

Figure 13.1 Family Planning Association campaign poster

'Mary had been on the pill for about fifteen years, but then the doctor said she couldn't carry on because she had high blood pressure. We looked at the alternatives, but they didn't seem very nice. She said maybe she should have a coil fitted, but I could see she was scared. She'd taken all the risks and responsibility for so many years, I felt it was time I did something.'

The majority of research into contraception has concentrated on female methods: in fact it has been calculated that, out of all the money spent on contraceptive research across the world, only about 8 per cent has been used to develop male contraceptives. Yet money has not been the only problem: there are real practical difficulties in the way of producing a contraceptive for men. To explain this, we need to look again, briefly, at the reproductive process in men.

The male reproductive process is directed by a hormone called either Luteinizing Hormone Releasing Hormone (LHRH) or Gonadotrophin Releasing Hormone (GnRH). (To simplify matters we will confine ourselves to the term GnRH.) GnRH is produced by an area in the brain called the hypothalamus; it passes to the pituitary gland, also in the brain, and stimulates the production of two hormones, Follicle Stimulating Hormone (FSH) and Luteinizing Hormone (LH). FSH and LH travel through the bloodstream to the testes, where FSH brings about the formation of sperm themselves, while LH causes the testis to produce another hormone, testosterone. (Testosterone is responsible for male libido (sex drive), and for male characteristics.) In summary, FSH prepares the sperm and LH and testosterone encourage the man to have sex, and thus pass them on.

Before sperm leave the body they spend around three months moving slowly down the production lines in the testis. They will travel through roughly a mile of small tubes before arriving at the epididymis, where they remain for some twelve days and then pass into the vas deferens, which enters the penis. At this stage they are still not fully active; this will only occur when they reach the woman's vagina and cervix.

It seems extraordinary that it has not so far proved possible to thwart the production of sperm at any of these many stages. One serious problem is that there are an enormous number of sperm: 100,000 are produced every minute (or between 1,000 and 2,000 per second!).

Since only one is required for a pregnancy to occur, effective contraception must mean destroying all of them. Even men with a 'low

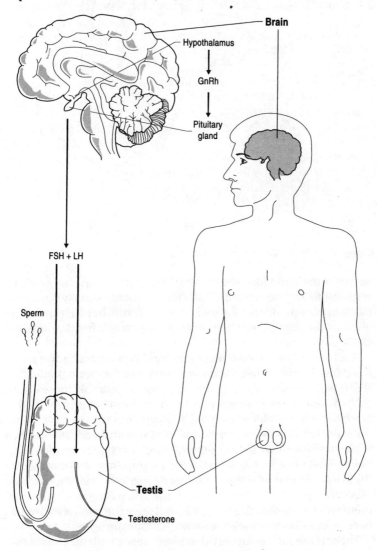

Figure 13.2 How reproductive hormones work in men

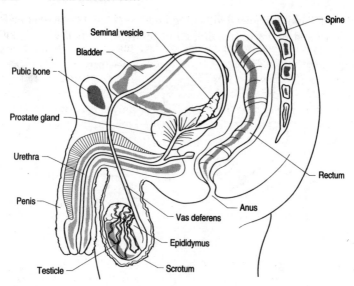

Figure 13.3 The male reproductive system

sperm count', provided they have no other problems, can easily be responsible for pregnancies. (Infertility in men is usually due to the fact that not only do they have a low sperm count, but their sperm are also not very mobile, or otherwise inactive, so that fertilization does not occur.)

Another problem with trying to create a male contraceptive is that it is difficult to block the hormone responsible for sperm production (FSH) without also affecting the hormone responsible for sex drive (LH). A contraceptive which prevents men from being interested in (and therefore capable of) sex will be of no use to anyone. Yet another difficulty is posed by the large number of sperm already in existence at any one time: any contraceptive method which prevents their production will not become fully effective for three months (that is, until the existing sperm have gone). During this period some other method of contraception must be used. Similarly, when pregnancy is desired there will be another three-month wait after the contraceptive has been stopped, before the sperm store has built up again.

There is the further anxiety that interference with the production of sperm may lead to abnormal ones being produced, and this in turn could lead to abnormal babies. Such a danger would be particularly acute during the first few months, while the contraceptive is beginning to take effect, and for a few months after stopping, when sperm are beginning to reappear. A contraceptive that works by making the sperm inactive faces the same problem: there must be no chance that some sperm could remain active but abnormal. Efforts have been made, however, to develop male contraceptives focused on both of these areas: that is, some have attempted to stop the production of sperm, and some to inactivate the sperm after they have been produced.

Methods which attempt to stop the production of sperm

There are a number of ways in which it is possible to interfere with sperm production, as can be seen from Figure 13.2. The obvious place to start is at the hypothalamus with GnRH. However, although stopping production of GnRH will prevent the production of sperm, it will also, as noted above, prevent the production of LH, which gives men their sex drive, so the man will become impotent. To compensate for this it would be necessary to give the man testosterone by some other means. A further problem is that products which discourage GnRH cannot be given by mouth, as they are destroyed rapidly in the stomach. The solution to this has been to develop methods such as nasal sprays; but this is expensive, and the need to supply testosterone at the same time adds to the expense and the awkwardness of the method. On top of this men who have been given GnRH blockers have been known to develop side-effects such as hot flushes, rather like the female menopause, so the overall prospects of this approach are not good.

It is also possible to reduce, although not to prevent, the production of GnRH by giving large doses of steroids: the female contraceptive pill would be an effective treatment, but unfortunately the doses of female hormones would cause men to begin to change into women. However, it does seem to be feasible to give the injectable Depo Provera together with testosterone in the form of monthly injections, since this both reduces GnRH production and provides 'hormone replacement' via the testosterone. Although this appears to be a fairly effective process, the prospect of monthly injections must reduce its desirability.

A further development of the method, designed to avoid this problem and also to make it possible for men to administer the hormone themselves, has led to the use of oral medroxyprogesterone combined with testosterone cream (it is impossible to give testosterone by mouth because it will be broken down in the stomach). This too was unsatisfactory, since not only was it less effective, but it produced a new side-effect: the women partners of men taking this treatment began to grow moustaches and to suffer from excess hair: remnants of the testosterone cream lingered in the men's skin and were being transmitted in sweat, which was then absorbed by their partners.

Giving testosterone by itself is not really satisfactory. Weekly injections are needed, and sperm production is not completely halted, merely reduced. Since there are so many sperm, as we said earlier, allowing even a few to get through is an unacceptable risk. The evidence so far is that only 50 per cent of men stop producing sperm altogether, while another 40 per cent have a reduced sperm count. However, one promising development concerns a variant of testosterone which is stronger and therefore lasts longer. This is still in the early stages of investigation, but preliminary studies have shown that the injections will last three weeks. An even longer-lasting approach is the use of injectable microspheres, tiny pellets which would slowly release hormone perhaps over a period of months.

The next target of contraceptive research is the pituitary gland, where the hormones FSH and LH are produced. As has been suggested, the difficulty here will be to halt the production of FSH while leaving LH alone. However, it does seem to be possible to achieve this. One way is through the use of the hormone inhibin. Long before this useful hormone was discovered its existence had been deduced by scientists; for our purposes it seems almost too good to be true. It is produced by the testis and specifically inhibits the production of FSH. Because it has no effect of LH it fulfils precisely the criteria that we set out above: it stops the production of sperm without having any effect on sex drive. It may even, apparently, be suitable for women, since in them it functions equally selectively to prevent ovulation. For this reason, it is sometimes referred to as the 'unisex' pill. However, although it seems to be the perfect answer, it is at present not practicable to produce inhibin in large quantities. It is a very complicated molecule (rather it consists of two molecules which do not necessarily have the same effects when separated), and at the moment it has not proved possible to synthesize it in a laboratory. Discovering inhibin in its natural state in the testis was merely a first step; until a satisfactory synthetic production process exists it cannot be marketed as a contraceptive, and this kind of research is liable to be both time consuming and expensive. All we can say so far is that inhibin has exciting possibilities.

Another method of targeting FSH alone is to try and produce a vaccine against it; but vaccines present their own problems. Responses to them vary, and so some men would need boosters much sooner than others. The only way to discover whether a booster was needed would be for each man to monitor his sperm count constantly, and this is not a reasonable option. In addition, the vaccine itself causes quite a nasty local reaction in the skin, and ulcers have been known to form. All in all the difficulties outweigh the advantages, especially since it is not even a dangerous disease that the man is being vaccinated against.

Methods which act directly against sperm production in the testis itself

Any drug which acts to poison the sperm-producing cells in the testis unfortunately tends simultaneously to poison the man, and this has been a constant problem in research of this nature. One famous example is a drug called gossypol. Its potential as a contraceptive came to light by chance, when it became apparent that, in one particular rural area of China, there was an above-average likelihood of men being infertile. This was a cotton-growing area, and after some research the effect was traced to the cottonseed oil containing gossypol, in which they fried their food. Since there is a major overpopulation problem in China this created great interest, and large trials in which men were treated with gossypol were initiated. The results suggested that the drug gossypol was rather too effective: about 10 per cent of the men became permanently infertile. Furthermore, gossypol is known to lower the amount of potassium in the body: initially this causes men to feel tired and weak, but it can eventually bring about total muscle paralysis (including paralysis of the heart). Research in this field is now focused on producing a derivative of gossypol which might be an effective, reversible contraceptive without the side-effects.

China is also the source of another potential contraceptive drug which, it is hoped, will present fewer problems than gossypol. This is an extract of the Thunder God vine, which has been in use in traditional Chinese medicines for many years, and is principally used to treat skin conditions and arthritis. Again the discovery was made by chance, when it became apparent that there was a higher incidence of infertility among men given medicines containing this extract. Since no other side-effects were noticeable, the drug appears promising, but we must await the results of the tests which are currently under way in China.

Methods which try to stop the maturation of sperm in the testis

Research is concentrating on the production of substitutes for certain sugars which seem to be necessary for the well-being of sperm while they remain in the epididymis. The substitute sugars would be designed to block rather than help sperm metabolism, and the advantage of interference at this point in the cycle is that it would affect the existing rather than the potential sperm and thus be fully effective within a few days, rather than in three months. Unfortunately, these substitutes are at present causing side-effects in the nervous system, which limits their potential.

Cyproterone acetate, an anti-androgen, seems to be able to affect the function of sperm in the epididymis, but it cannot be used for contraception in men because it reduces their sex drive. (This drug became notorious when its use in high security prisons to decrease the sex drive of inmates was discovered.) Combined with oestrogen, however, it can be used as a contraceptive for women, because it is good at clearing up acne.

Methods of inhibiting sperm function after their release

If any method of achieving this were to be introduced, it would of course have to be used by women (as are existing spermicides). As stated above, sperm only become fully functional when they arrive inside the woman's vagina, so it is possible to attack them there. One drug, propranolol, which is used in the treatment of high blood pressure, may have potential in this field. In normal use the tablet would be swallowed, but if, instead, it is placed inside the vagina, it appears to slow down the movement of sperm. Once sperm reach the womb they can survive there for up to a week, but if their stay in the vagina can be sufficiently prolonged, they will die, because the acidic environment is uncongenial to them.

Another possibility is a drug called sulphasalazine. This is principally used to treat ulcerative colitis, a condition of the bowel, but it can also reduce sperm motility and thus men taking it can become infertile. It is unsuitable as a contraceptive in its present form because not all men are affected by it, and it is not easily reversible; but is may be possible to find a more satisfactory derivative.

Anti-sperm antibodies, which would destroy any sperm they met, may also eventually prove viable, although, bearing in mind the problems of trying to produce vaccines which can be used by men, this would probably be most effective if it could be arranged for the antibodies to be present in the woman, waiting to attack the sperm as soon as they entered. Some infertile men, and some who have had a vasectomy, have been found to carry antibodies which attack and destroy their own sperm (this reduces the success rate for vasectomy reversal). This area is looking hopeful at present, since researchers have actually managed to develop anti-sperm antibodies which are much more potent at immobilizing sperm than conventional spermicides. In addition, there is work going on to develop a similar system which would release antibodies against sexually transmitted infections, such as herpes, chlamydia, gonorrhoea, and HIV. The antibodies could be added to, for example, a progestogen-releasing vaginal ring or an IUD and would be slowly released.

In summary

Clearly there is no likelihood of a male hormonal method of contraception being developed in the near future. One of the most promising developments, the anti-sperm antibody, might even need to be taken by women. However, it is important that male involvement in contraception generally should be encouraged, since the research and the funding will not be available unless it is plain that a genuine need exists.

Other ideas

One extremely odd attempt at male contraception is based on the fact that the testes are deliberately sited outside the main body so that they can remain at a slightly lower temperature than the rest of the body. Research has shown that in hot weather fewer sperm are produced, so the concept of 'scrotum warmers' was invented to try and reduce fertility. These can hardly be regarded as a serious option, since they are unreliable, uncomfortable, and unattractive.

Ultrasonic waves appear to damage the ability of the testes to produce sperm. Most of this work has so far been done on rats, in which the ultrasound seems to cause permanent infertility. It is possible that it would act for a shorter term in men, perhaps lasting two or three years. However, it is unlikely that it would be reversible within that time. Ultrasound is not well conducted by air or skin, but it is well conducted by water. So far, the rats tested have been made to swim in a bath of water through which ultrasound waves are passing. It has been suggested that men could sit for a few minutes with their testes immersed in a bowl of water for the treatment. This research is, however, still in its very early stages.

Of course, the final male method is vasectomy, which is discussed in detail in the next chapter.

CHAPTER 14

Sterilization and Vasectomy

> *'Well, the doctor said I couldn't take the pill any more, I'd had trouble with the IUD in the past, and neither of us really fancied the condom or the cap, so I thought, "what else is there?" '*

In Britain sterilization is now the most popular method of contraception for couples over 35. No doubt this is at least partly because it is such a simple procedure both in men and in women. But is it really the answer? At the same time as its popularity has been increasing, so have divorce rates, and so have requests for sterilization reversal. This would not be such a problem if reversals were easy and guaranteed: in practice, they often involve quite major surgery, much heartache, and limited success. Unlike the other contraceptive options we have looked at, sterilization is a permanent method and should always be viewed as irreversible when you take the decision.

Both men and women can be sterilized (the operation for men is called a vasectomy), so not only do you need to think about the concept of sterilization in general, you may also need to consider which of you should actually have the operation done.

> *'I felt really awful, going to the doctor. Three children, two abortions, and there I was pregnant again. He agreed to refer me to the hospital and then suggested they could sterilize me at the same time. I would have said yes to anything. I just went home so happy to know I was saved. I hardly thought about it at all. I wish I had now. Tom left me a year later. Now I've met Robert and I hope he might want to marry me. But I won't be able to give him a child, and I know he'd like one.'*

> *'I was carrying my second child and it had been a dreadful pregnancy. I had so many complications, put on so much weight, felt so ill. The final straw was the doctor saying the baby was still the*

*wrong way round and I would have to have a Caesarean. Jack
and I agreed that I should be sterilized at the same time so that
we didn't have to go through all this again. It seemed like the simplest solution. Sammy was a beautiful baby and no trouble.
Everyone said he was so good, slept through the night so quickly.
Then one morning he wasn't breathing when I went in. I couldn't
believe it. We were both devastated. At first we could only think
about losing him. But now part of the problem is knowing we
can't try again.'*

How would you feel if your relationship ended, through either divorce
or death? Do you think you might want another child if something
happened to one you already have? If you have even the slightest
doubt about these questions, you should not opt for sterilization yet.

*'Things hadn't been going too well in our marriage, but I wasn't
quite sure why. Perhaps it was the disruption of having the kids
around? Maybe he was worried about my becoming pregnant
again? Whatever the reason, he didn't seem interested in me like
he used to be. I decided to be sterilized, thinking it might take
some of the pressure off. He didn't really get involved, said it was
my decision. I felt OK after the operation and for a while things
really did seem a little better. But six months later he told me he
was in love with someone else and he was going to move in with
her. She was pregnant.'*

*'John started having trouble with premature ejaculation and
counselling hadn't helped so far. I thought maybe if I was sterilized he wouldn't be anxious about getting me pregnant, so it
might help. But he got worse. He said afterwards he felt I had
really rejected him, that I wanted to make sure I didn't have any
more children by him.'*

*'Lucy hadn't been very interested in sex since our last child. She
always seemed worried by this or that. She was having trouble
with the pill and wanted to stop it. But she didn't know what to
use. We didn't want any more children, two were enough. I
thought it would be my chance to do something positive, so I had
a vasectomy. Lucy thought it was a good idea too, at the time. But
after I had it done she completely went off sex. We went for coun-*

selling and she realized that she enjoyed the risk-taking, the
chance that a pregnancy might happen after all. So much for
that. What do we do now?'

Sterilization is never the answer to problems in a relationship. Do not think it will solve your lack of interest in sex, his lack of interest, stop you quarrelling, make you happier. Sterilization will only improve your sex life if that is founded on a good relationship: then removing anxieties about pregnancy or side-effects of contraceptives may indeed be beneficial.

'I was told to stop the pill because of my age and because I smoke.
I didn't know what to use. Sterilization seemed an easy option.'

Have you considered alternative methods of contraception? Just because one does not suit or has been taken away does not mean there is nothing left. Get hold of some leaflets, talk to your doctor, read the other chapters in this book. You might well find something that will suit without being a permanent method. Why not keep your options open for as long as possible?

'I know I haven't had any children, but I don't want any. I've
never met any man I thought I'd want a child by.'

Yes, but he might just turn up tomorrow. Doctors are generally very reluctant to sterilize women or men who have not had any children, especially if they are young and not in a stable relationship. You may be quite sure now that you do not want children, but can you be certain you will say the same in ten years' time? Remember the things you were convinced about when you were 20. Some of those memories almost certainly embarrass you now. And although you may now be much more mature, much more developed, people of 40 often think differently from when they were 30. Circumstances change. Priorities change. You may think now that you could not be happy with a partner who wanted children. In a few years you may not feel so strongly; you might be willing to compromise for the sake of the person you love. Is there no reversible method you could use for a while longer?

'Alec had a vasectomy when things were going really badly. We had a large mortgage, little Sally had to be fed, clothed, kept in nappies. We had to think of the future, she would go on needing things. There was no point in my going back to work for a few years because of the cost of child-minding. His firm started to do badly, there was a rumour about redundancies. We both panicked a bit, I suppose. About a year after he had it done he was promoted. He's such a worrier he hadn't realized that he had been making a good impression all along. Interest rates fell. I was offered typing I could do at home, so that brought money in. Suddenly we were much better off and much more secure. I started to think how nice it would have been if Sally could have had a brother or sister.'

Would a change in your circumstances have an effect on your decision? If so, think again.

'Both Jane and I were sure sterilization was a good idea. We had two lovely children, we felt that fifteen years was long enough for Jane to have been on the pill. I said I would have a vasectomy, it was my turn to do something. Everything went well, I had my sperm count checks, and then Jane came off the pill. It was a complete disaster. Her periods were very painful, she ended up having to lie in bed for two days. They were also very heavy, which embarrassed her: once we came out of the cinema and I realized she had a red patch on her skirt. And she was so irritable and touchy in the week before her period. Effectively, both our lives were completely disrupted for nearly two weeks every month. In the end, she decided go back on the pill. Why did I bother?'

It is important to think carefully about how sterilization would affect your lives in other ways. Many women who have been on the pill for a long time forget what it was like to have 'normal' periods and premenstrual tension. It is not always true that periods get better as you get older, so it is dangerous to assume that will be the case. Sometimes it is worth coming off for a couple of months as a trial, to see what your periods might be like.

'We had decided sterilization was the best option for us, and that

I would have a vasectomy. Sandra already had heavy, painful periods and she had heard that they could get worse after a sterilization. When we went to see the doctor, she said she wanted to examine Sandra. It turned out that she had fibroids [a kind of swelling of the wall of the womb]. *They were quite big, the doctor said. She referred Sandra to a gynaecologist. We both went along and discussed what would be best to do. In the end, Sandra decided to have a hysterectomy, which solved both problems.'*

Before deciding on sterilization, it is always worth checking that there are no gynaecological problems which might need treatment. It is very frustrating to have a sterilization, only to find yourself having a hysterectomy shortly afterwards.

'I was 39 and Sean was 42. We had three children and were very happy. Sean was devoted to them, I've rarely seen a man so good with children. We discussed sterilization: I was quite sure that I wouldn't want to go through another pregnancy, no matter what happened. Anyway, soon I would be too old to have children safely. So I said I would have the operation: that way, if anything happened to me Sean could still have children with someone else.'

For women childbearing has a limited possible duration: by the time a woman is 45, her chances of having a baby are very small. However, a man continues to be fertile sometimes even into his seventies. This needs to be considered when deciding which of you should be sterilized. A man who is widowed or divorced in his late forties will often go on to form a new relationship with a woman considerably younger than himself. She may not yet have had children and is likely to be disappointed when she finds he has had a vasectomy. A woman in the same position could not have children any more anyway, so she is less likely to regret her sterilization. Similarly, if a man is married to a woman much younger than himself, it would often be more sensible for him to have a vasectomy, since he may die while she is still young enough to have more children.

What does having a sterilization involve?

Before making a final decision about which partner should be sterilized, you need to know what the two types of operation involve, and about their advantages and disadvantages.

Female sterilization

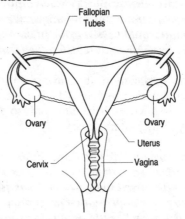

Figure 14.1 The points at which the Fallopian tubes are cut

The basic principle behind female sterilization is to stop the egg getting to the womb. The Fallopian tubes, which connect the ovaries and the womb, must be removed, cut, or destroyed. Obviously, if you have the tubes completely removed (a salpingectomy) there is no chance of anything happening again. However, this requires a fairly big operation and is nowadays usually only performed if there is a medical reason for doing so.

The most common operation carried out today is the laparoscopic sterilization. This can be done under either general or local anaesthetic. A laparoscope is simply a telescope designed to be used inside the pelvis. It therefore has to have its own fibre-optic light source, or it would be too dark to see anything. The laparoscope is inserted into the abdominal wall through a small incision usually around the umbilicus, or tummy button. In order that this can be done safely, the abdomen is first filled with carbon dioxide gas, so that there is plenty of space, and the operating table is tilted backwards, so that most of the 'unnecessary' organs lean over towards your head end. The main danger of laparoscopy is that the surgeon has to push the instrument in 'blind'—he cannot see what is underneath. This is why so much care is taken to try to make sure that nothing is in fact there.

Once in, the other instruments can either be passed down the laparoscope itself, or they can be inserted through a separate small incision further down, near the bikini line. Since the cuts are both so small, it really does not matter much which is done from your point of view, and will depend on the individual surgeon's preference.

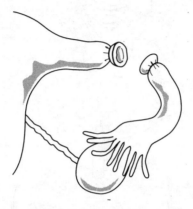

Figure 14.2 Tying the ends after the tubes have been cut

There are several options for dealing with the tubes. They can be electrically burnt, a procedure called diathermy. This destroys a lot of tissue and has the added risk of burning something else unintention-ally, such as the bowel. For this reason it is not a very commonly used method. The tubes can be cut and the ends tied (see Figure 14.2). Many surgeons now also make sure the ends are left in separate, non-communicating tissue areas so that there is the least possible chance of them meeting up again. Unfortunately, the separated ends of the tubes seem to have a great desire to rejoin each other, and will do so given the slightest opportunity.

Another method is to draw a section of tube up into a tiny ring (called a Falope ring) made of silastic (see Figure 14.3). This is much the same principle as an elastic band. The section inside the ring dies. The newest idea is the use of clips which simply flatten the tubes between their jaws (see Figure 14.4). There are two main types in use, the Hulka and the Filshie clip. Of the two, the Filshie clip does less

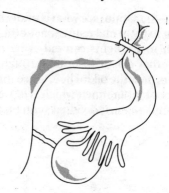

Figure 14.3 Falope ring

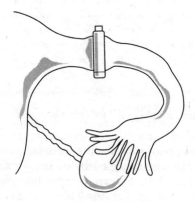

Figure 14.4 Filshie clip

damage to the tube. Indeed the Filshie clip is the most effective of all the laparoscopic methods available. Clips also give a better chance of being reversed successfully.

Once the sterilization has been performed, the instruments are removed and the tiny cuts sewn up. After a laparoscopic sterilization you may be allowed to go home the same day, if only a local anaesthetic was used. In fact, this is increasingly the case even if you have a general anaesthetic, provided there are no unusual problems and you have someone who can take you home and look after you.

'I was fine except that I felt as though I had been kicked several times in the stomach. Even laughing was painful. But it wore off after a couple of days.'

Unfortunately, the stretching caused by the gas, and the effect of the clips on the tubes themselves causing cramps, make the first few days after the operation uncomfortable. If you had a general anaesthetic you may also feel a little sick and 'woozy'. However, most women are back to their usual selves and can be back at work or full normal activities in three to four days.

Not everyone is suitable for a laparoscopic sterilization. If, for example, you are rather overweight, or have had previous pelvic surgery, it may not be considered safe. In such cases an operation called a mini-laparotomy is usually carried out. This involves a bikini-line scar and means that the surgeon can see exactly what is happening. The operation can also be carried out under either local or general anaesthetic and does not take very much longer than a laparoscopy. Obviously, there is a slightly larger scar and you may feel 'delicate' for a little longer, perhaps up to a week. Any of the methods of obstructing or cutting the tubes can be used, as described above. Nowadays it is unusual to have a full operation (called a laparotomy) just for a sterilization procedure. This requires a much larger incision and is a bigger operation altogether. It would only be done if there were some other reason for wanting to have an extensive look at your pelvis, such as another medical problem.

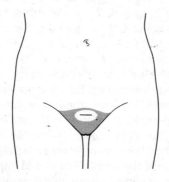

Figure 14.5 Bikini line cut

Whichever type of sterilization procedure you have, it is now common for the surgeon to perform a D & C (dilatation and curettage) of the womb as well, to make sure there is no chance of a pregnancy arising from intercourse prior to the operation. Women have been known to have a sterilization and turn up amazed a couple of months later, pregnant, because there was already a fertilized egg sitting in the womb when the procedure was done. The D & C (or 'scrape', as it is often called), helps to make sure that does not happen.

Recently there has been increasing interest in the idea of performing sterilization from within the womb. This has the advantage of leaving no scar at all and, once perfected, could even be done in the out-patient clinic. However, it is technically quite difficult to manipulate an instrument with so much accuracy actually inside the womb. We will discuss this again towards the end of the chapter.

We should perhaps mention hysterectomy, although to remove the womb just for the purpose of sterilization would be a little extreme. It is a much bigger operation, and requires a general anaesthetic, a week in hospital, and usually a couple of months to recover fully. As we mentioned before, however, you should make sure that a hysterectomy is not on the cards for some other medical reason, because then a separate sterilization would be pointless.

After the operation

In the long term the most important thing to watch out for is an ectopic pregnancy (a pregnancy in the tube). Sometimes the cut ends of the tube do manage to join together again, but are damaged. This is likely to result in fertilization taking place actually within the tube because the egg cannot properly make its way into the womb. A pregnancy in the tube is dangerous because the tube will eventually burst and peritonitis can develop. So if you notice any unusual pain, especially if it is one-sided, and whether or not you also have any symptoms of pregnancy (for example, nausea and breast tenderness), always see your doctor and remind her that you have had surgery on your tubes. It is also possible for a pregnancy to occur in the normal way, inside the womb. This could happen if the ends of the tubes joined up or if in fact the operation was carried out incorrectly and the wrong structure was cut or clipped. This does not happen often, but is possible. That is why you have to sign about this on the consent form (see below).

It does appear to be true that some women find their periods are heavier and more painful after sterilization. Partly this may be because they have come off the pill and notice the difference, but some cases are just coincidences of two now common things (having heavy periods and being sterilized).

The one thing a sterilization does not do is affect your sex life in any way. It does not interfere with the hormones which make you feel interested in sex, nor does it make you age prematurely.

How effective is female sterilization?

The two main factors here appear to be the age at which a woman is sterilized and the way in which the operation is performed. Obviously, if you have a hysterectomy or the tubes completely removed there is really no way the operation can fail. However, recent studies have shown that sterilization is often not as effective as we used to think, especially in women under the age of 28. In addition, there seems to be an increasing failure rate with time, so the longer it is since a woman was sterilized, the greater the failure rate is likely to be. In fact, whatever the failure rate is at two years, it will be double that by ten years.

Diathermy and Filshie clips are very effective, but even there the failure rate in young women is around two to three per thousand in the first year, reducing to about one per thousand in those over 34 years old. The variation in failure rates can be quite large depending on the method used.

The other thing which is worth noting is that one-third of pregnancies which do occur after sterilization are ectopic (i.e. outside the womb). As an ectopic pregnancy is a dangerous condition, this could be a worry especially if you are young and therefore more at risk of a sterilization failure.

An advantage of female sterilization over vasectomy is that it is effective from the moment you leave hospital. This is not the case with vasectomy, where you often have to wait several months before being given the 'all clear'. Let us now look at vasectomy in more detail.

Male sterilization: vasectomy

Vasectomy is in many ways an easier operation than female steriliza-tion. This is mainly because the male genital organs have been so conveniently positioned outside the abdomen. The principle is simply to cut the vas, the tube which connects the testicles to the penis. This can easily be done under local anaesthetic and it is unusual for the operation to require general anaesthesia.

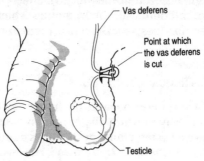

Vas deferens

Point at which the vas deferens is cut

Testicle

Figure 14.6 How a vasectomy is done

'It was all so simple really. The worst bit was having to shave: my wife lent me some of the cream she uses for her legs. She said I looked so nervous I might start the operation off myself . . . I had to lie on an operating table, covered in green cloth, all except—well, you can imagine. I felt more stupid than I've ever felt in my life. The injection hurt a bit, but I think the thought of it made it worse. Then the doctor chatted to me for a few minutes, asked if I'd brought someone with me, did I have some Y-fronts. I guess he was waiting for the anaesthetic to work. Then I felt him washing me, but it was all numb, rather like when you go to the dentist, you can still feel things, but they don't actually hurt. They asked if I'd like to watch in a mirror, but I was so nervous I was feeling a bit sick. So I just lay back and tried to think about other things. It only took a couple of minutes and he was saying, 'You can get up now.' Jane was waiting outside. They gave us a cup of coffee and off we went.'

During the operation the surgeon finds the vas, which is a tube just under the skin of the scrotum, and grips it firmly. He makes a small cut over it, pulls it out, then cuts the vas itself. Some surgeons like to send a small piece to the pathology laboratory to be sure that they have cut the correct tube. The two cut ends are tied off or heat-sealed and may be replaced in different tissue layers in order to try to minimize the chance of them rejoining. Then the skin incision is stitched up and it is all over. Obviously, this has to be repeated on the other side, since each testicle has its own vas.

In recent years a 'no scalpel' technique has been introduced which seems even quicker and easier. This involves the use of a special pair of forceps which can puncture the skin over the vas and immediately be used to grip the tube. The main advantages seem to be the speed with which the operation can be done and the fact that there is no incision requiring stitches. If anything there seem to be fewer problems after the operation than with conventional surgery, so although this is still a new technique, it is gradually being more widely used.

Following the operation, firm support, such as a pair of Y-fronts, is important even in bed at night for the first two or three nights; lying flat for the first 12 to 24 hours helps and any kind of strenuous exercise (including sex) should be avoided for a week.

Things to watch out for

Infection can occur, and if this happens you will notice some pus coming out of the wound. Antibiotics should clear this up quite quickly. A penalty for overdoing things, though it can occur anyway, is that you may develop a large bruise called a haematoma. This can be very sore and swollen and cause great alarm. Most of the time, with rest and support it will get better, but very occasionally it may be large enough to require drainage in hospital. Sperm can leak out of the cut ends of the tubes and cause an inflammatory reaction. This is harmless but may cause a small swelling or lump, called a sperm granuloma. This is not a problem unless it becomes painful, in which case it can be removed.

Having a vasectomy has absolutely no effect on a man's ability to have sex—unless it affects him psychologically. This is one of the reasons why it is so important to think through the decision very carefully. The ejaculate looks exactly the same as it did before. In fact, no one can tell a man has had a vasectomy unless they get out a microscope and look for sperm.

How effective is vasectomy?

Like female sterilization, vasectomy is not guaranteed 100 per cent effective (the main cause of failure is that the two cut ends of the vas can occasionally join up again), but the failure rate is very low, at between one and two per thousand cases. However, unlike female sterilization, vasectomy is not effective straight away. This is because at any given time there are huge numbers of sperm throughout the vas system 'downstream' from the cut. These have to be flushed out before it is safe to have otherwise unprotected sex. The number of ejaculations to achieve this varies greatly between men, which means that unless you go into overdrive it is likely to take three or more months before the operation can be assumed to have taken effect. (At the Margaret Pyke Centre the first sperm test is done about fifteen weeks after the operation.) Two successive clear sperm counts (that is, not containing any sperm) are required before the 'all clear' can be given. So be sure that you have made arrangements to use an alternative form of contraception until then. Even after two completely negative sperm counts very rare failures of vasectomy, even years later, have been reported.

Long-term consequences of vasectomy

Many men develop antibodies to sperm after a vasectomy, which is only of importance if they want to have the operation reversed (see below). Otherwise these antibodies are completely unnoticeable. There was some publicity a few years ago about an increased risk of atherosclerosis (hardening of the arteries) in monkeys which had had a vasectomy. Although this caused a panic at the time, research on humans has consistently shown no link between vasectomy and arterial disease.

At one time there was a slight suggestion of a possible increase in the risk of cancer of the testis in vasectomized men, but further research showed this was not the case. However, in 1993 two reports appeared of carefully conducted research suggesting an increase in the risk of cancer of the prostate in men who had had a vasectomy. Prostatic cancer is very common in older men: indeed, by the age of 75 about thirty-nine out of every thousand men will have been diagnosed as having this type of cancer. The cancer is rare under the age of 65 and becomes more common with increasing age. It is also often very slow growing and in many cases can be removed with no further problems.

The studies suggested that the risk of prostate cancer could go up by about 60 to 85 per cent in men who had had a vasectomy. So if currently about thirty-nine out of every thousand men develop the cancer by the age of 75, for vasectomized men the figure could be up to seventy-two in every thousand. The risk appeared to be highest in men who had had the operation a long time ago, reaching a maximum in men who had been operated on twenty years previously. However, you should note that, even taking the highest estimate of seventy-two in a thousand, this still means that 928 men out of every thousand who have a vasectomy will not develop prostate cancer.

One of the problems in interpreting these studies is that we actually have no idea of what causes prostate cancer, although smoking has sometimes been implicated. The men in these studies were unusual because they were all health workers themselves or were married to nurses. The studies were in fact originally designed to look at the health of the women, and the male data were incidental. So it is possible that this particular group of men had some other risk factors which made them more likely to develop prostate cancer, and the vasectomies were just a coincidence. Certainly there is no obvious biological explanation of why a vasectomy should increase the risk.

In America, it is recommended that men over the age of 50 have a yearly rectal examination to check the size of the prostate, and also that they undergo a yearly blood test (for prostate specific antigen) which can detect the cancer. However, these tests have a tendency to cause false alarms and therefore unnecessary surgery and anxiety, so they are not yet recommended here. If you are very worried it might be worth asking about the tests, but bear in mind that you may get a positive result which will turn out to be wrong. You may be wondering whether having a vasectomy reversed would reduce the risk: however, since we do not understand how it could increase the risk in the first place there is no obvious reason why a reversal should affect the risk either. We do not have any studies which have looked at this aspect, so it is impossible to predict what would happen. Further studies are under way to try to answer all these questions, but pending their results each man will have to make a decision about vasectomy based on his perception of the risks and benefits. Many continue to take the view that the convenience and effectiveness of the operation outweigh the uncertainty about a small increase in prostate cancer risk during old age.

Sterilization reversal

'I was married at 18 and had three children by the time I was 25. I was so fed up, stuck at home, watching my friends having a good time. I really felt I would never want any more children. My husband felt the same, so when I was 27 I went for the operation. I had no problems afterwards, everything was fine. The children started to get older: Janie, the oldest, is 17 now and Bobby, my youngest, is 13. When Bobby was 9 I decided I could try and find a job; I wasn't going to stay at home any more. Maybe that was a mistake, but it's too late now.

I started working as a secretary in a PR company. It was so exciting, all the activity. Sometimes famous people I had seen on TV would come in. Peter and I started to grow apart, his job seemed so boring, he had nothing to talk about. I made friends with other people in the office and they were all so much more sophisticated and interesting. That's how I met James. He couldn't believe I already had a grown-up daughter when we were almost the same age. We started going for lunch, then I pretended to Peter that I had to stay late quite often to help with a big event. I think he must have guessed long before I actually told him. James and I are getting married just as soon as the divorce comes through. He's 36 and never been married before. Although I don't want a child yet, I do feel that in a couple of years we'll want one of our own. That's why I think I should have the operation reversed now, to give myself the best possible chance.'

The number of requests for sterilization reversal is constantly increasing. Now that one in three marriages ends in divorce, more people who are still young are remarrying and want to set up another family. However, sterilization reversal is not without its problems and has no guarantee of success. This is why it is so important to think carefully about the original decision to have a sterilization operation. The success of female sterilization reversal depends greatly on how the original operation was performed. Obviously, if the tubes have been completely removed there is no possibility of reversal. Equally, the diathermy technique often damages the tubes so much that the chances of success are very small. The best results are usually obtained when the original sterilization was performed using Filshie clips (see above).

A sterilization reversal is a much bigger operation than a laparoscopic sterilization. The surgeon needs to have the best possible access to the tubes, so a mini-laparotomy or even a laparotomy may be necessary. The operation is usually done by a microsurgical technique, is very fiddly, and therefore takes a relatively long time. A general anaesthetic is always required. But the surgery itself is not the end of it. Usually the male partner will have to provide a semen sample for analysis beforehand—after all, if he is infertile there is not that much point performing a complicated operation on the woman. Then there is an increased risk that a pregnancy will be ectopic because of the surgically damaged tubes. This can be a life-threatening condition so there is considerable anxiety involved. Nevertheless, success rates of up to 90 per cent have been achieved following the use of clips, though with other sterilization techniques the success rate of reversals is usually more in the region of 50 per cent.

'Sarah and I were married when we were both 23. We had two lovely children, Richard and Louise. Sarah had a lot of trouble with the pill and I hate condoms, so in the end I said I would have a vasectomy. We were a very happy couple and a close family. Until the accident. Sarah was driving the children home after a day out. Both Sarah and Louise were killed instantly. Richard was OK, thank God. He was 14 when it happened, so it wasn't so difficult for me to cope with work and looking after him on my own: we grieved together.

Two years ago I met Pamela. She's quite different from Sarah, but something about her attracted me almost straight away. I hadn't really been interested in looking for another relationship. Richard liked her too, in fact he positively encouraged me. He's 19 now and has girlfriends of his own. Pamela gradually became part of my life and last month we decided to get married. She's ten years younger than I am, only 35. She's not been married before and I know she'd like at least one child. It must be worth a try, even if there's only a small chance it can be reversed.'

Vasectomy reversal is in theory easier than reversal of female sterilization. The vas is easily accessible and all that has to be done is to reconnect the two cut ends. However, in practice, the success rate of vasectomy reversal is only around 50 per cent, and lower still if the operation was done more than ten years earlier. Sometimes this is because of technical problems with the operation, but often it is due to the formation of anti-sperm antibodies. Antibodies are like warriors against things the body considers foreign. They fight bacteria and viruses, for example. Unfortunately, sometimes they can be produced inappropriately: the body thinks something is foreign which actually is not. This is what seems to happen in many men following a vasectomy. For some reason which is not understood the body suddenly thinks that the man's own sperm are foreign and produces antibodies, ready to pounce on any stray sperm that might appear. When the vasectomy is reversed and many sperm are let loose, the antibodies simply destroy them before they have a chance to go anywhere. What is even more intriguing is that some men who have been shown to have antibodies still manage to be fertile, while others do not. Again, the difference is unclear. It does however mean that having antibodies to sperm is not definitely the end of all hope.

The future of vasectomy and sterilization

Most of the new advances in sterilization techniques are designed either to make the operation more easily and more successfully reversible, or to make an irreversible procedure simpler. For women, an instrument called a hysteroscope is being viewed with great interest. This is rather like a laparoscope, but it is inserted actually into the womb and allows the surgeon to perform operations inside the womb. This has the advantage of not requiring any scar and could be done in the out-patient clinic. Various materials are being investigated which could be used to block the Fallopian tubes through the openings into the womb. One of them is methylcyanoacrylate, better known to most of us as 'Superglue'. This has been injected into the tubes and basically glues them together. The success rate so far has been between 88 and 94 per cent. This type of sterilization would not be reversible. Various other destructive agents could be injected into the tubes in this way, but again their main disadvantage is their irreversibility.

Theoretically, the vas could also be injected with a destructive chemical and indeed zinc has been used with some success in dogs so far. As always the worry in men is that the chemical, if not 100 per cent effective, might allow damaged sperm to get through and bring about an abnormal baby. Since clips have already been used successfully in women, why not use them to do vasectomies? Indeed, a new instrument called the Vasocclude is designed to place metal clips onto the vas. The operation is otherwise similar to a surgical vasectomy, but might be easier to reverse. So far, tests have shown a 96 per cent success rate and a new design due soon is expected to increase the efficacy to 99 per cent. Preliminary trials are under way and, if successful, the technique could be available by the year 2000.

Plugs made of silicone are being investigated for both male and female sterilization. The major advantage of these would be their reversibility. This idea has progressed further as a vasectomy technique so far, and could also be available in the next ten years.

In summary

The most important aspect of male or female sterilization is to make your decision very carefully. If there is any doubt, wait a little longer. Truly reversible sterilization is not yet available and, until it is, the procedure should always be viewed as irreversible. Having said all that, sterilization is highly effective, relatively simple, and can be an excellent solution for many couples.

CHAPTER 15

The Future

It takes a long time for new methods of contraception to become available to the public, since exhaustive monitoring and research are necessary to ensure that the methods are safe, effective, and free of damaging side-effects. Contraceptives are not judged like other medicines because the people who use them are not ill. If you are at risk of having a stroke because of high blood pressure, you will be very pleased that there is a medicine which lowers your blood pressure. This medicine may have some side-effects, like making you feel giddy or tired, but that is nothing compared to being an invalid after a stroke. So this medicine will continue to be available because, despite its side-effects, it prevents worse suffering and saves lives.

The same is not automatically true of contraceptives. People who use them are generally well, and the only thing the contraceptive prevents is pregnancy. If the contraceptive has health risks or side-effects of its own, it may make a previously healthy person ill. So the risk-benefit equation must depend on how risky it is for a woman to be pregnant. The risks inherent in pregnancy are fortunately very low in developed countries, so women will be less willing to accept side-effects and health risks merely to avoid it. Licensing of contraceptives also varies greatly from country to country, and in some European countries the methods described in this chapter have already been in use for several years, although they have not yet been approved in Britain. The American approval committee, the FDA, is the most cautious of all, and American women are always the last to acquire a new method of contraception and the first to lose it (because of the potentially enormous legal costs) if evidence of problems, or even adverse publicity, should arise.

Predicting the length of time a new method will take to arrive on the market is almost impossible, since it may be delayed by all manner of problems: in particular there may be unforeseen technical difficulties in manufacture or a side-effect which unexpectedly comes to light. Some of the methods which we will describe have been 'just around the corner' every year for the last five years.

Hormonal methods

Most potential new methods of hormonal contraception are not designed to be swallowed. Because all pills need to pass through both the stomach and the liver before they can begin to work, they are bound to be affected by stomach upsets or by any other condition which influences absorption from the stomach. Then, as the pill travels through the liver, the oestrogen and progestogen contained in it affect any other proteins and hormones in the vicinity, while the liver itself attempts to destroy the pill. This conflict in the liver is called the 'first-pass effect'; consequences of it include a weakening of the pill (which means that a higher-dose pill is needed to compensate for the wastage) and changes in blood-clotting factors, lipids, and various other substances. Since these latter changes are usually for the worse, any method of contraception which circumvented them would be preferable.

Avoiding both the stomach and the 'first pass' through the liver entails using one of the various non-oral routes employed by most new contraceptive methods. The principal advantage is that it is possible to give lower doses of hormones, since there will be no need to allow for wastage, as described above. A lower dose, naturally, means fewer side-effects and fewer health risks.

The other feature of the majority of new methods is that they do not contain oestrogen (that is, they are progestogen-only methods). In part this is a result of the fears expressed about the combined pill in the early 1980s, since research is planned and started long before its results actually affect the market. Since confidence in the pill has revived there has been a renewal of interest in oestrogen-containing methods; but the results of the relevant research will of course take equally long to become available.

Vaginal rings

One very interesting and easy-to-use new development is the vaginal ring. These are hollow, flexible, one-size rings intended to be inserted into the vagina and left there. They slowly release hormone, which is absorbed through the vaginal skin. Since they can be inserted and removed easily by the woman herself, they permit complete control over the method of contraception.

> *'This is the best thing I've ever tried. I don't have to remember to take pills. I don't have any side-effects—my periods were a bit irregular when I first started, but they settled down after a few months. I can't feel it inside me—I really don't know it's there.'*

Among the various types of ring currently under consideration, the progestogen-releasing ring contains the progestogen levonorgestrel encased in silastic. It is 5.5 centimetres in diameter and less than one centimetre thick. After it has been introduced into the vagina it can remain in place for up to three months. (Like the progestogen-only pill (POP) there is no need to remove it for periods.) This does not mean that it is a permanent fixture: it can be removed for a short period of time, for example for cleaning, or even for intercourse if either partner finds its presence off-putting. At present the opinion is that removal for up to three hours will not impair its efficacy. Since this ring functions in a similar way to the POP it has a comparable failure rate of three per hundred woman-years. More than 50 per cent of users continue to ovulate normally, so, like the POP, its success is based on thickening the cervical mucus so that sperm cannot penetrate it and on making the lining of the womb thin so as to prevent implantation of the fertilized egg.

Only 20 micrograms of levonorgestrel are released each day. It will be noticed that this is a lower dose than in the POP (Microval, the levonorgestrel POP, contains 30 micrograms), but this is because a lower dose is possible in contraceptives that are not taken by mouth. Despite this, the main side-effect also resembles that of the POP, in that the ring causes irregular bleeding, particularly during the first few months. (This will usually settle down as time goes on.) The ring may occasionally be expelled, especially during straining at stool, but then it can just be washed and reinserted.

Basically, using the ring is like taking the POP without the need to remember to take pills. (This is a particular advantage since the POP requires such a strict timetable.) Along with this, the user will have all the advantages of the POP: there will be no oestrogen-related health risks or side-effects. Studies in many countries, including the UK, have confirmed its popularity (indeed, women taking part in these studies were often reluctant to give it up when the trial came to an end).

Unfortunately, shortly before the ring was due to come onto the market, a problem came to light. A study was being carried out in England which was expected simply to confirm the acceptability and efficacy of the ring before a licence was granted. During routine vaginal examinations, it was noticed that a small proportion of women had reddened areas around the cervix or in the vagina. The women had not noticed any particular problem themselves and were mostly very happy with their rings. To be on the safe side, another examination was then carried out and where a red area was seen a little pinch was taken from it, called a biopsy. This meant that it could be looked at more closely in a laboratory.

The biopsies from these reddened areas mostly showed the same features: a thinning of the epithelium (skin covering) and marked inflammation. These women were asked to stop using the ring and were monitored. Gradually, the reddened areas disappeared and the thinning and inflammation improved. The finding of these reddened areas has considerably delayed the marketing of this ring. The strict control of new contraceptives means that it now has to be proved that these areas pose no risk to the woman. Changing the ring's dimensions and flexibility may perhaps almost stop them appearing. All this new research means that this ring is unlikely to be available for some considerable time.

Trials are also taking place on a second progestogen-releasing vaginal ring, one which releases desogestrel. Desogestrel is one of the newer, more specific progestogens, which have a less marked effect on blood fats and sugars and a low incidence of side-effects, so there are high hopes for this contraceptive. One should, however, be aware that the dose used in all rings is extremely small so it is unlikely that one progestogen will have any particular advantage over another in this respect. This ring may induce slightly more regular bleeding, which would be an improvement; but it is at a very much earlier stage in development than the levonorgestrel-releasing type and may suffer delay for the same reasons.

For women who are breastfeeding a ring releasing progesterone is under development. Since progesterone is a natural hormone, whereas the progestogens are synthetic, this will, it is hoped, be a more satisfactory option: there will be no chance of synthetic hormones passing into the milk. However, research here too has a long way to go, especially since this ring does seem to cause more bleeding problems than the others.

A further possibility is a combined oestrogen-progestogen ring, and several are now under development. The furthest advanced contains 15 micrograms of ethinyloestradiol and 120 micrograms of desogestrel. If this should be viable it will give a lower dose than the lowest-dose combined pill, Mercilon, which contains 20 micrograms of ethinyloestradiol and 150 micrograms of desogestrel. The combined ring will need replacing only every three months, but it works on the same system as the combined pill with its pill-free week: every three weeks the ring will be taken out to permit withdrawal bleeding. The bleeding pattern should be regular, as on the combined pill, but the advantage of the ring is that it would contain a lower dose, so there should be fewer side-effects and health risks, and again no tablets to remember. There is still, however, much work to be done before it will be on the market.

Biodegradable implants

Research is now under way into the possibility of biodegradable implants: that is, implants which would not need to be removed at the end of their life but would simply dissolve. (This would deal with one of the disadvantages inherent in Norplant.) One version which may be available in the relatively near future is called Capronor. It consists of a single capsule containing levonorgestrel, the same progestogen as is used in Norplant. The capsule is similar in size to the Norplant ones, and a small incision is required for its insertion in just the same way. It continues to act for about eighteen to twenty-four months, after which time the capsule is gradually absorbed.

Another type of biodegradable implant uses extremely small pellets containing progestogen. These have the advantage over Norplant of being virtually invisible and can hardly be felt at all, although four pellets will be required. Their protective effect will last for a year. However, the disadvantage of this method is that once the pellets have been inserted you have only a limited time in which to change your mind; after this time they cannot be removed, so you will have to accept their effect until it comes to a natural end.

Hormone-releasing intrauterine devices (IUDs)

The levonorgestrel-releasing intrauterine system (Mirena) has been discussed in Chapter 8. At present, it is licensed only for contraception, but it is hoped that it will soon be licensed for other uses. For example, it would be of enormous benefit to women who suffer from heavy periods, even if they do not need contraception. In addition, it has great potential for use in hormone replacement therapy, as discussed in Chapter 12.

A desogestrel-releasing intrauterine system is also under trial. Although progestogenic side-effects, such as acne, are already unusual with the Mirena, the newer progestogen should help those women who may still be troubled by even a very low dose of levonorgestrel. It is hoped that this device may be available within the next few years.

Injectable contraceptives

The various advantages of injectable contraceptives, such as Depo Provera, are discussed in Chapter 7 above. The principal disadvantage associated with this means of contraception is irregular bleeding, and various attempts are being made to improve this. One of the more promising is Cyclo-Provera, or Cyclofem, a monthly injection of 25 milligrams of Depo Provera plus 5 milligrams of oestradiol cypionate which has proved extremely effective: its failure rate is less than one per hundred woman-years. Unfortunately Cyclofem contains oestrogen as well as progestogen, so it is possible that using it may entail some oestrogenic side-effects and health risks. Like other injectables it has the advantage that the woman does not need to take pills, and that a small dose can be given because non-oral methods avoid the destructive agents in the stomach and liver. Furthermore, it gives fairly regular cycles and, because it is a monthly dose, it is easier to stop quickly than Depo Provera. It also appears that fertility will return sooner after it is given up: most women become pregnant within three months of stopping the method. However, for some women having to attend a clinic or make an appointment with their doctor every month may be a disadvantage.

The 'once-a-week' pill

This method is being developed primarily by the Indian Ministry of Health. The pill, Centchroman, is a new compound which works mainly by preventing implantation. The tablet is taken twice weekly for the first three months and once weekly thereafter. Side-effects appear to be mainly related to some irregularity of the menstrual cycle. The failure rate is about twelve per hundred woman-years, making it less effective than either the combined pill or the POP. Some women may find it more difficult to remember to take a pill just once a week, since there is less of a routine. Its main advantage seems to be the lack of side-effects, but large-scale trials are still needed.

More effective emergency contraception

Mifepristone (formerly RU486), which is currently being used as an 'abortion pill', has also been shown to be very effective when a single dose is given within 72 hours of unprotected sex. Under these conditions it works by preventing implantation. It seems to have an advantage over the conventional emergency pill in that it causes less nausea. Although it is not currently licensed for use as an emergency contraceptive, trials are proving very successful and provided there are no legal or regulatory problems it could be available in the near future.

The 'unisex' pill

Interesting possibilities are raised by the current attempts to develop a pill which could be used by both men and women, based on the use of the hormone inhibin. This hormone is found in both men and women, and is connected with the production of sperm and eggs. High doses of inhibin are likely to prevent the production of eggs in women and sperm in men, and its great advantage is that there will probably be few side-effects, since inhibin appears to have no other functions.

Nasal spray contraception

The use of nasal spray for contraception came to the fore a number of years ago. The spray works on the same principle as the combined pill, in that it stops ovulation, but it interferes at an earlier stage in the process. Only a very small dose of hormone is required, and since it is very easily absorbed through the nasal skin, it is given in the form of a spray. This also has the advantage that it avoids the stomach, where it would be completely destroyed. However, it does produce one completely unacceptable side-effect: since it prevents oestrogen from being produced, it induces a menopause, complete with hot flushes. As a result it has been necessary to abandon this method until some means of avoiding this effect can be found. One of the possibilities is to give natural oestrogen replacement, as in hormone replacement therapy. However, then the woman would also need to take progestogen to protect the womb from cancer of its lining. The idea of using nasal sprays in combination with pills, patches, and even possibly a progestogen-releasing IUD is obviously rather 'over the top', but if the concept could be simplified it might be useful.

Hormone-releasing patches

There is a great deal of interest in patches for use in hormone replacement therapy at the moment. The patch, which resembles a sticking plaster containing hormone, needs only to be stuck on to the skin, and the hormone will gradually be absorbed through the skin. This method too avoids the stomach and liver, where a good deal of any oral hormone dose can be destroyed. Of course, allergies to sticking plaster are not uncommon, and women have been known to react adversely to the hormone patches, but they are generally very popular. One early problem was that although it was easy to give oestrogen through patches, the combination of oestrogen and progestogen was a more complicated proposition; but it seems that research is currently overcoming this difficulty. If the combination turns out to be possible we should be able to use patches for contraception, and this will dispense with the need for pills or the discomfort of injections or implants. A disadvantage is that patches would probably last only for a week, so the woman would need to remember to replace her patch regularly. Nevertheless, this would almost certainly be a popular method if it became available.

Non-hormonal methods

Barrier methods

New condoms for men are being developed, designed to be loose-fitting and therefore hopefully to improve sensation. The condom would be loose but would have an elasticated base, so that it did not come off. Plastic is also being investigated as a possible material for condoms. Plastic is stronger than latex, not damaged by oil-based lubricants, and less sensitive to the effects of heat and humidity (a point of special interest for those in tropical countries).

There is also a novel idea for another female condom. This is called the 'bikini condom' and consists of a latex panty with a built-in rolled pouch that fits over the opening of the vagina. Before intercourse, the woman pushes the pouch into the vagina. No doubt this would prove fascinating for rubber fetishists, but it will be interesting to see how acceptable it is to the general population.

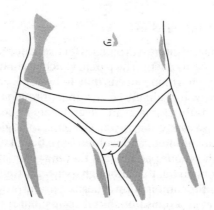

Figure 15.1 The bikini condom

Variants on the theme of the cervical cap are also being tested. Lea's Shield is made of silicone and fits snugly over the cervix, held on by suction. It contains a one-way valve to allow cervical secretions and blood out, but ensure that sperm do not get in. The device is pliable and adapts its shape to suit each person, so that 'one size fits all'.

The device can be left in place for 48 hours and is easily removed by means of the loop (see Figure 15.2). There are as yet few studies as to its efficacy and acceptability.

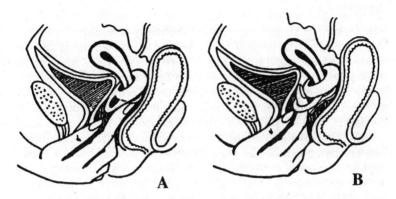

Figure 15.2 Lea's Shield

The Femcap is another variant on the cervical cap theme, also made of silicone. Again it stays in place by suction, but because of its unusual physical design (with side brims) it is expected to give effective contraceptive protection. It comes in two sizes, a small one for women who have not had a baby and a larger one for those who have. Like the Lea's shield a loop on the underside is designed to faciliate easy removal.

There is considerable interest in finding new spermicides. The antiseptic chlorhexidine has been shown to thicken cervical mucus, preventing the passage of sperm. This and other vaginal substances being researched could have an extra benefit in perhaps also protecting against HIV infection if they are also shown to inactivate or destroy the virus. Gossypol, the Chinese drug derived from cottonseed oil, is also being tested as a vaginal contraceptive gel. Although when taken orally it has unpleasant effects (see Chapter 13), it seems well tolerated in the vagina and appears to be very effective at immobilizing sperm. A derivative of the drug propranolol, which is used to lower blood pressure, also seems to work as a spermicide. A tablet is placed in the vagina and temporarily immobilizes sperm for up to 24 hours, which means they are likely to die in the hostile, acidic, vaginal environment. Although some of the drug will be absorbed, the form being studied is inactive in the circulation.

Contraceptive vaccines

Vaccines are an attractive idea, since they would eventually be cheap, simple, very effective, and potentially reversible. Two types are currently under study. The idea behind any vaccine is to make the body think something is 'foreign'. Each of us has an 'army' in the blood-stream, ready for a potential attack. These are the immune cells: when an invader is registered they multiply and rush to the scene. Their job is to seek and destroy anything they do not recognize as part of their own body. Once the immune cells have won, a small group of cells is allocated the job of remembering the exact nature of the invader, and how best to deal with it. If the same invader comes again, these cells suddenly become alert, start reproducing them-selves very rapidly, and produce huge numbers of specifically trained fighters called antibodies which rush to the scene.

Vaccines capitalize on this 'memory'. They stimulate the immune cells into remembering a particular type of attacker, so that the next time they come across it, they react in force. Thus, when you have a typhoid vaccine, you often feel quite ill for a day. In effect, you are suf-fering a very mild case of typhoid in order for your immune cells to remember what the typhoid 'attacker' is. The next time your body is invaded by a typhoid infection, it will be the real thing, but your immune cell antibodies are ready and waiting.

Two types of contraceptive vaccine for women are currently under study. (We discuss the possibility of an anti-sperm male vaccine in Chapter 13.) The first is a vaccine against the covering of the egg, the zona pellucida. The effect of such a vaccine is to make the body pro-duce antibodies against the zona pellucida. Whenever an egg is released, the antibodies wake up and rush over to attach themselves to it. They do not actually destroy the egg, but because they remain in the way no sperm can get through to fertilize the egg.

The other type of vaccine is against the hormone Human Chori-onic Gonadotrophin (HCG). This is a hormone produced by the embryo once it has embedded, or implanted, in the wall of the womb. Essentially, its function is to stop the shedding of the lining of the womb at the end of the month, because then the embryo would be washed away. Normally, if no pregnancy has occurred, the ovaries shut down production of progesterone about a week after ovulation and the lining drops off. The job of the HCG hormone is to inform the ovaries that an egg has been fertilized and that continued supplies of progesterone are needed. The vaccine works by making the immune cells think that HCG is an invader. They attach themselves to it and prevent it from passing its message to the ovaries. So although the embryo is producing quantities of HCG, this is all in vain. The ovaries are unaware that progesterone is needed and the lining, complete with the embryo, is shed at the end of the month. This type of vaccine is in fact causing an abortion, since it acts after the fertilized egg has implanted in the wall of the womb. It seems that one injection lasts about six months.

The problem with vaccines is that we have to be quite sure that they do not cause any permanent damage, and also that, if they fail or wear off, any resulting pregnancies will not be harmed. Trials are under way, but achieving a good menstrual cycle in users is proving difficult and there is still quite a long way to go.

What about the male pill?

This is discussed in Chapter 13, but seems unpromising at present.

In general, it is not advisable to become overenthusiastic about any new method until it actually reaches the market. There are so many possible disasters along the way: a new side-effect or health risk becomes suddenly apparent, the material used to hold the hormone is found to be dangerous or unstable, the company discovers something else which they find more exciting and simply stops putting money into the older product—these are just a few. Nevertheless, it is good to know that research is going on, since none of the methods we have at present could be described as 'perfect' by a long way. The more choices there are available, the greater the likelihood of finding one that suits.

Further Reading

Adler, Michael, *ABC of Sexually Transmitted Diseases* (BMJ, 1990). Written for doctors but comprehensible to the general reader.

Cochrane, John, and **Szarewski, Anne,** *The Breast Book* (Macdonald Optima, 1989).

Delvin, David, *The Book of Love* (New English Library, 1975).

Filshie, Marcus, and **Guillebaud, John,** *Contraception: Science and Practice* (Butterworths, 1991). For the very interested, and those who have some scientific background. Written for doctors in the family planning field.

Flynn, A., and **Brooks, M.,** *A Manual of Natural Family Planning* (Unwin Hyman, 1990). All the most advanced techniques for assessing fertile and non-fertile phases in the cycle in order to avoid or plan a possible pregnancy.

Guillebaud, John, *Contraception Today* (Martin Dunitz, 1997). A brief look at all aspects of contraception—written for doctors but not too technical.

——*The Pill* (5th edn., Oxford University Press, 1997). A comprehensive guide to the combined pill and the progestogen-only pill, written in terms anyone can understand.

Hayman, Suzie, *Vasectomy and Sterilization* (Thorsons, 1989), Sensible, balanced, and easy-to-read guide for the general reader.

Leathard, Audrey, *The Fight for Family Planning* (Macmillan, 1980). The history of the birth control movement in Britain from 1921.

McLaren, Angus, *A History of Contraception from Antiquity to the Present Day* (Blackwell, 1990). A fascinating look at the development of the family, sexuality, and social relations through the ages.

Quilliam, Susan, *Positive Smear* (2nd edn., Letts, 1992). Experiences of having an abnormal cervical smear presented from the woman's viewpoint. Written by a counsellor who has interviewed dozens of women.

Szarewski, Anne, *The Cervical Smear Test* (Vermilion, 1994). A comprehensive guide to the meaning of an abnormal smear, treatment options and future possibilities.

Useful Addresses

UK

The Health Education Authority
Hamilton House
Mabledon Place
London WC1H 9TX

0171 383 3833

Provides information and leaflets on all aspects of family planning.

Health Authority Board for Scotland
Woodburn House
Canaan Lane
Edinburgh EH10 4SG

0131 447 8044

Similar to the above.

Health Promotion Wales
FFYNNON-LAS
Ty-Glas Avenue
Cardiff CF4 5DZ

01222 752222

Health Promotion Agency for
Northern Ireland
18 Ormeau Avenue
Belfast BT2 8HS

01232 311611

The Family Planning Association
2–12 Pentonville Rd.
London N1 9FP

0171 837 5432
Helpline 0171–837 4044

FPA Wales 01222 342766
FPA Scotland 0141 2118138
FPA Northern Ireland 01232 325488

Gives advice on all aspects of family planning, sexual and reproductive health, etc. A good source of information about other clinics and services available throughout the United Kingdom. They have a bookshop and also have free leaflets on many topics.

Margaret Pyke Centre for study and
    training in family planning
73 Charlotte St.
London W1P 1LB

0171 530 3600
Helpline 0171 530 3636

The largest centre in Europe, dealing with all aspects of family planning, counselling, and screening.

Brook Advisory Centres
(Head Office)
165 Grays Inn Road
London WC1X 8UD

0171 713 9000
recorded information helpline 0171
    617 8000

Specialize in young people's problems (under 24). Provide family planning, screening services, and counselling.

British Association for Counselling
1 Regent Place
Rugby
Warwickshire CV21 2PJ

01788 578328

Useful source of nation-wide information about clinics which provide counselling.

Relate (formerly National Marriage
  Guidance Council)
Head Office
Herbert Gray College
Little Church St.
Rugby
Warwickshire CV21 3AP

01788 573241

*Nation-wide network of clinics providing
psychosexual and marriage guidance
counselling. Local branches can be found
in telephone directories.*

Scottish Marriage Guidance
  Council
26 Frederick St.
Edinburgh EH2 2JR

0131 225 5006

Similar to Relate.

Association of Sexual and Marital
  Therapists
PO Box 62
Sheffield S10 3TS

Terence Higgins Trust
BM AIDS
London WC1N 3XX

0171 833 2971/071 278 8745
Helpline 0171 833 2971

*Information, support groups, and coun-
selling about AIDS.*

The Women's National Cancer
Control Campaign
Suna House
128 Curtain Rd.
London EC2 3AR

0171 729 4688

*Information and free leaflets on all aspects
of women's cancers.*

Women's Health Concern
Alexandra House

Oldham Terrace
London W3 6NH

0171 938 3932

*Practical help with women's health
problems, especially those relating to
the menstrual cycle and the
menopause.*

Action on Smoking and Health
(ASH)
Devon House
12–15 Dartmouth St.
London SW1H 1BL

0171 233 1800

Private Family Planning Clinics

British Pregnancy Advisory
  Service
Austy Manor (Head Office)
Wootton Wawen
West Midlands B95 6BX

01564 793225

*Will provide lists of all their clinics and
services.*

Marie Stopes House
The Well Woman Centre
108 Whitfield St.
London W1

0171 388 0662/2585

Marie Stopes Centre
10 Queen Square
Leeds LS2 8AJ

01532 440685

Marie Stopes Centre
1 Police St.
Manchester M4 7LQ

0161 832 4250

Eire

Irish Family Planning Association
(Head Office)
36–7 Lower Ormond Quay
Dublin 1

003 531 872 5033

*Provides a similar service to the FPA
within the confines of Irish law.*

United States

Planned Parenthood Federation of
America (head office)
2010 Massachusetts Avenue
NW Suite 500
Washington DC 20036

202 785 3351

Western region:
333 Broadway
3rd Floor
San Francisco
California 94133

415 956 8856

Southern region:
303 Peachtree Rd.
NW Room 303
Atlanta
Georgia 30305

Northern region
2625 Butterfield Rd.
Oak Brook
Illinois 60521

312 986 9270

Australia

Australian Federation of FPAs
Suite 603
6th floor

Roden Cutler House
24 Campbell St.
Sydney
NSW 2000

New Zealand

The New Zealand FPA Inc.
PO Box 68200
214 Karangahape
Newton
Auckland

South Africa

FPA of South Africa
412 York House
46 Kerk St.
Johannesburg 2001

**Pharmaceutical Companies
Manufacturing Contraceptives**

These companies usually have information departments, which you
may find helpful if you have a query
relating to one or more of their products.

Gold Cross/Searle Pharmaceu-
ticals
PO Box 53
Lane End Rd.
High Wycombe
Bucks. HP12 4HL

01494 521124

*(combined pills: Conova 30; POPs:
Femulen)*

Janssen-Cilag Ltd.
PO Box 79
Saunderton
High Wycombe

Bucks. HP14 4HJ

01494 563541

(combined pills: Cilest, Neocon, Ovysmen, Ortho-Novin 1/50, Binovum, Trinovum, Trinovum ED; POPs: Micronor; IUDs: e.g. Ortho Gynae T 380; diaphragms and caps; spermicides)

Lamberts (Dalston) Ltd.
Dalston House
Hastings St.
Luton
Beds. LU1 5BW

01582 400711

(cervical caps)

London Rubber Company
LRC Products Ltd.
North Circular Rd.
Chingford
London E4 8QA

0181 527 2377

(condoms, diaphragms)

Organon Laboratories Ltd.
Cambridge Science Park
Milton Rd.
Cambridge CB4 4FL

01223 423650

(combined pills: Marvelon, Mercilon; combined oestrogen-progestogen vaginal ring; IUDs, e.g. Multiload, desogestrel IUD; desogestrel implant)

Parke-Davis Medical
Lambert Court
Chestnut Ave.
Eastleigh
Hants SO5 3ZQ

01703 620500

(combined pills: Loestrin 20, Loestrin 30)

Pharmacia-Upjohn Ltd.
Davy Avenue

Knowlhill
Milton Keynes MK5 8PH

01908 661101

(injectable contraceptive: Depo Provera)

Roussel Laboratories Ltd.
Broadwater Park
North Orbital Rd.
Uxbridge
Middx. UB9 5HP

01895 834343

(progestogen-only vaginal ring, Norplant, Mifepristone)

Schering Health Care Ltd.
The Brow
Burgess Hill
West Sussex RH15 9NE

01444 232323

(combined pills: Eugynon 30, Femodene, Triadene, Microgynon, Logynon, Logynon ED; POPs: Neogest, Norgeston; post-coital pill: PC4; injectable progestogen: Noristerat; IUDs, e.g. Nova T; Lev-onorgestrel-releasing intrauterine system: Mirena)

Syntex Pharmaceuticals Ltd.
Syntex House
St Ives Rd.
Maidenhead
Berks. SL6 1RD

01628 33191

(combined pills: Brevinor, Norimin, Norinyl-1, Synphase; POPs: Noriday; spermicide: Staycept)

Unipath Ltd.
Norse Rd.
Bedford MK41 0QG

01234 347161

(Persona)

Wyeth Laboratories
Huntercombe Lane South
Taplow
Maidenhead
Berks. SL6 OPH

016286 4377

*(combined pills: Minulet, Tri-Minulet,
Ovran, Ovran 30, Ovranette, Trinordiol;
POPs: Microval)*

G. H. Zeal Ltd.
8 Lombard Rd.
Merton
London SW19 3UU

0181 542 2283

(fertility thermometer)

Index